The Campus History Series

EDINBORO UNIVERSITY

On the Front Cover: Most of the student body stands in front of the west wing of Normal Hall around 1925, when enrollment was between 300 and 400 students. The dates on the building—1860 and 1890—represent the year Edinboro applied to become a normal school and the year the west wing of Normal Hall was constructed, respectively. The original portion of Normal Hall was erected in 1875. The building burned to the ground in 1969. (Photograph courtesy of Edinboro University Archive.)

On the Back Cover: This aerial view of campus looks from the southeast to the northwest around 1969. To the right is Hendricks Hall, built in 1968. Darrow Road extends downward and is faced by three dormitories: Rose Hall, Earp Hall, and Dearborn Hall. (Photograph courtesy of Edinboro University Archive.)

The Campus History Series

EDINBORO UNIVERSITY

DAVE OBRINGER

ARCADIA
PUBLISHING

ISBN 978-0-7385-9277-0

Published by Arcadia Publishing
Charleston, South Carolina

Printed in the United States of America

Library of Congress Catalog Card Number: 2012935820

For all general information, please contact Arcadia Publishing:
Telephone 843-853-2070
Fax 843-853-0044
E-mail sales@arcadiapublishing.com
For customer service and orders:
Toll-Free 1-888-313-2665

Visit us on the Internet at www.arcadiapublishing.com

This book is dedicated to my family:
Janice, Sean, Michael, Ruth, Bill, John, and Edna.

CONTENTS

ACKNOWLEDGMENTS

This book would not have been possible without the support of Friends of the Baron-Forness Library. Members of this group include Dr. Mary Paniccia Carden, Dianne Howard, Dr. Donald Swift, Prof. Jack Braun, Dr. James Drane, Dr. Cynthia Legin-Bucell, Janet O'Dessa, Jeff Pinski, Dr. Sandra Waite Stupiansky, Barbara Kantz, Courtney Tedesco, and Dr. Donald Dilmore. I especially want to acknowledge the work of Dr. Carden, president of the Friends, and Dr. Dilmore, associate vice president for University Libraries. Without their perseverance in negotiating the approval process, this book would have been stuck in a bureaucratic bog.

In a larger sense, this book is only possible because of the many students, faculty, managers, and other employees who are a part of Edinboro's history. Many people have invested a career at Edinboro and have done remarkable work. For those whose photographs or names do not appear, I can only plead space limitations.

All images appear courtesy of Edinboro University of Pennsylvania.

INTRODUCTION

The goal of this publication is to convey to all who read it a sense of Edinboro University's history. Students who spend their college years here and faculty who invest their careers here see a small portion of the school's history. The span of events we witness is measured on a long timeline not visible in our daily activity. Hopefully, this book will bring to light some of that history.

A work such as this is not intended to be comprehensive; it is like the highlight reel of a football game. As fans watch the footage, they wonder why other plays were not included. For more in-depth coverage, there are two comprehensive books written in different formats: Russell Vance's *A Portrait of Edinboro: From Private Academy to State College, 1856–1976* and Roy Strausbaugh's *Edinboro University: An Administrative History, 1963–1993*.

This book is a visual stroll through Edinboro's past with an explanation of interesting events. The images convey a feeling for the times as well as any text could. With images dating from the founding of the school to photographs today's visitors will recognize, this book provides the historical background of the school.

Edinboro was not founded as a state-owned school; it was purchased by the state nearly 60 years after opening. As a normal school, Edinboro provided the state with much-needed qualified teachers. When the state moved to require college degrees, Edinboro changed its curriculum to confer bachelor's degrees. When graduate degrees gained importance, Edinboro added those to the curriculum. In short, Edinboro has mirrored the development of public higher education in Pennsylvania.

The school has also witnessed the Civil War, World War I, the Great Depression, World War II, the Vietnam War, and the Civil Rights Movement. Enrollment has dipped and peaked to reflect the economy and the needs of the military.

Just as the school has had four stages of development, this book is divided into four chapters covering the normal school years, the state teachers college years, the state college years, and the university years. Each designation represented a significant change in curriculum and in degrees conferred.

The first and longest chapter shows the least visible part of Edinboro's history and presents the foundations upon which the school sits. The connection between the community and school were built here, before it became a college. As an academy and then as a normal school, Edinboro taught students to become teachers in a time before teachers needed a college degree. To many, these schools were considered akin to a trade school.

Chapter two establishes the post-secondary school years. Until the state started requiring a bachelor's degree for teaching, a normal certificate was all one needed. To keep up with the change in requirements, Edinboro became a state teachers college and was able to confer college degrees. In 1928, the Board of State Teachers Colleges approved a curriculum revision that established 136 credit hours for a bachelor's degree, transforming the state normal schools into colleges.

Perhaps the era producing the most growth was its time as a state college. President Tom Miller grew the campus from just over 500 students to nearly 3,000, the grounds expanded to more than 500 acres, and the number of faculty increased from less than 50 to more than 180. Following Miller as president was Chester McNerney, who continued the growth and improved the credentials of the faculty.

The chapter covering the most recent events since Edinboro became a university in 1983 has caused me the most angst. Many people have different ideas on what has been most important in these years. It is, by design, the shortest chapter, and I choose to comment as little as possible on current events. It is a time period that has yet to have sufficient historical context for us to judge it. I have included the obvious, but otherwise, I am ready to hear the opinion of others.

Much has taken place in the last 155 years. The school has shined as a provider of affordable and quality education for the people of Pennsylvania. It has met the needs of the state while weathering a number of challenges, including wars, depressions, and continuous reductions in state support. The school has persevered because it has a character and life born from its history—a history all members of the Edinboro University community continue to build upon.

All of the materials for this book have come from the archives and special collections department of the Baron-Forness Library.

One

Academy and Normal School Years 1857–1927

Edinboro was a much different place in 1856. There was a sawmill, a grain mill, a few dirt roads, and farmland. The town center offered three stores: a grocery, a dry goods store, and a general store. There were three physicians and a veterinarian. For travelers, the Robinson House offered rooms for rent. One-room schoolhouses dotted the countryside, usually on a farmer's property. Transportation was by horse-drawn carriage, and oxen were used for pulling plows.

For the people of Edinboro, education beyond the primary years was available in the next town at Waterford Academy. Some of the leading citizens of Edinboro, including James Reeder, Isaac Taylor, and Andrew Proudfit, had children attending Waterford Academy. Traveling 10 miles to Waterford was, at the very least, an inconvenience.

To address the problem, town leaders agreed to form a corporation for the purpose of establishing an academy. A charter was drawn up and approved by the court of common pleas in 1856. After that, it was necessary to raise the funds to build a school and hire teachers. A subscription from the community was initiated to secure the money. Each person who gave money became a stockholder and was entitled to vote for or even hold office as a trustee of the school.

Once the money was raised, Nathaniel Austin was hired to build what is known today as Academy Hall. Joel Merriman, who had been teaching in Waterford, was brought on as the first principal, and the school opened on December 15, 1857.

The school progressed under the governance of the elected trustees until 1914. Up to that time, the school had received support from the state by way of tuition reimbursements for the students. Direct support did not come until the state purchased the property from the shareholders in 1914. While this represented a watershed in governance, the mission of the school would not change until 1927, when Edinboro State Normal School became Edinboro State Teachers College.

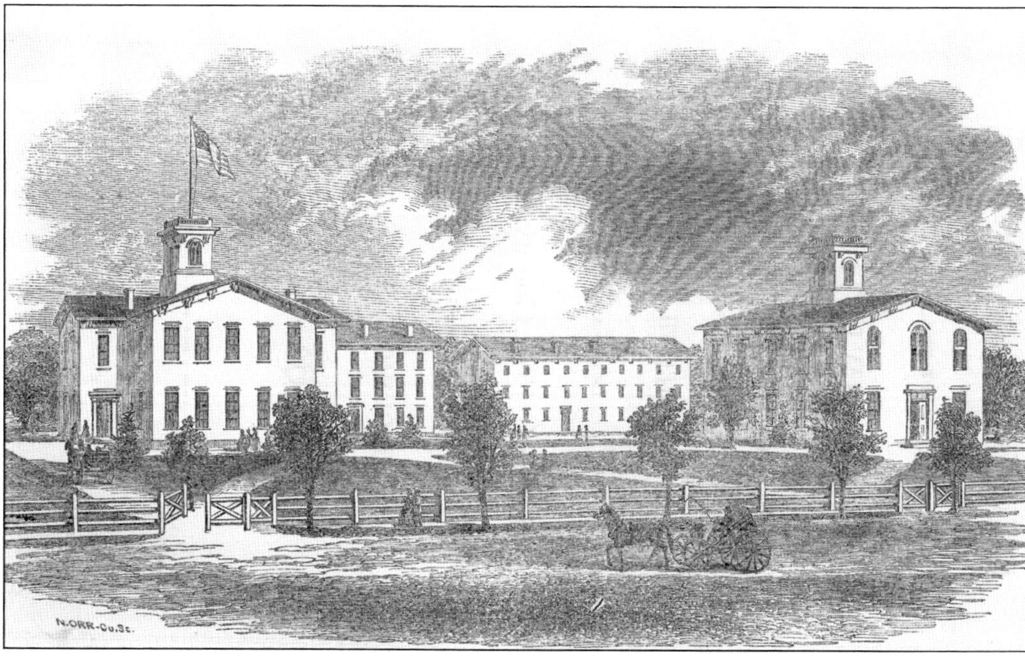

This woodcut of the Edinboro campus is from the 1861–1862 catalog. It shows Academy Hall (originally named Austin Hall after the builder) in its original position facing Meadville Street. To the right, or south, is Assembly Hall. The North and South Hall dormitories are behind. In all, there were four buildings and 10 acres.

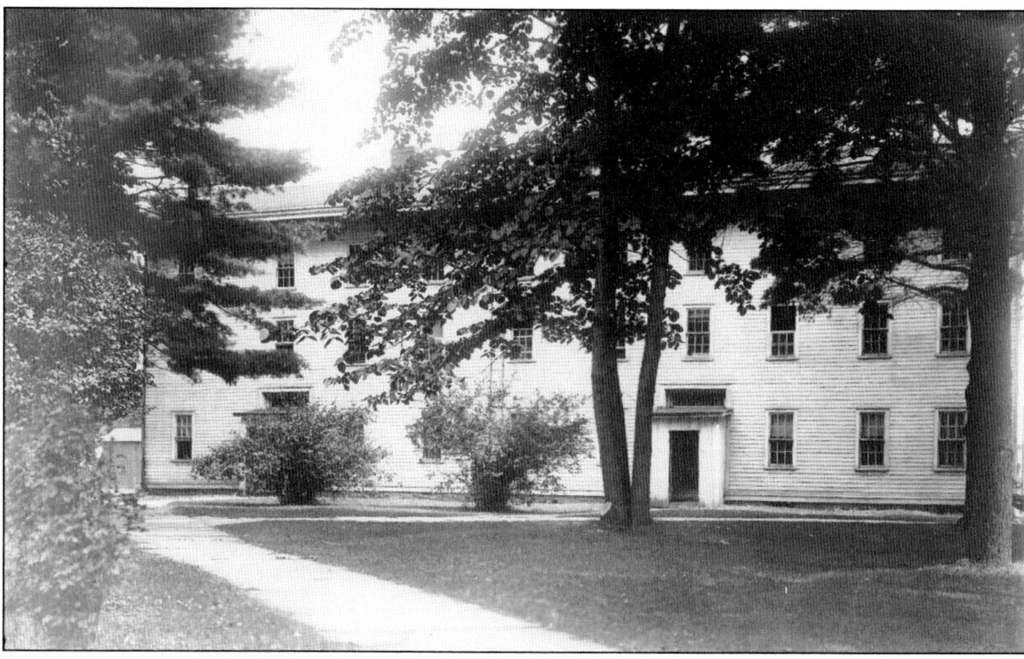

North Hall is seen here around 1916. Originally built in 1858 to meet the requirements of becoming a state normal school, North and South Hall were mirror images of one another. When built, the rooms were heated by small woodstoves, which also served as small cooking stoves.

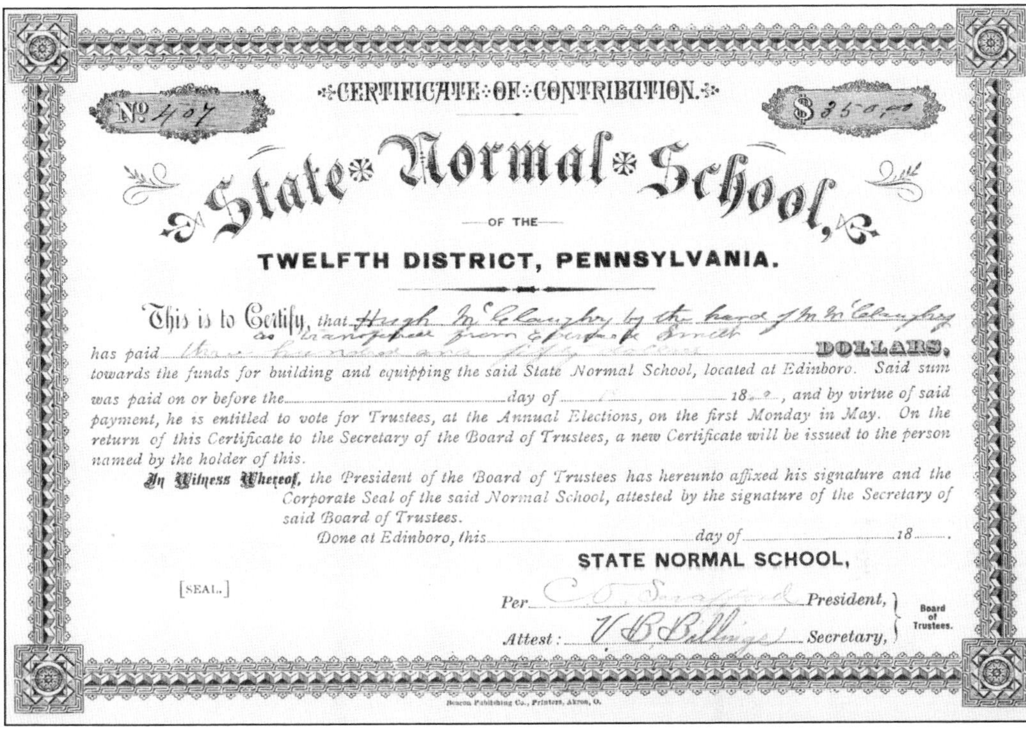

CERTIFICATE OF CONTRIBUTION.

№ 407 $350

State Normal School,

OF THE

TWELFTH DISTRICT, PENNSYLVANIA.

This is to Certify, that ________ has paid ________ DOLLARS, towards the funds for building and equipping the said State Normal School, located at Edinboro. Said sum was paid on or before the ________ day of ________ 18__, and by virtue of said payment, he is entitled to vote for Trustees, at the Annual Elections, on the first Monday in May. On the return of this Certificate to the Secretary of the Board of Trustees, a new Certificate will be issued to the person named by the holder of this.

In Witness Whereof, the President of the Board of Trustees has hereunto affixed his signature and the Corporate Seal of the said Normal School, attested by the signature of the Secretary of said Board of Trustees.

Done at Edinboro, this ________ day of ________ 18__.

STATE NORMAL SCHOOL,

[SEAL.]

Per ________ President, } Board of Trustees.

Attest: ________ Secretary, }

Beacon Publishing Co., Printers, Akron, O.

This Certificate of Contribution was the stock receipt Edinboro citizens received when they contributed to the school. This one was issued in 1892. As a stockholder, a person was eligible to vote and run for board of trustees of the school.

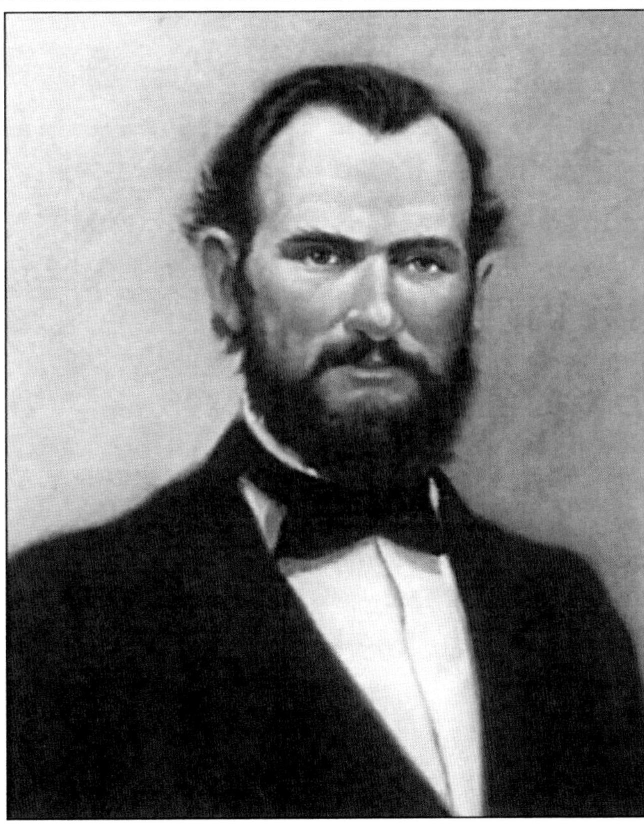

Edinboro Academy's first principal was Joel R. Merriman, recruited from Waterford Academy, where the children of some prominent Edinboro citizens attended. The school opened December 15, 1857, with 110 children and teenagers attending. Merriman left the school in 1860 to pursue the Baptist ministry.

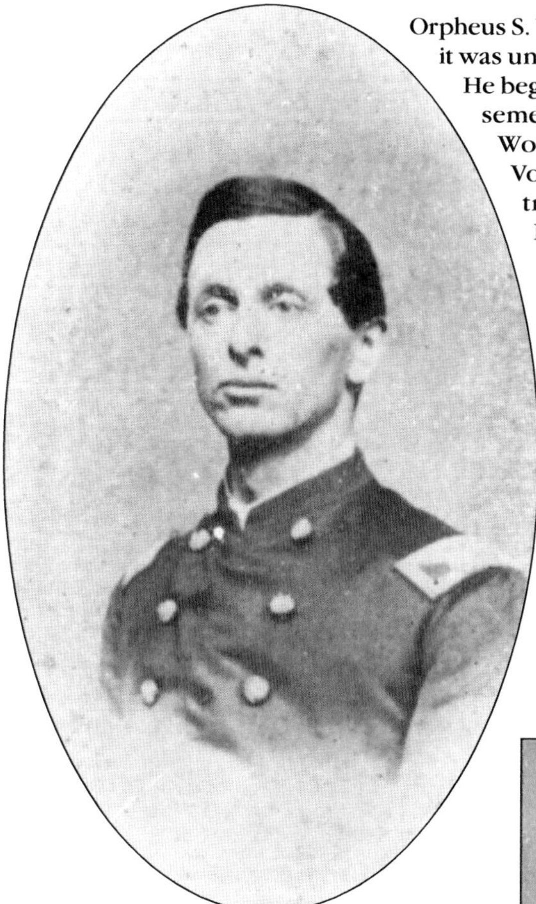

Orpheus S. Woodward entered Waterford Academy while it was under the direction of principal Joel Merriman. He began teaching at Edinboro in 1858, and for one semester (spring 1860), he served as principal. Woodward joined the 83rd Pennsylvania Volunteers in 1861 as a captain, leading his troops at Gettysburg into the fighting at Little Round Top after Col. Strong Vincent was fatally wounded. Together with the 20th Maine and 44th New York, they held the flank, which was critical to the success of the Union. Woodward was promoted to colonel after the Mine Run campaign and to general after the Battle of Wilderness, where he lost a leg.

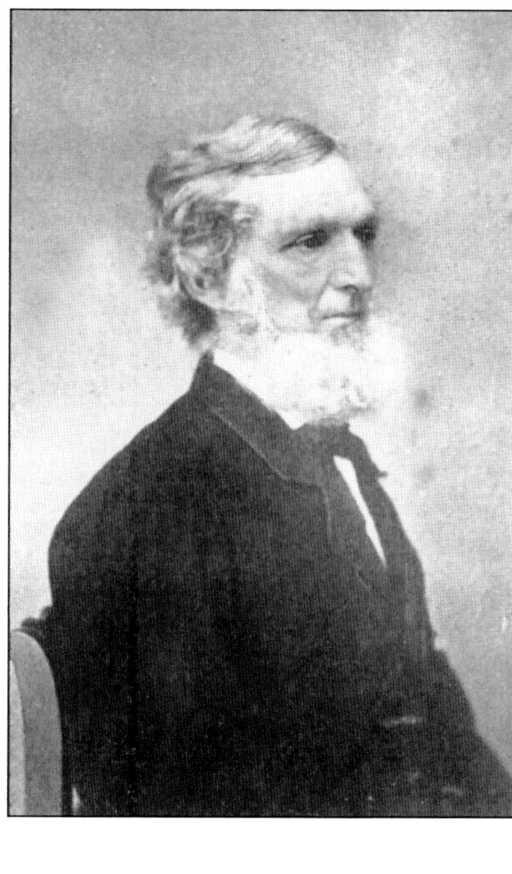

James Thompson became principal of Edinboro Academy in fall 1860. The school was recognized as a state normal school in 1861, and the name was changed to Edinboro State Normal School. Thompson remained principal until 1863.

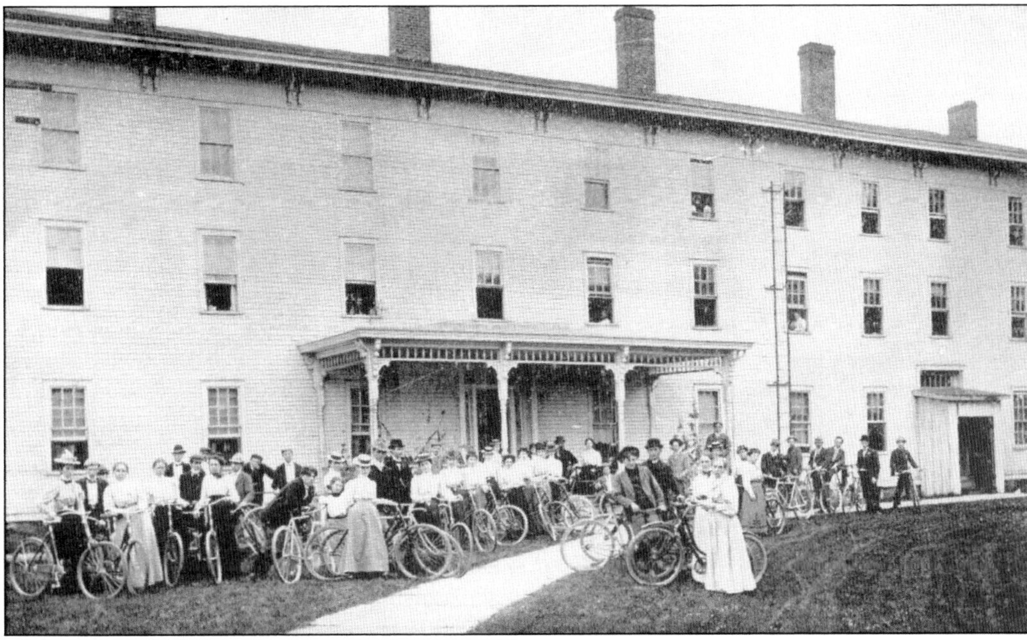

Bicycling was a popular pastime in the late 1800s, and Edinboro students formed a club around the activity. Here, a large group of cyclists poses in front of one of the dormitories. Modesty dictated that the women in skirts had bloomers underneath.

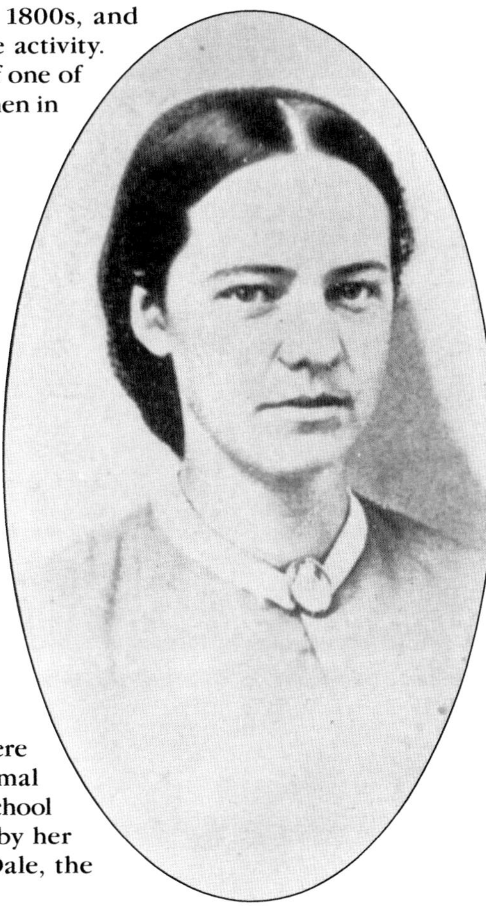

Sallie Reeder, seen here, and her sister Louise were the first two graduates of Edinboro State Normal School in 1862. They both taught in the normal school for three years. Sallie's career was cut short by her untimely death. Louise married Charles H. Dale, the county superintendent of Venango schools.

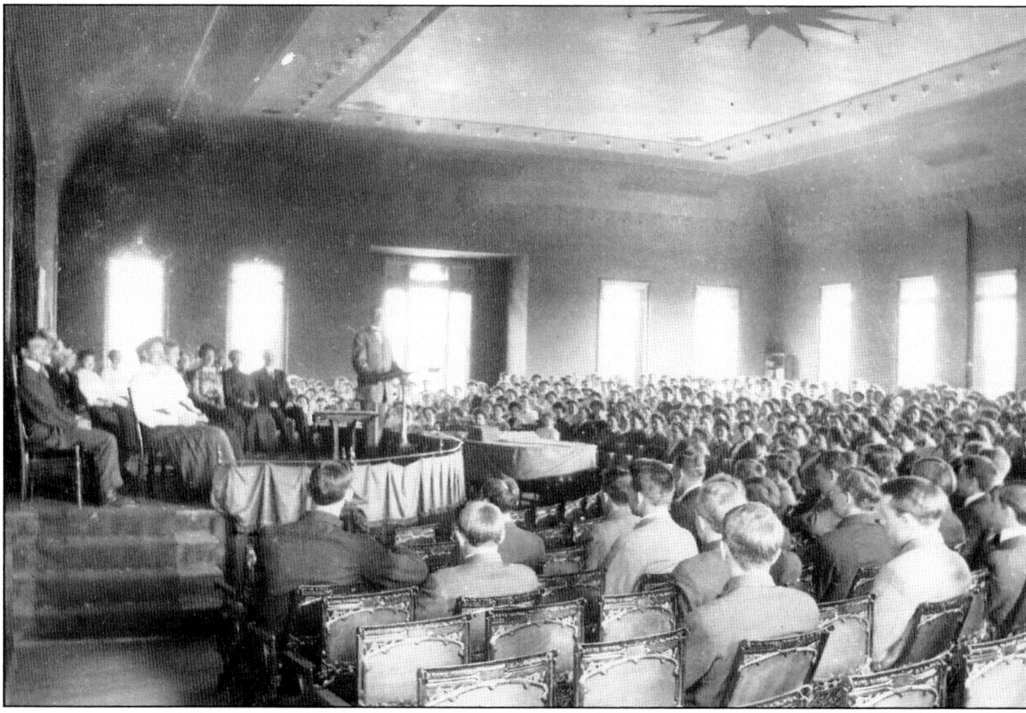

In the earliest years, students were required to attend chapel every day for the opening exercises. According to the 1877 school catalogue, "Students are required to attend a daily chapel service at 8 a.m. and are invited to attend a half-hour prayer meeting at 6 p.m." These were held in Normal Hall's auditorium, with the faculty sitting on the stage and the students in their assigned seats. Notice that the men and women were seated apart in this photograph from around 1910.

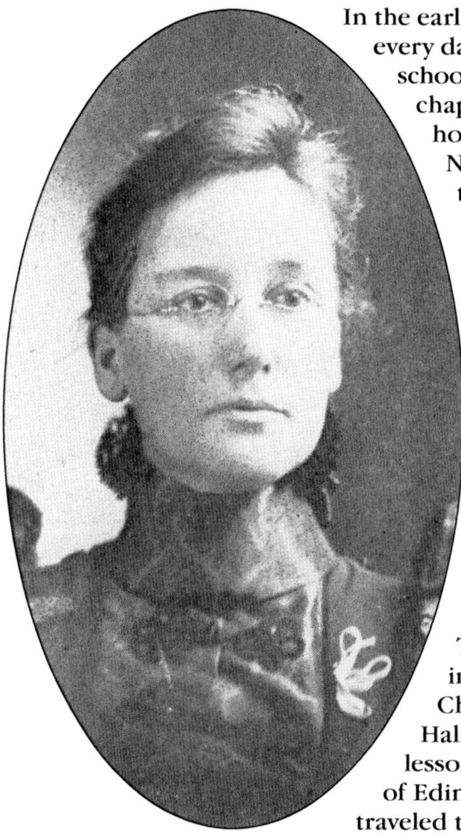

The temperance movement was very much alive in Edinboro. In 1886, a convention of the Women's Christian Temperance Union was held in Assembly Hall. Rachel Benn gave a demonstration of a temperance lesson with a group of kindergarten children. A graduate of Edinboro, Benn went on to get a medical degree and traveled to China to do missionary work.

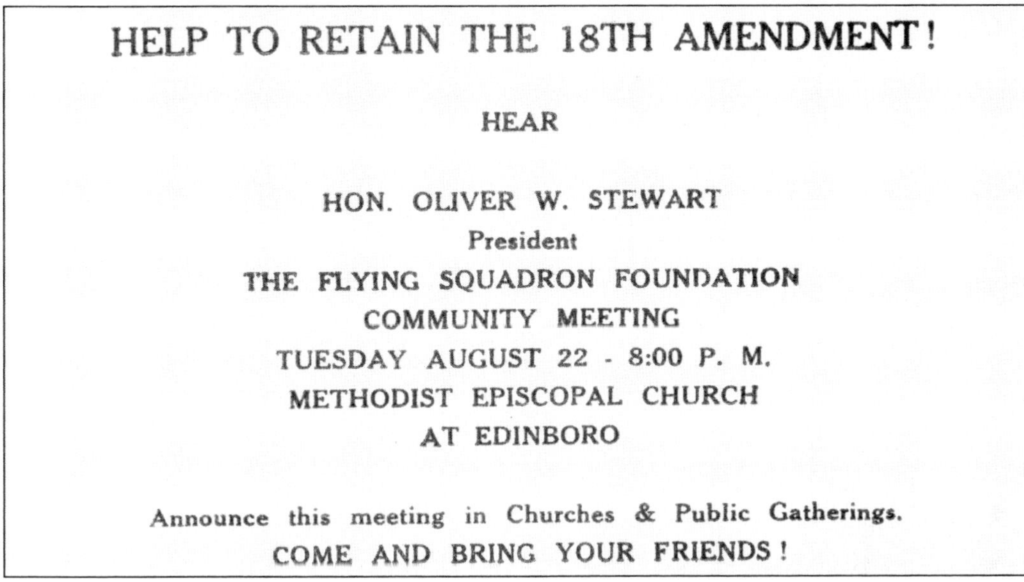

HELP TO RETAIN THE 18TH AMENDMENT!

HEAR

HON. OLIVER W. STEWART

President

THE FLYING SQUADRON FOUNDATION

COMMUNITY MEETING

TUESDAY AUGUST 22 - 8:00 P. M.

METHODIST EPISCOPAL CHURCH

AT EDINBORO

Announce this meeting in Churches & Public Gatherings.

COME AND BRING YOUR FRIENDS!

In the 1880s, the school had a student branch of the Women's Christian Temperance Union. Nancy Taylor, the wife of one of the school's trustees, was president of the Erie County Temperance Union from 1887 to 1889. Trustees John Proudfit, Henry Lewis, and Isaac N. Taylor were involved in the effort to establish a county constitutional temperance amendment.

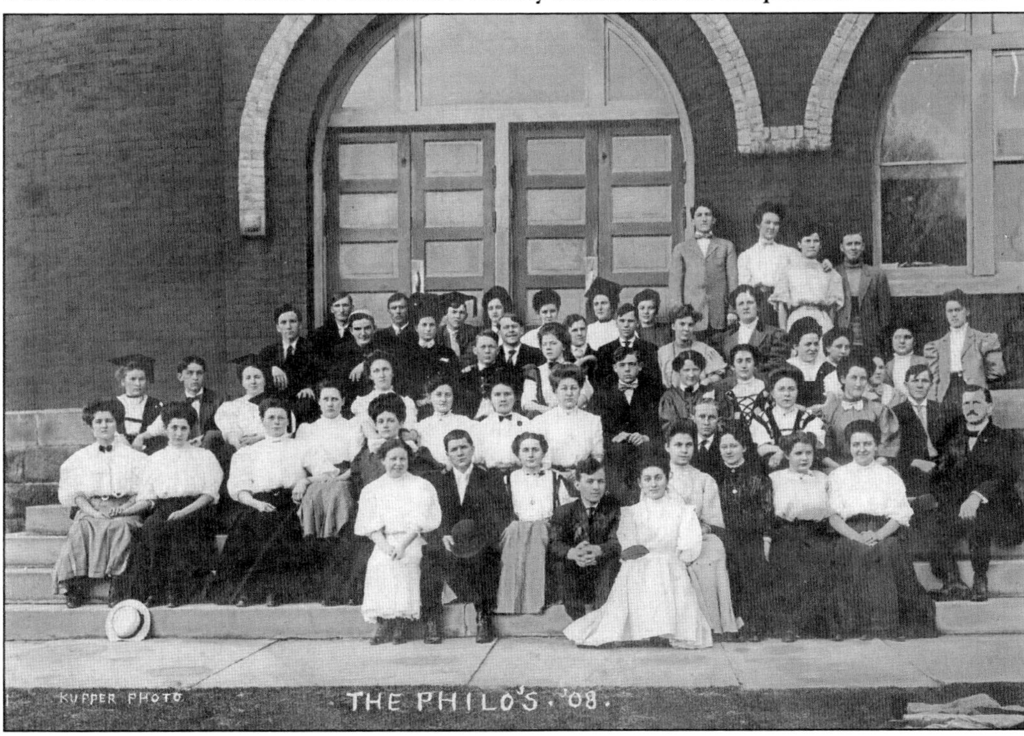

Literary societies were popular on college campuses from the mid-1800s to the early 1900s. The Philos were founded by Samuel Myron Brainerd, who later partnered in a law office in Erie. In 1882, Brainerd was elected to the 48th Congress, serving one term. This photograph shows the Philo Everett Society in 1908.

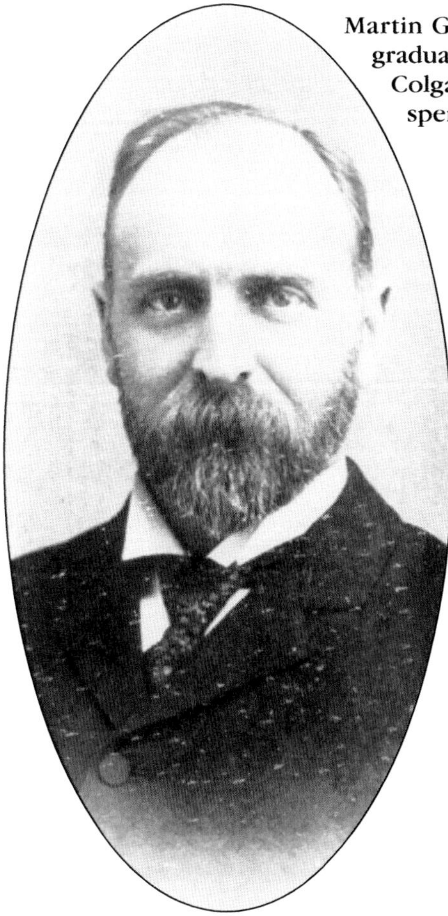

Martin G. Benedict took the reigns of the school in 1892. A graduate of Allegheny College, Benedict received a PhD from Colgate University. Before becoming principal, Benedict spent time as a teacher in the normal school.

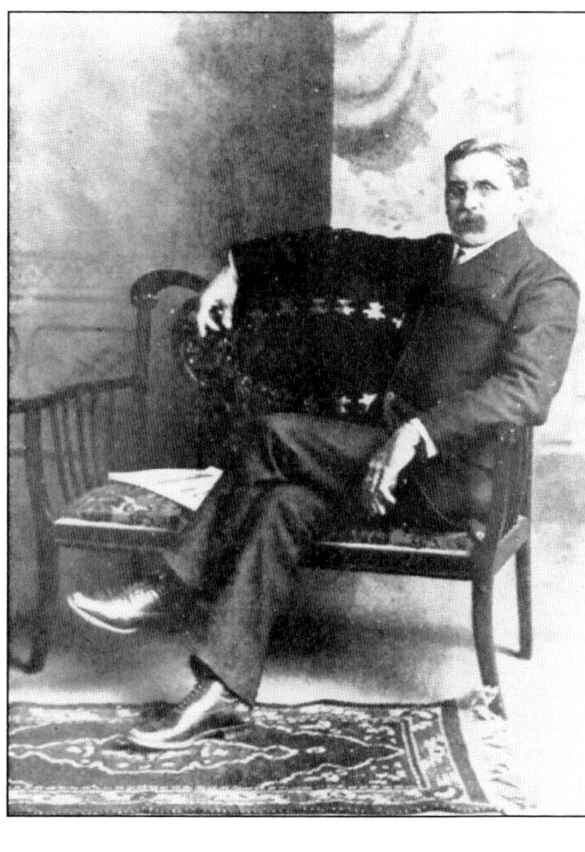

John R. Flickinger became principal in 1896 after receiving his master of arts degree from Princeton University. During the short time he was at Edinboro, Flickinger received a salary of $2,250 plus housing. He left Edinboro on January 1, 1900, to become the principal of Central Normal School at Lock Haven.

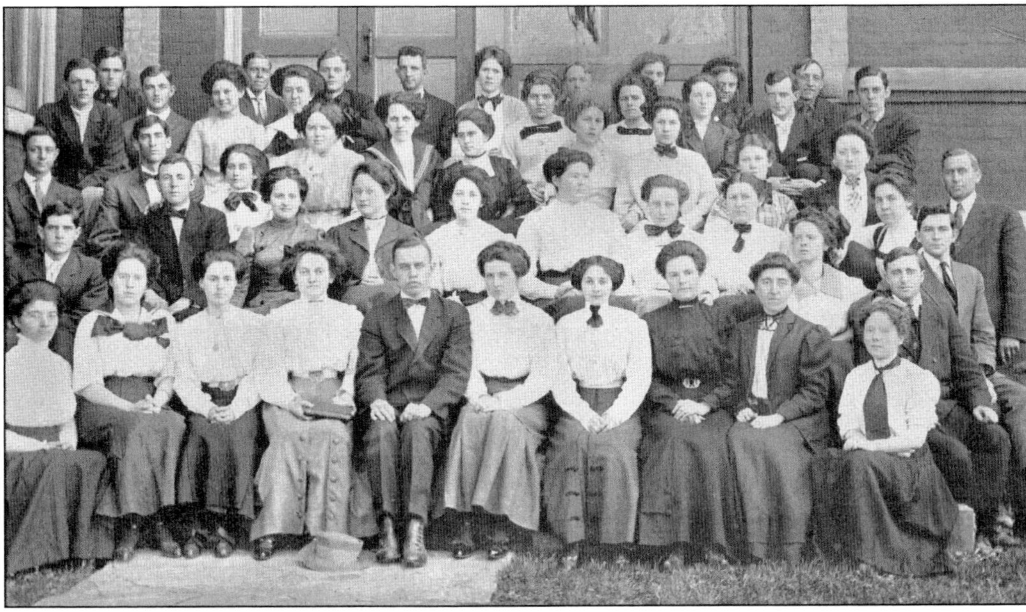

The Potter Literary Society was established in 1862, just one year after the school became a state normal school. Regular meetings were held on Saturday afternoons until about 1901, when they moved to Monday evenings. The meetings consisted of readings, oratories, and music. As part of the normal school curriculum, students had a required number of recitations to give. The literary societies provided a platform for them. This 1910 photograph shows the membership with one person in front symbolically holding a book.

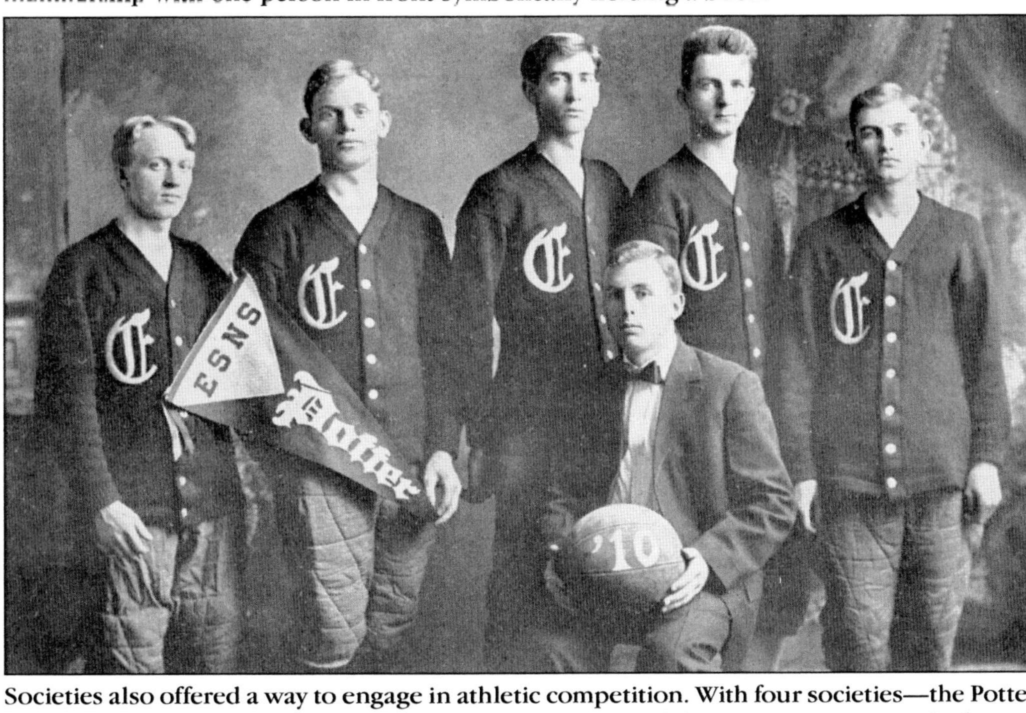

Societies also offered a way to engage in athletic competition. With four societies—the Potter Society, the Philo Everett Society, the Clionian Society, and the Agonian Society—the league was small, but winning carried hefty bragging rights.

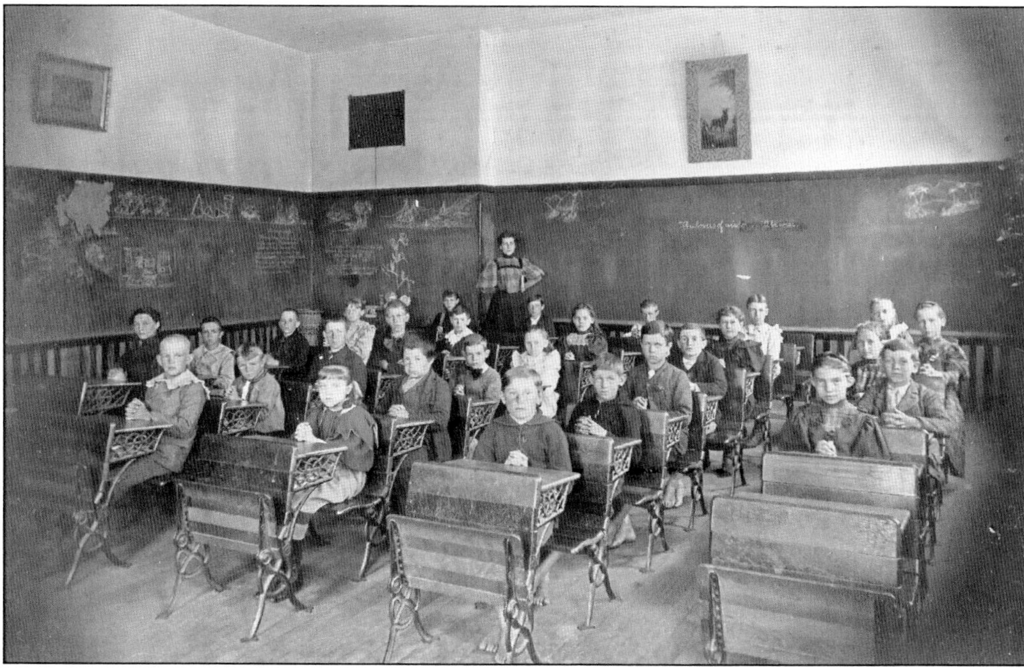

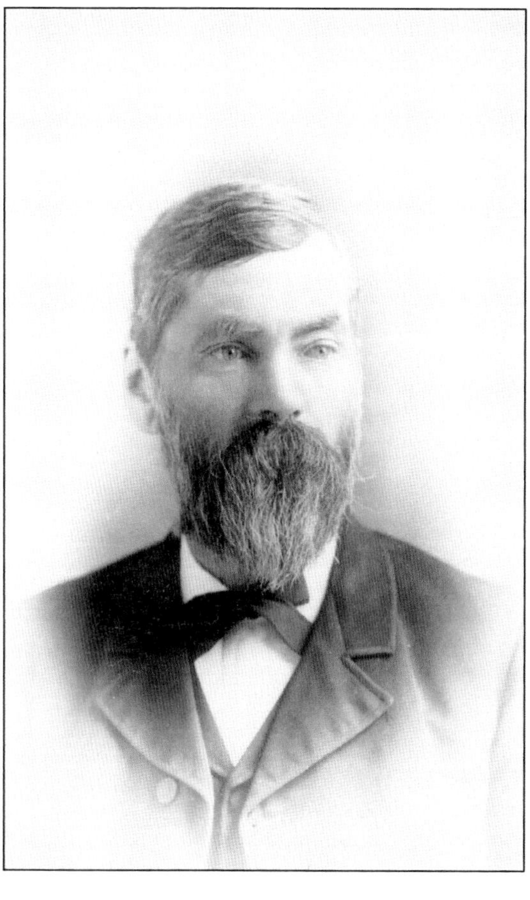

As a normal school, or a teacher training school, students were required to have student teaching experience. Travel options at the time meant that Edinboro needed a model school to accommodate this requirement. This 1880 photograph shows the youngsters in their classroom in Normal Hall. The model school was housed in Academy Hall before being moved to Normal Hall, referred to at the time as "New Building," in 1875. Notice the barefoot boys seated in the second row from the right.

Joseph Cooper served as principal of Edinboro Normal School from 1863 to 1892. Beloved by the students and faculty, his tenure ended poorly with the board of trustees accusing him of "acts and conduct of an immoral character." According to Cooper, he was accused of stealing $2,000. Six faculty members who supported Cooper were also dismissed, but they refused to leave and held the board to their contracts. The students left en masse, with many transferring to Clarion. In 1892, there were 240 students; the next year, there were only 83.

Accused of misdoings, principal Joseph Cooper was dismissed in 1892, after 32 years of service to the school. He was accused of mishandling funds and stealing $2,000 out of the school safe. Cooper strongly defended himself, pointing to numerous inaccuracies in the charges against him and shifting blame to other possible thieves; nevertheless, his dismissal caused a deep chasm in the community for years between pro-Cooper and anti-Cooper contingents.

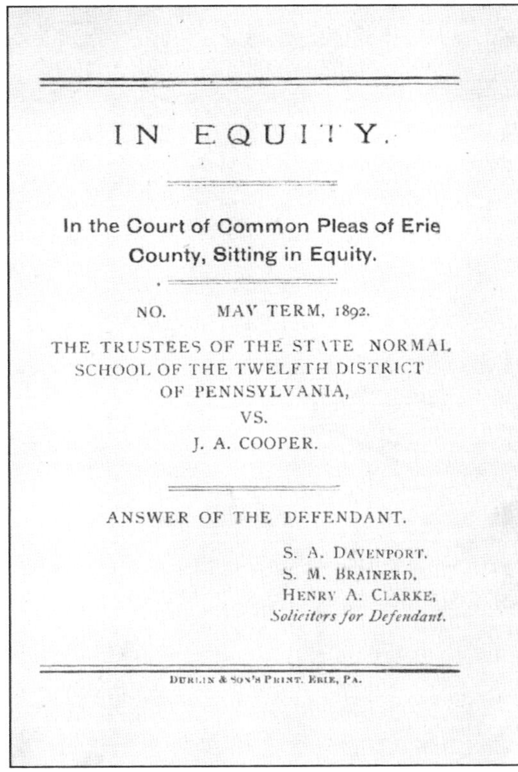

IN EQUITY.

In the Court of Common Pleas of Erie County, Sitting in Equity.

NO. MAY TERM, 1892.

THE TRUSTEES OF THE STATE NORMAL SCHOOL OF THE TWELFTH DISTRICT OF PENNSYLVANIA,
VS.
J. A. COOPER.

ANSWER OF THE DEFENDANT.

S. A. DAVENPORT,
S. M. BRAINERD,
HENRY A. CLARKE,
Solicitors for Defendant.

DURLIN & SON'S PRINT, ERIE, PA.

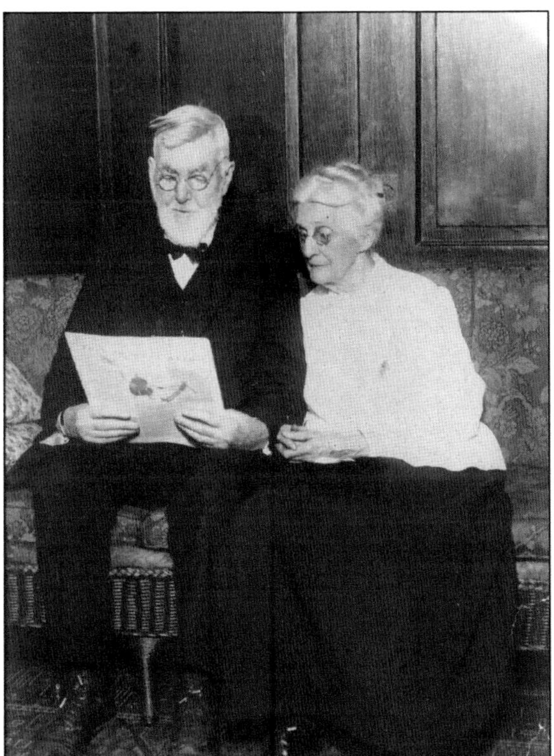

Principal Joseph Cooper and his wife, Lydia, are seen here around 1920. Some years after his dismissal, the Edinboro Student Association, led by alums judge Thomas Prather and Isaac Ketler, bought Cooper a house at 300 Erie Street. Ketler later founded Grove City College.

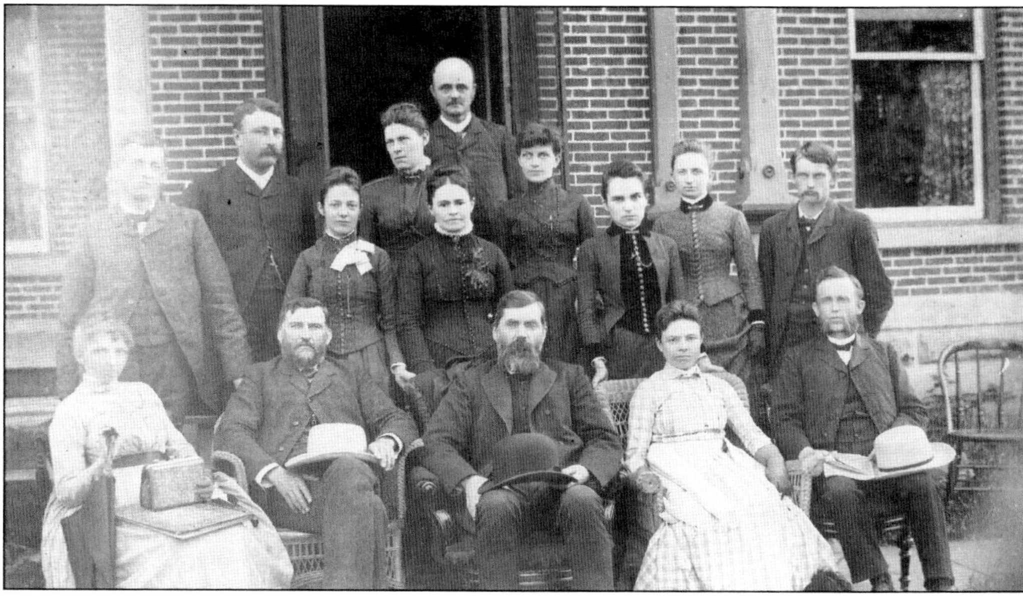

In 1887, the faculty was a small group. Principal Cooper is in the center of the first row, holding his hat. On the far left holding an umbrella is Margaret Compton. This is the only photograph identifying her. Today, there is a building named in her honor.

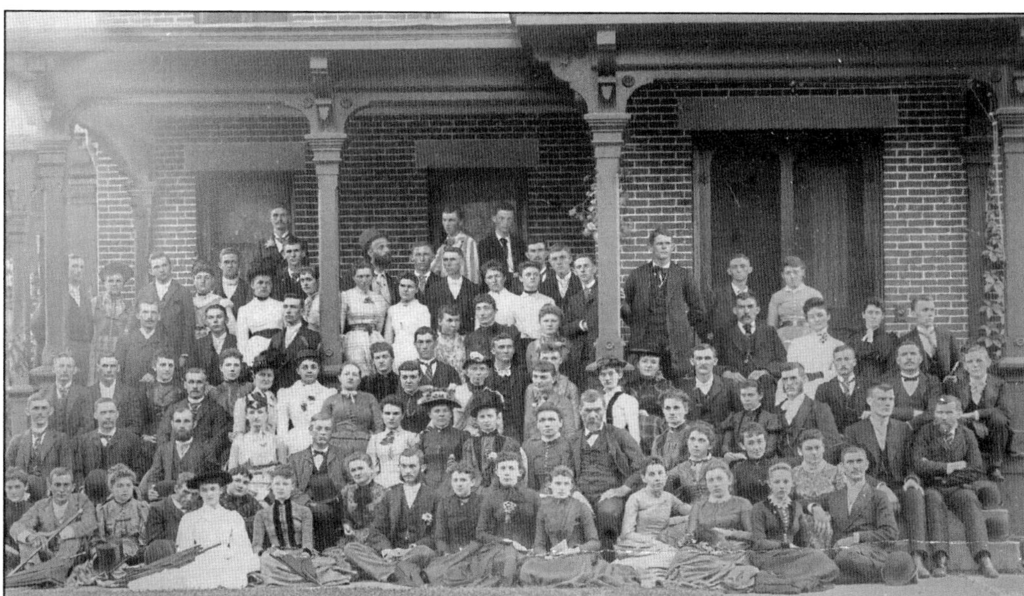

The junior class is seen here in 1890. The school offered two tracts at this time: an elementary course and a normal scientific course. The elementary course was expected to take two years. Graduates of a high school, seminary, or advanced academy could complete the course in one year. It took an additional two years for the scientific course. Before being admitted to the senior class, students had to pass an examination by the state board of examiners.

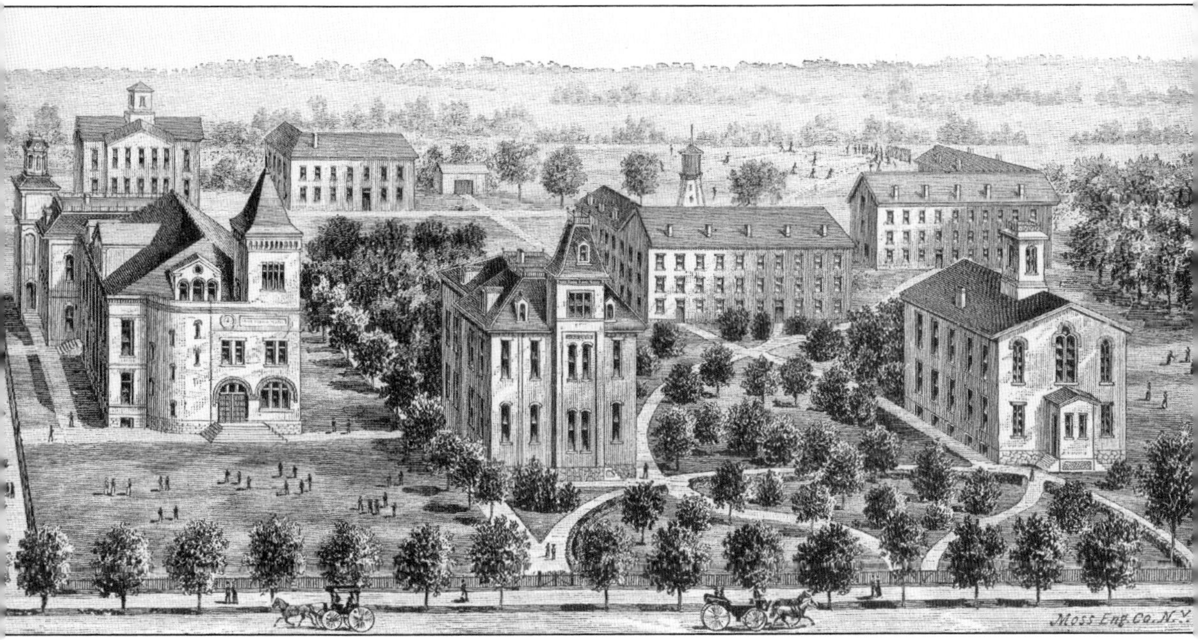

This 1893 view of campus shows significant changes from the original wood cut. Academy Hall was moved back and is behind Normal Hall in this image. Normal Hall was built in two phases, with the original building erected in 1875 and the west wing, the more prominent portion, added in 1890. Standing to the right of Normal Hall is Recitation Hall, the building designed by Principal Joseph Cooper. The numerous chimneys on the dormitories in the upper right of the picture were necessary for the venting of the woodstoves. In the far upper right portion of this engraving, a baseball game is taking place, and a croquet match is in progress in front of Normal Hall.

Schedule of Examinations

Edinboro State Normal School

June 9-10, 1919

SENIORS N-5		JUNIORS N-6
Monday, June 9		
	9:00-10:30	
History of Education Superintendent Jones		U. S. History Superintendent Etters
	10:30-12:00	
Methods in English Superintendent Butterworth		Methods in Geography Superintendent Plasterer
	1:00-2:30	
Arithmetic The Department		Methods in Reading Principal Hertzog
	2:30-4:00	
Methods in Arithmetic Principal Hertzog		Methods in History Superintendent Rapp
	4:00-5:30	
Agriculture and Nature Study Superintendent Rapp		Psychology The Department
Tuesday, June 10		
	9:00-10:30	
Public Speaking Superintendent Jones		School Hygiene Superintendent Butterworth
	10:03-12:00	
Primary Methods Superintendent Etters		Geography Principal Hertzog
Grammar Grade Methods Superintendent Plasterer		
	1:00-2:30	
Grammar Review Superintendent Plasterer		Physiology and Sanitation Superintendent Butterworth
	~~2:30-4:00~~	
Methods in Drawing Superintendent Etters		Principles of Education Superintendent Jones

The state board of examiners arrived on campus in June. Members of the board included the state superintendent of common schools, a deputy, the school principal, a principal from another state normal school, and two superintendents of county schools. Two types of tests were given: one for graduation and the other for advancing to the next grade. Edinboro administered a test beforehand to recommend only those they thought would pass for examination.

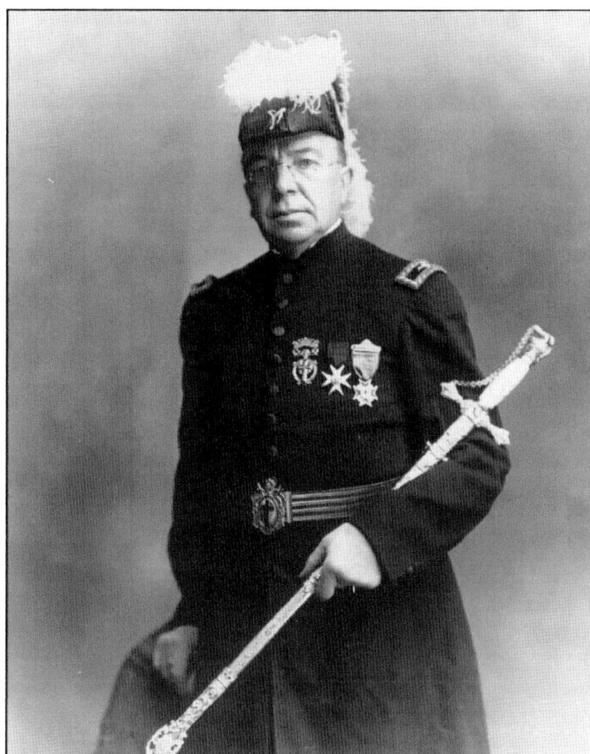

Born in Germersheimer, Germany, in 1864, Lawrence Kupper came to America in the late 1870s or early 1880s. He worked his way across New York as a teacher of shorthand and other commercial subjects and had made his way to Edinboro by 1890, where he took up the photography business. His work documented life in rural Pennsylvania in the late 19th and early 20th centuries. Kupper was also closely allied with the school in a couple ways: he took all the class and yearbook photographs and was on the board of trustees from 1901 to 1904.

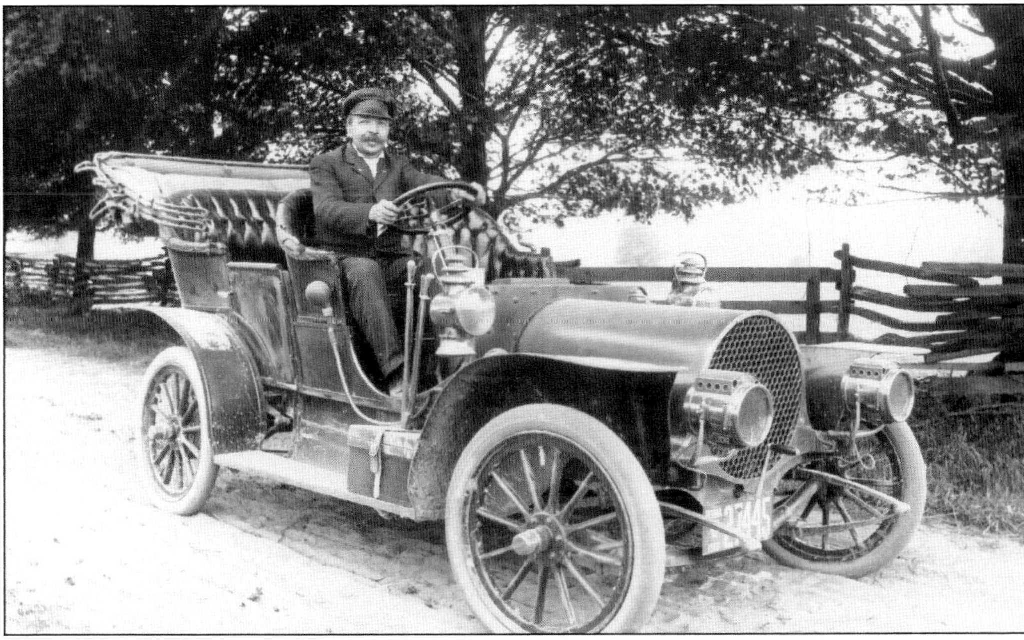

The early roads were rough, but that did not stop Lawrence Kupper from taking this drive. Kupper was a local photographer who did much to document the town and the school; early school catalogs and yearbooks have numerous Kupper photographs.

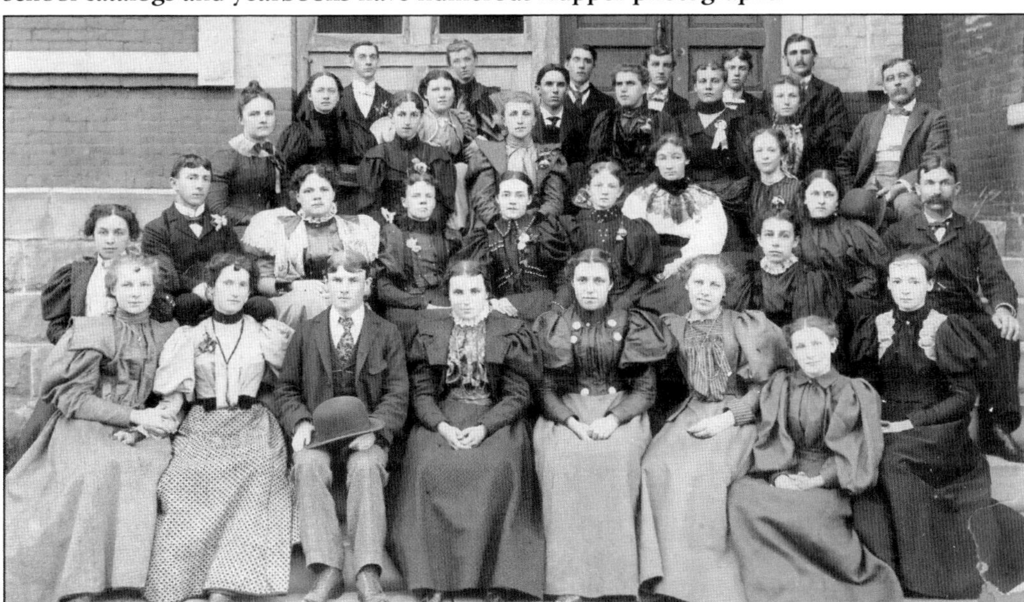

The Normal Guards were formed in 1888, around the same time this class photograph was taken. According to the 1888 catalog, "The battalion consists of three companies. Its officers are elected by the members at the beginning of each term. The armory, which is well filled with the necessary arms and equipments, is under the library . . . This organization has done great good for its members by giving them a more graceful gait in walking, straightening rounded shoulders, developing the military principles of courtesy and discipline, and giving practice in military drill."

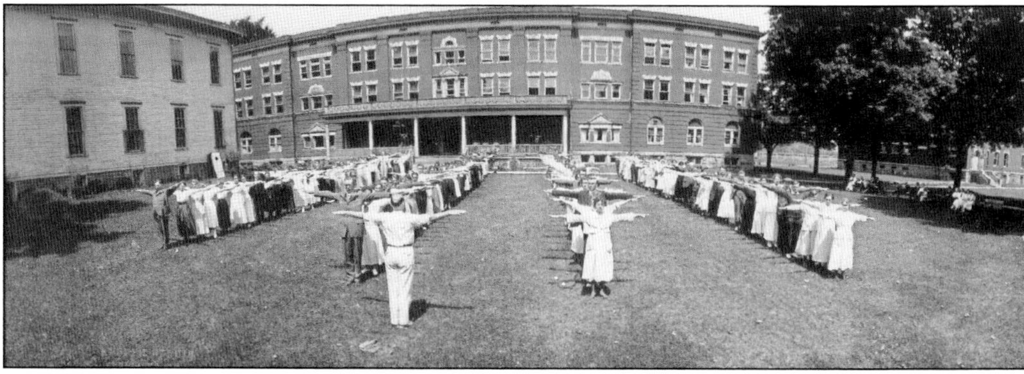

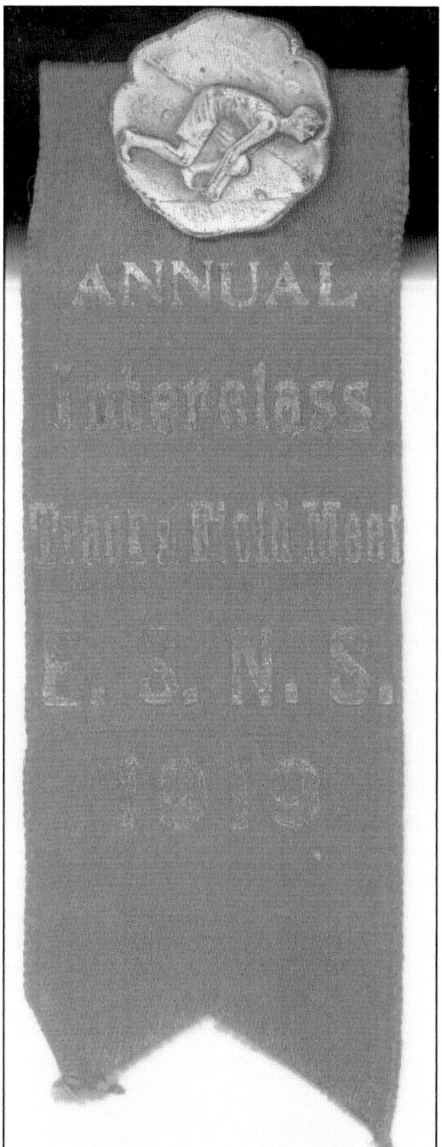

Edinboro has long valued fitness. The 1881 catalog reads, "A thorough and complete education ought to preserve and increase the pupil's bodily health and strength; give him command of his own muscular and mental powers; increase his quickness in perceiving through his five senses, and quicken his mental perception." These fitness exercises took place in front of the ladies dormitory around 1915.

This ribbon and medal is for the annual interclass track and field meet. Medals were given for a number of events as part of Edinboro's philosophy of promoting a healthy mind and body.

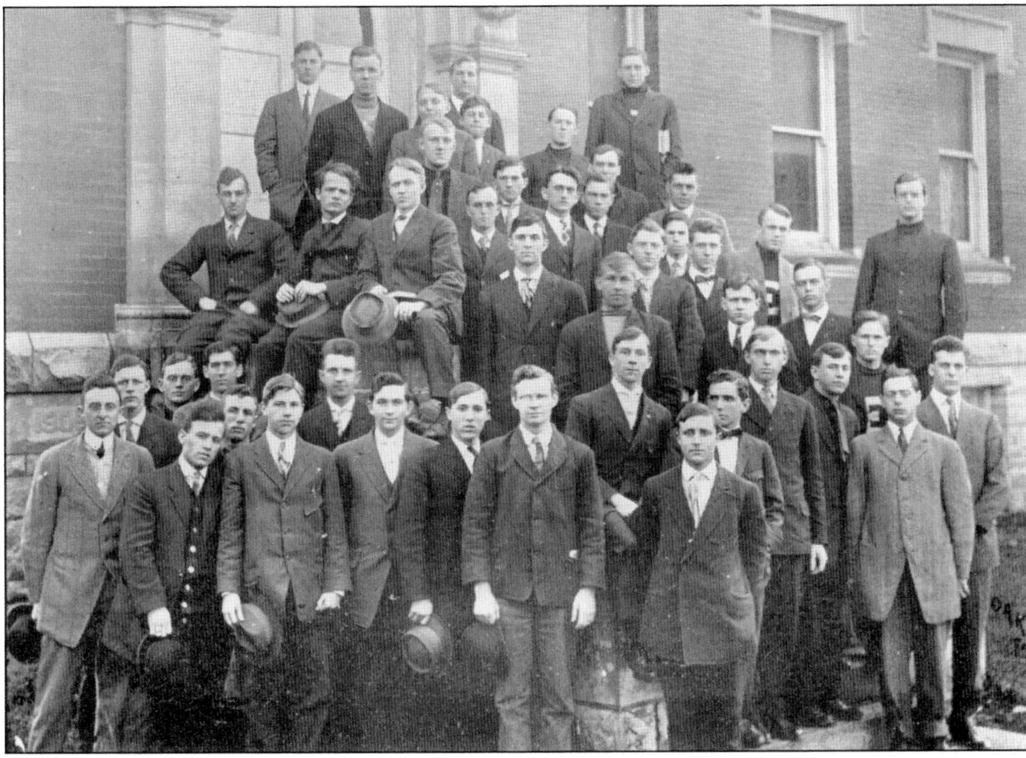

Latin teacher Celia Sherman first organized a YMCA chapter on the Edinboro campus in 1868. Their daily prayer meetings were in addition to the students prayer meetings held every Sunday evening in Normal Hall. The YMCA held their meetings on the first floor of what is now Academy Hall.

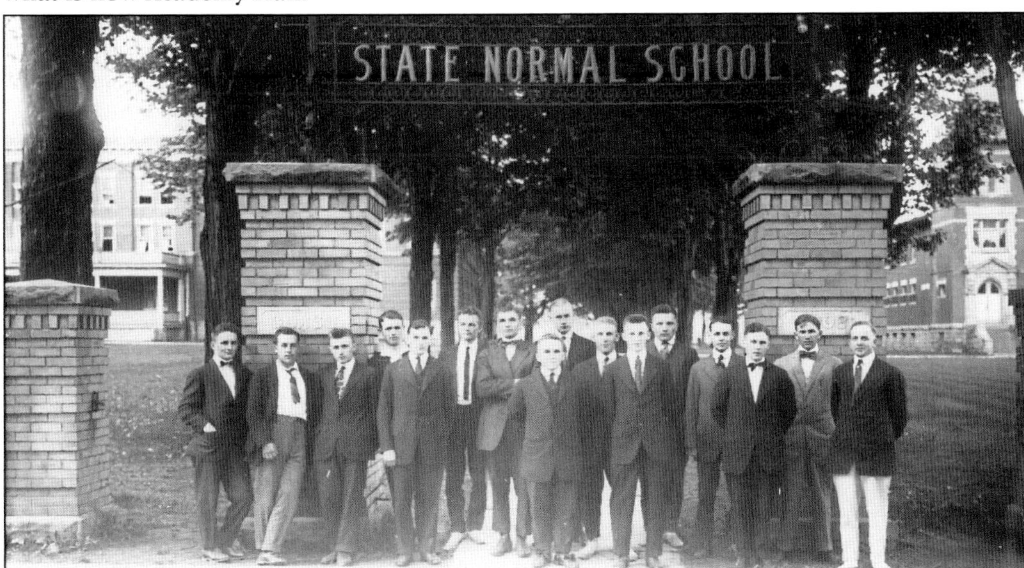

Standing in front of the entrance pillars donated by the class of 1908 is the YMCA, a popular organization among the students. The pillars remain in place, but the "State Normal School" sign is gone.

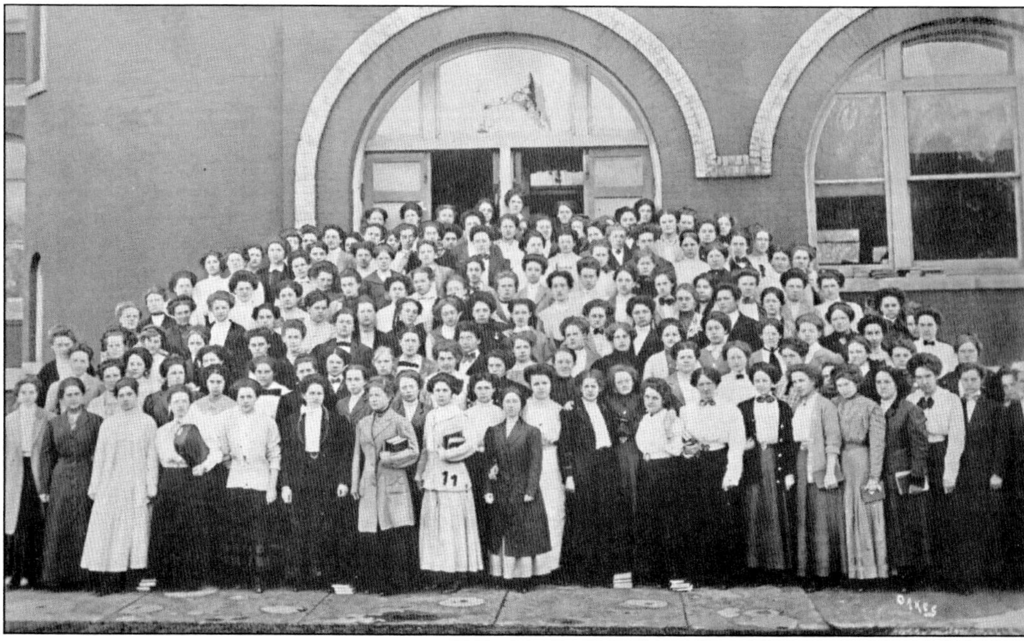

Membership in the YMCA was open to all students and faculty. In fact, it was common to have a faculty member elected president of the organization. By 1880, Edinboro boasted the largest membership of any of the state's normal schools. In 1883, it was decided that a YWCA be carved out of the YMCA.

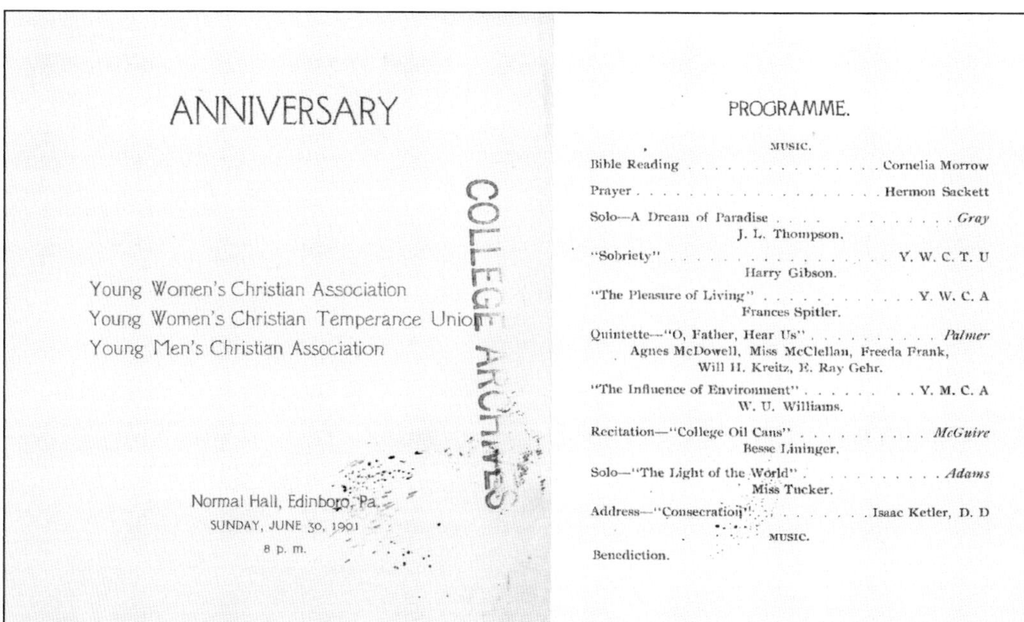

ANNIVERSARY

Young Women's Christian Association
Young Women's Christian Temperance Union
Young Men's Christian Association

Normal Hall, Edinboro, Pa.
SUNDAY, JUNE 30, 1901
8 p. m.

PROGRAMME.

MUSIC.

Bible Reading . . . . Cornelia Morrow
Prayer . . . . Hermon Sackett
Solo—A Dream of Paradise . . . . *Gray*
J. L. Thompson.
"Sobriety" . . . . Y. W. C. T. U
Harry Gibson.
"The Pleasure of Living" . . . . Y. W. C. A
Frances Spitler.
Quintette—"O, Father, Hear Us" . . . . *Palmer*
Agnes McDowell, Miss McClellan, Freeda Frank,
Will H. Kreitz, E. Ray Gehr.
"The Influence of Environment" . . . . Y. M. C. A
W. U. Williams.
Recitation—"College Oil Cans" . . . . *McGuire*
Besse Lininger.
Solo—"The Light of the World" . . . . *Adams*
Miss Tucker.
Address—"Consecration" . . . . Isaac Ketler, D. D

MUSIC.

Benediction.

Today's YMCA programs show little resemblance to this 1901 program. At this time, the activities revolved around the religious. This particular program was a combined program with the YWCA and the Young Women's Christian Temperance Union.

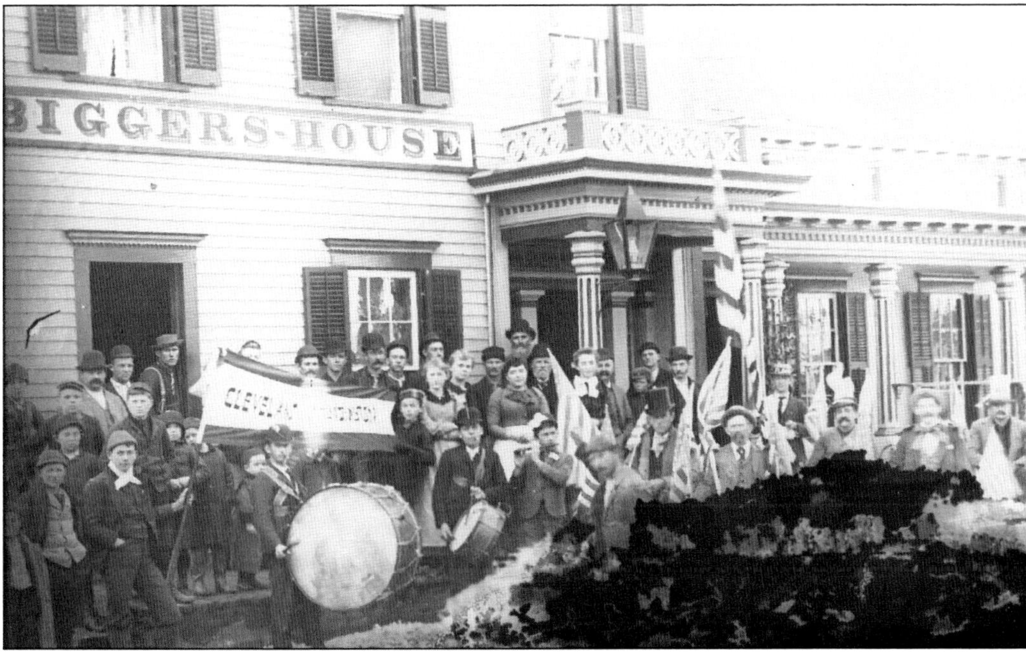

In 1892, Grover Cleveland and Adlai Stevenson ran for president and vice president, and Edinboro joined in the political season with this rally at the Biggers House. Today, the Biggers House holds Edinboro's graduate and grants offices.

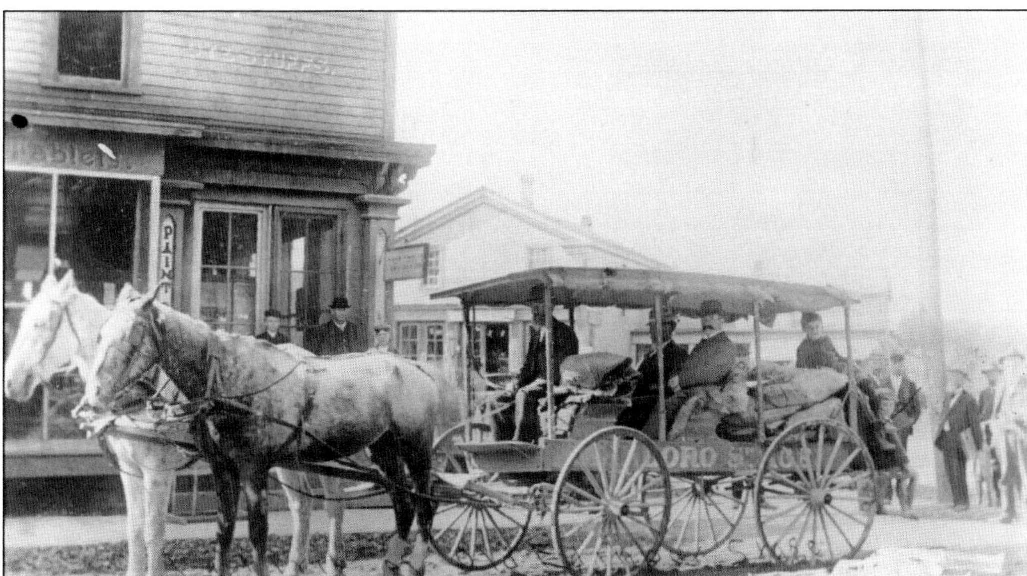

Intercity trolley service came to Edinboro in 1900 and lasted until 1928. Until then, stage and hackney were the mode of transportation in and out of Edinboro. A trip to Erie, 18 miles to the north, took three hours, and a trip south to Cambridge Springs lasted one hour and cost 50¢.

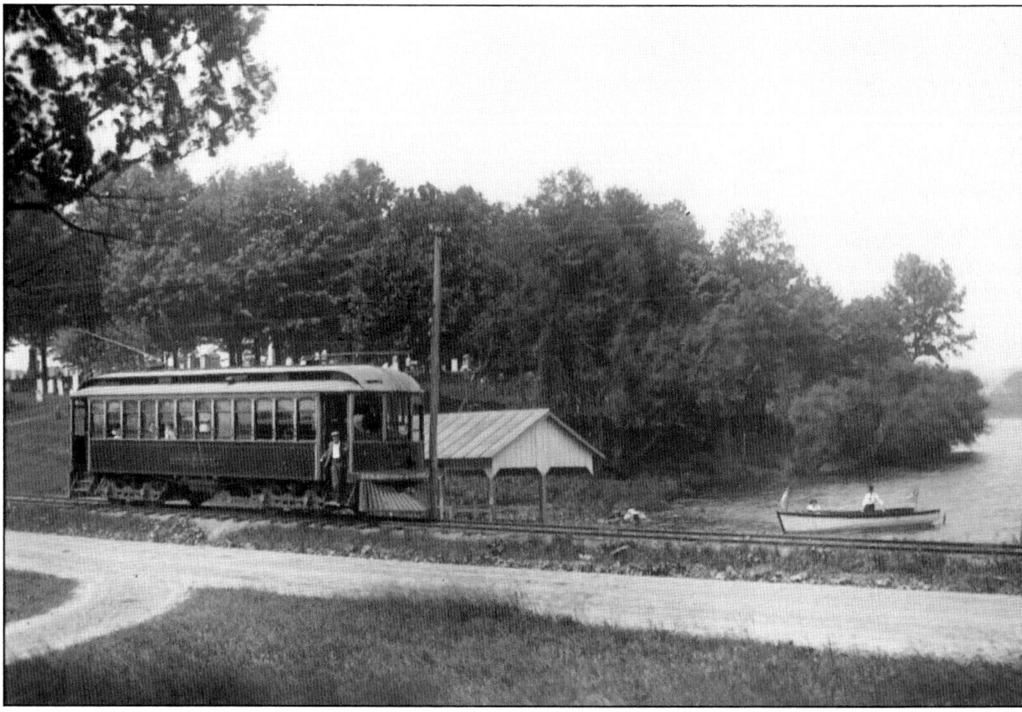

With the introduction of the electric trolley in 1900, it was possible for students to commute from several miles away. Here, the trolley goes north to Erie and passes Edinboro Lake.

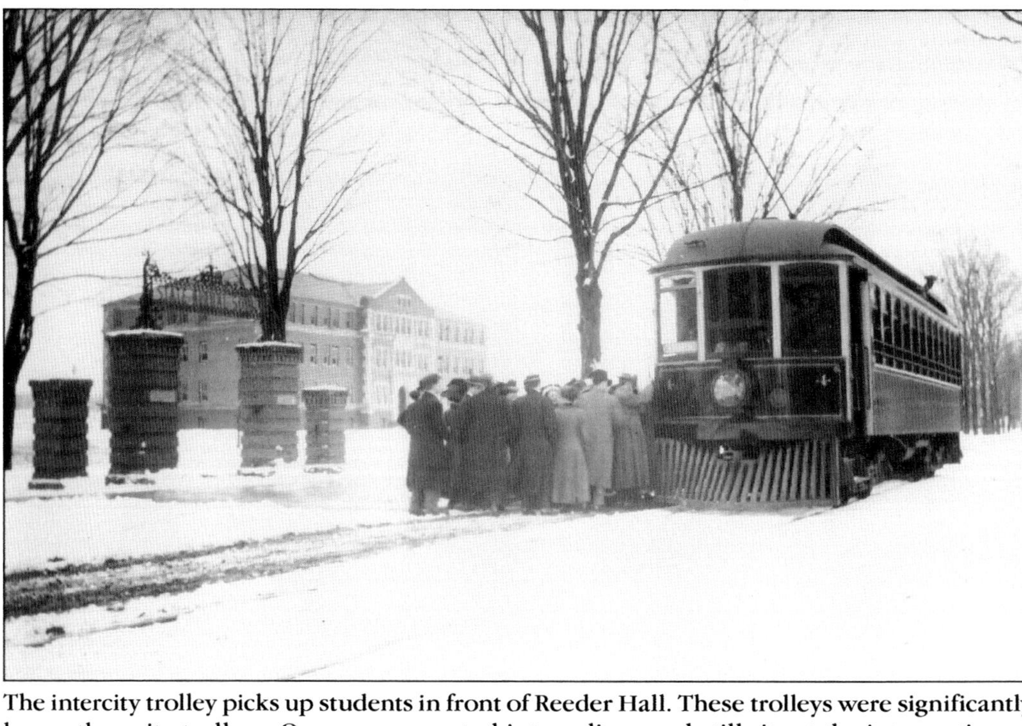

The intercity trolley picks up students in front of Reeder Hall. These trolleys were significantly larger than city trolleys. One was converted into a diner and still sits at the intersection of Route 6N and Route 99.

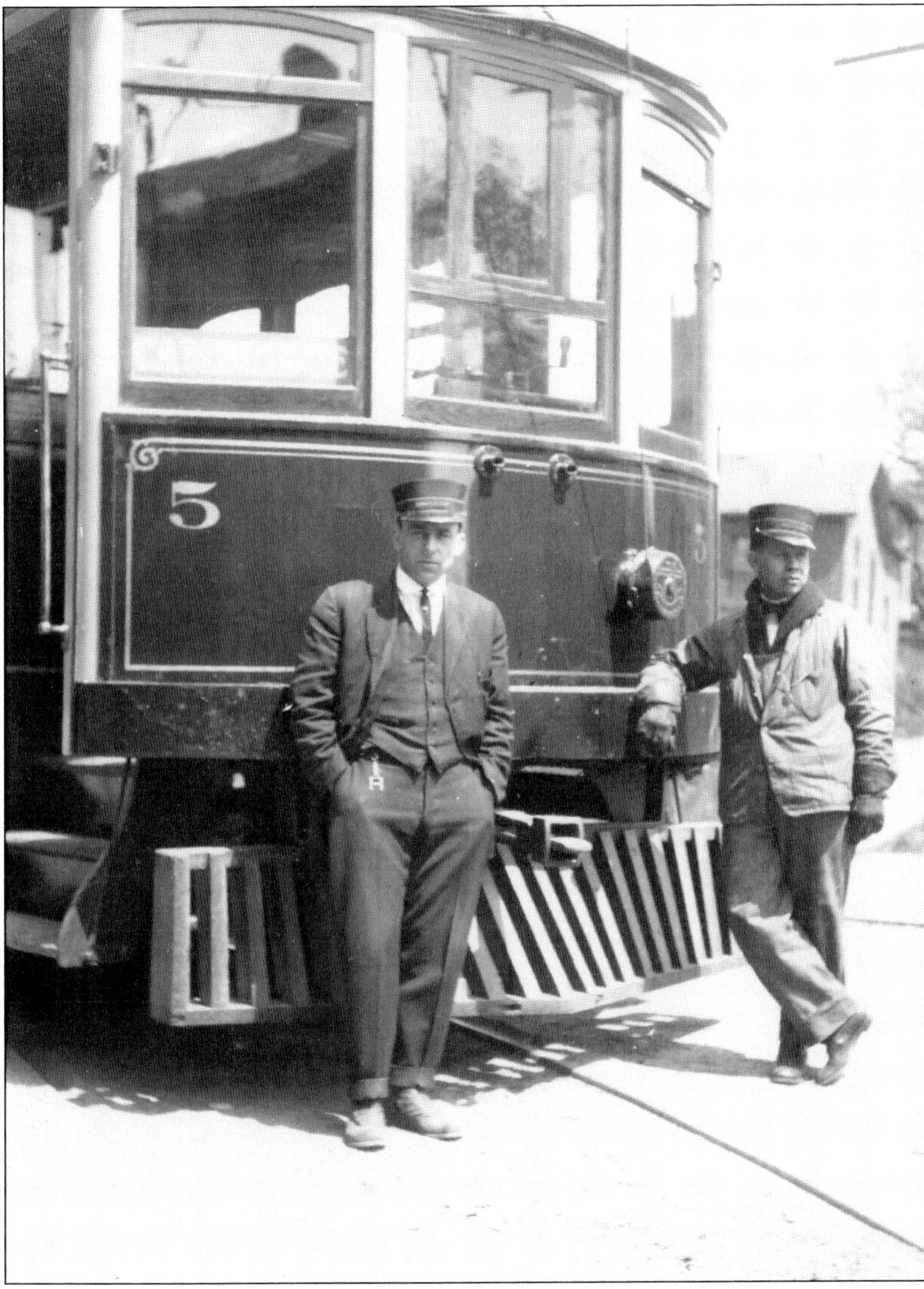

When not coaching Edinboro sports teams, B. Regis "Sox" Harrison (left) was a streetcar conductor. Harrison was an enterprising man, also opening Sunset Camp for boys and girls close to Edinboro Lake on the current site of the Sunset Heights subdivision. Motorman "Blink" Morgan stands next to Harrison.

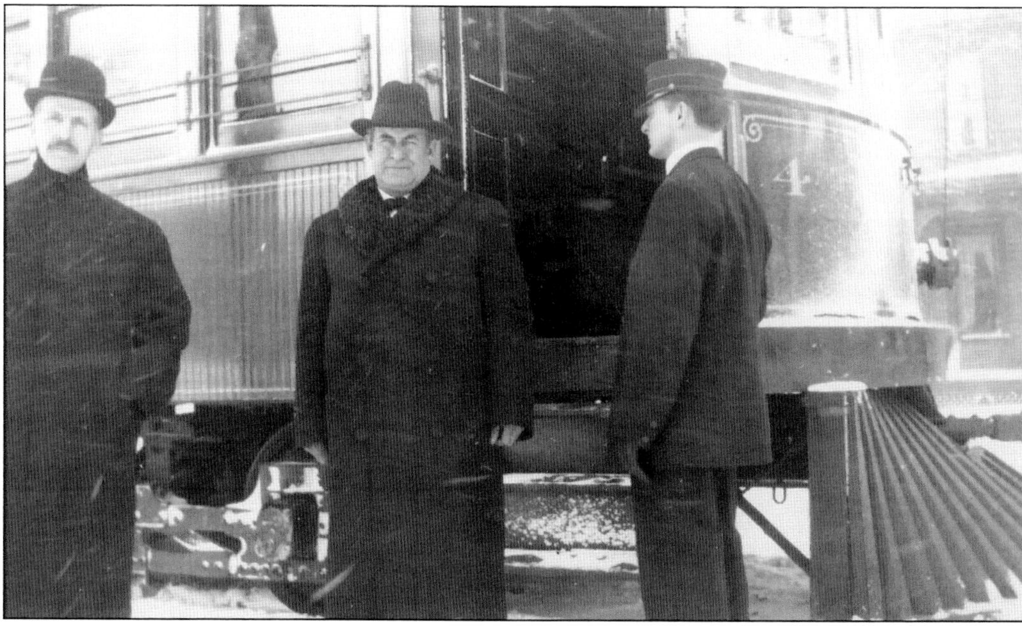

On March 15, 1911, William Jennings Bryan arrived in Edinboro on the intercity trolley. The three-time presidential candidate, best known for his "Cross of Gold" speech, spoke to the students on religion. He was joined on the auditorium stage by four Catholic priests, several Presbyterian ministers, and representatives of other denominations. His speech, titled "Prince of Peace," was delivered again later that day at Erie's Central Presbyterian Church.

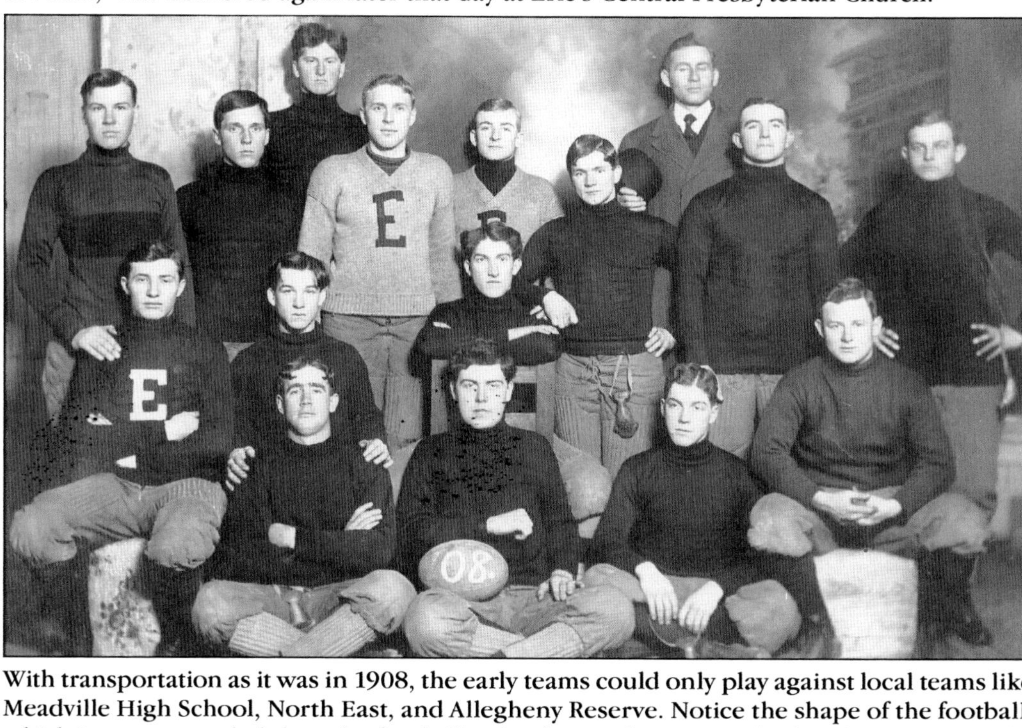

With transportation as it was in 1908, the early teams could only play against local teams like Meadville High School, North East, and Allegheny Reserve. Notice the shape of the football, which is more rounded than the footballs of today. With some quilted padding around the knees and shoulders and a leather helmet, they were ready to go.

Haven Hall was built in 1903 as the ladies dormitory. At the time, rules governing interactions between male and female students were quite strict. As the catalog states, "Young women shall not be permitted to receive calls from young men, whether they are connected with the school or not, without the consent of the principal . . . no prolonged conversation between the sexes must take place in the buildings or upon the grounds, except in the performance of school duties or by permission . . . no student attending this institution will walk or ride with students of the opposite sex except by permission from the principal."

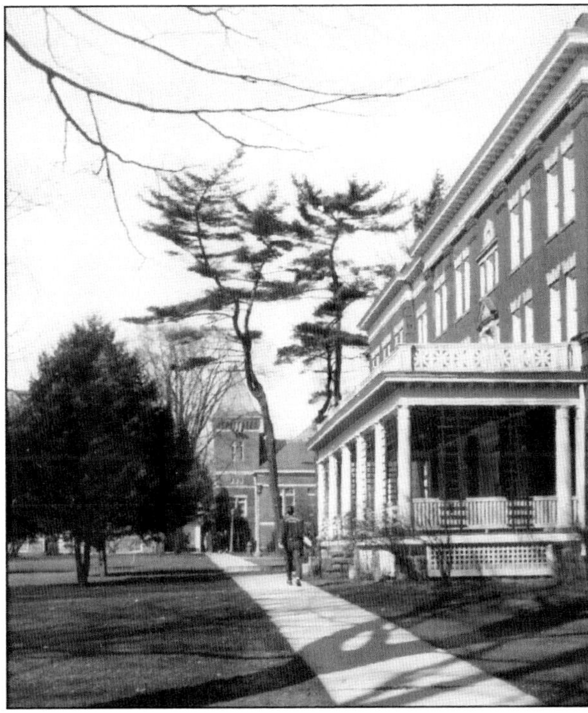

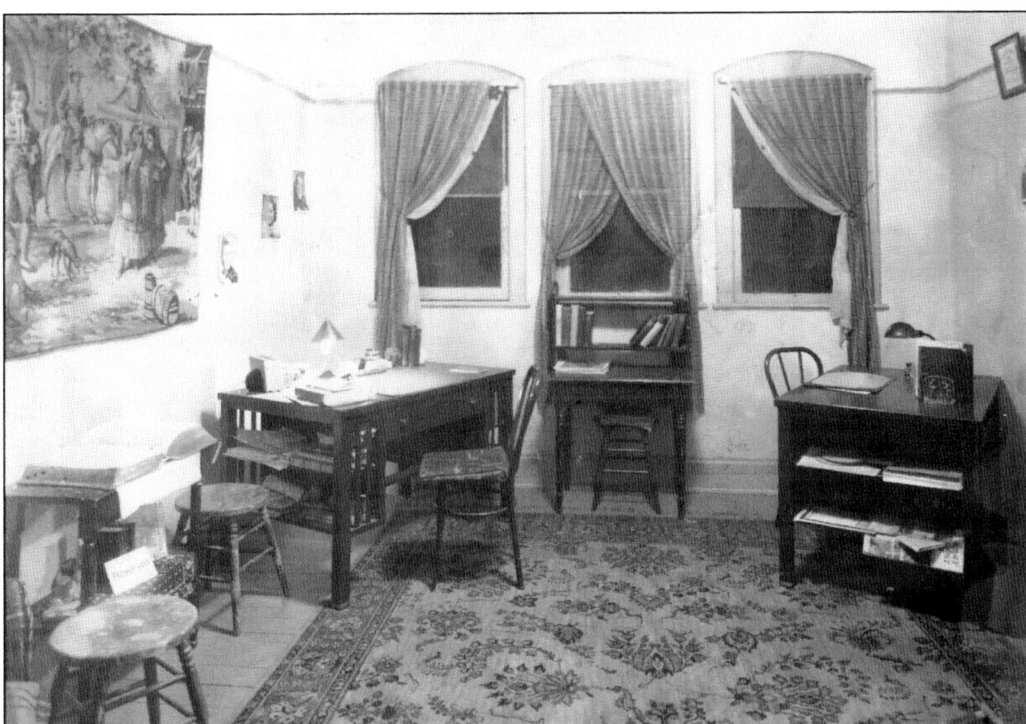

Reeder Hall was built in 1908 as a men's dormitory, named in honor of the Reeder family of Edinboro, who played a critical role in the founding of the school. This is a study room in Reeder Hall.

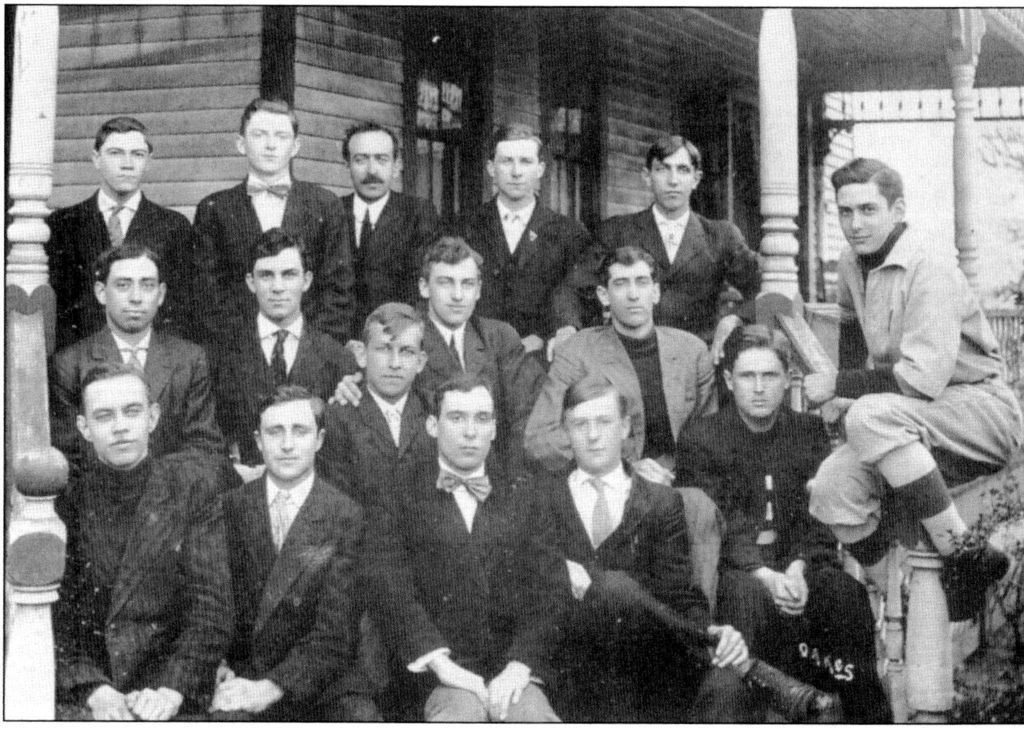

Boarding off-campus was a common practice, as seen here with the Oakes Club, which took its name from the owner of the boardinghouse. The club was not short on confidence; in the 1910 yearbook, they wrote: "The Oakes Club is noted for its great amount of intelligence, ability and influence."

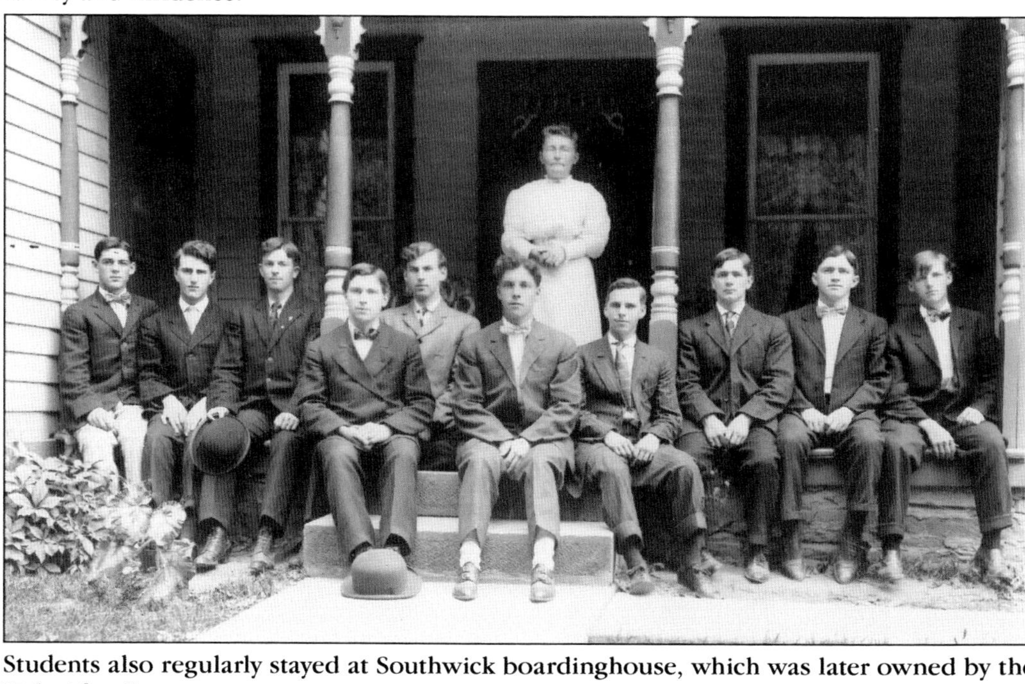

Students also regularly stayed at Southwick boardinghouse, which was later owned by the Halmi family.

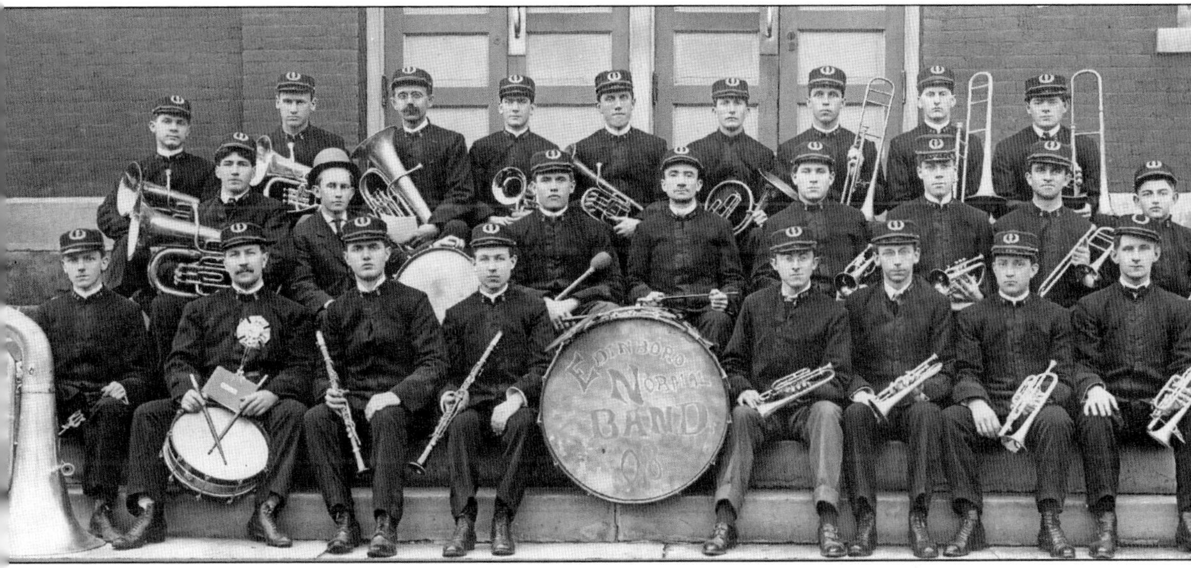

The Edinboro Normal Band is seen here in 1908. Music has long been a part of Edinboro's curriculum. In the 1880s, the school issued a separate *Catalogue of the Normal Musical Conservatory*, naming Frank W. Atwater as director and teacher and Jessie McGill as a teacher. Music Hall, known later as White Hall and no longer standing, was built in 1878. In 1889, there were 97 music students, which was a good portion of the total student body.

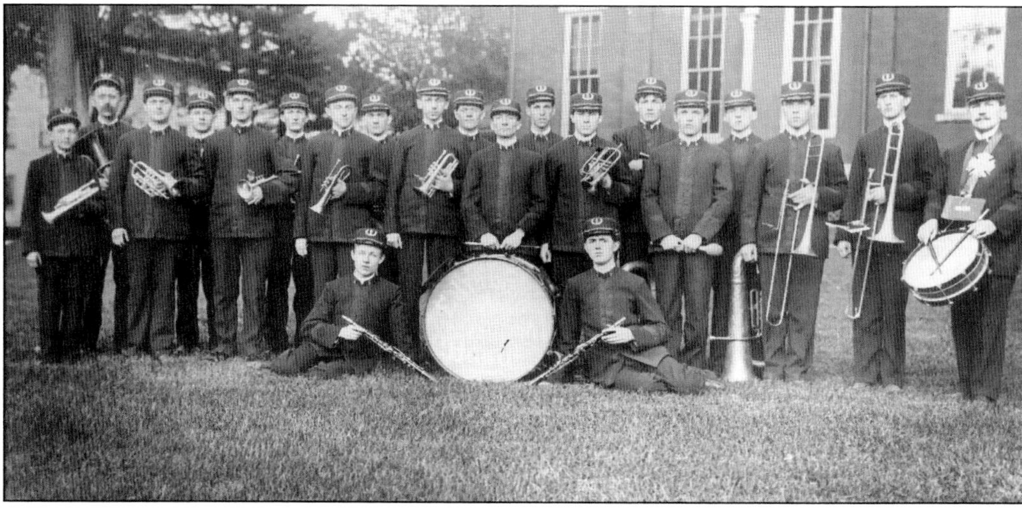

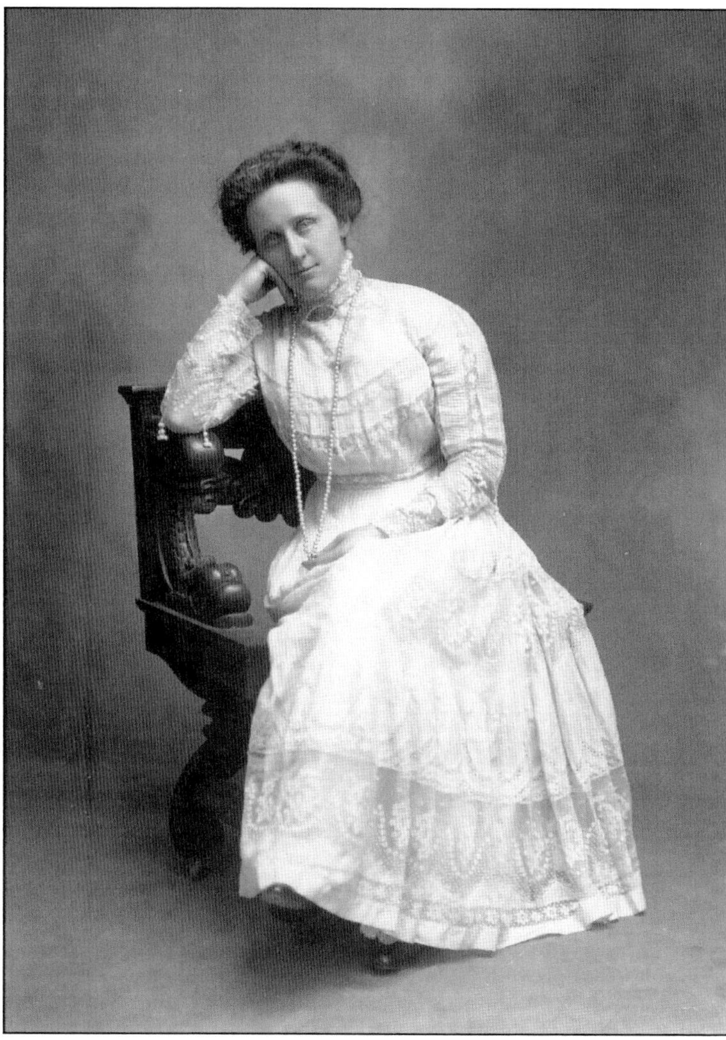

This photograph of the Edinboro Normal Band appeared in the *Pittsburgh Gazette Times* in July 1907. They were advertising the use of a particular brand of musical instrument. In later years, the band played at the halftime show of the Pittsburgh Steelers and at the capitol building in Harrisburg.

Olivia Thomas, the head of the music department, graduated from Thiel and Dana Institute. She taught piano and voice from 1909 to 1919. Music was a big part of student life; all the literary society programs, YMCA programs, and just about every other school gathering included some musical performance.

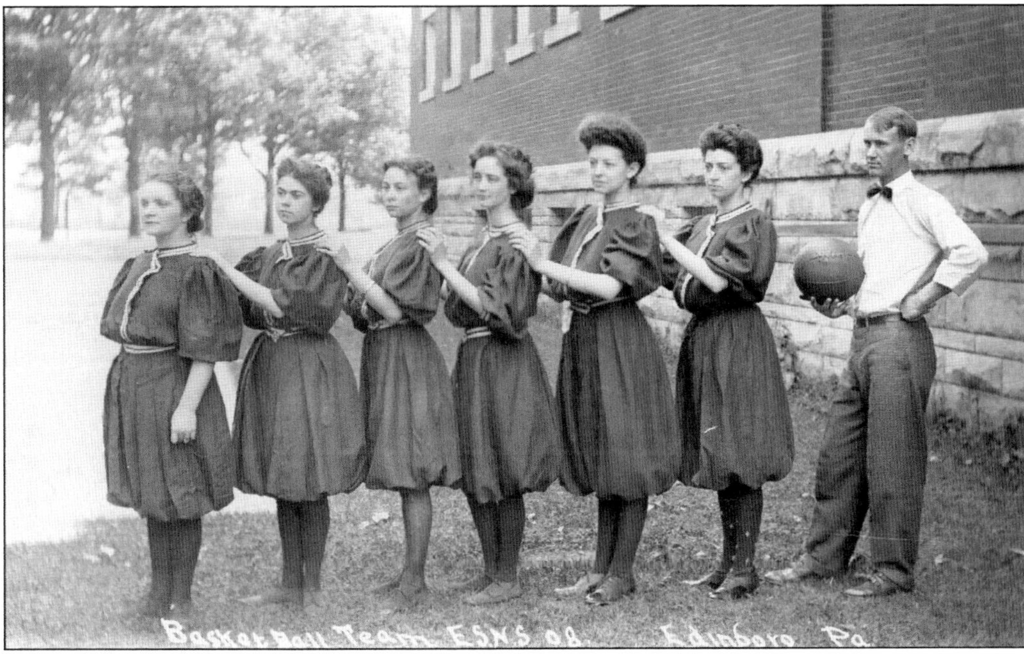

Only recently freed from corsets, the 1908 Edinboro ladies basketball team stands ready to play. Women were still escaping the confines of the Victorian era at the time, and many would have considered running after a ball and yelling to their teammates undignified and unladylike. In 1892, Senda Berenson Abbott adapted James Naismith's 1891 game for women and introduced basketball at Smith College. Edinboro was not far behind.

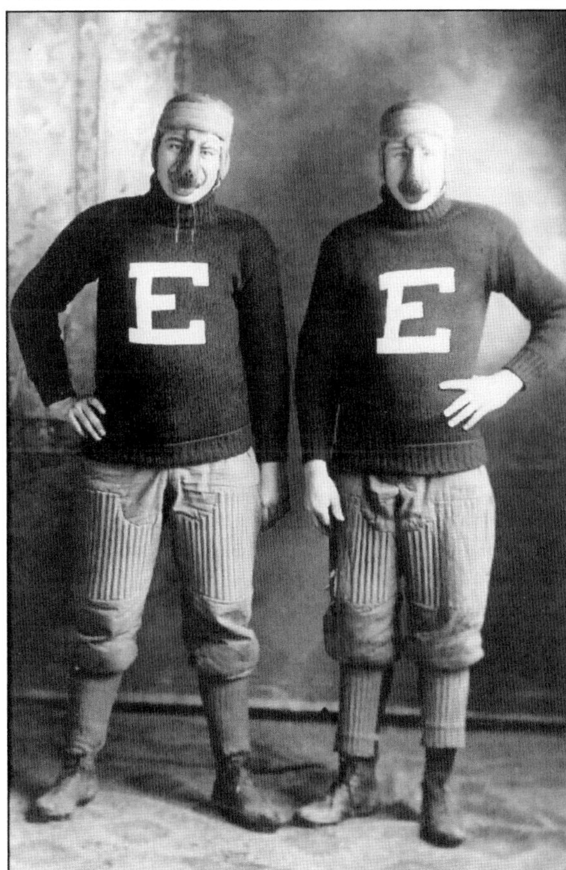

Football equipment has changed considerably since 1908. These two titans of the gridiron sport just leather helmets and noseguards.

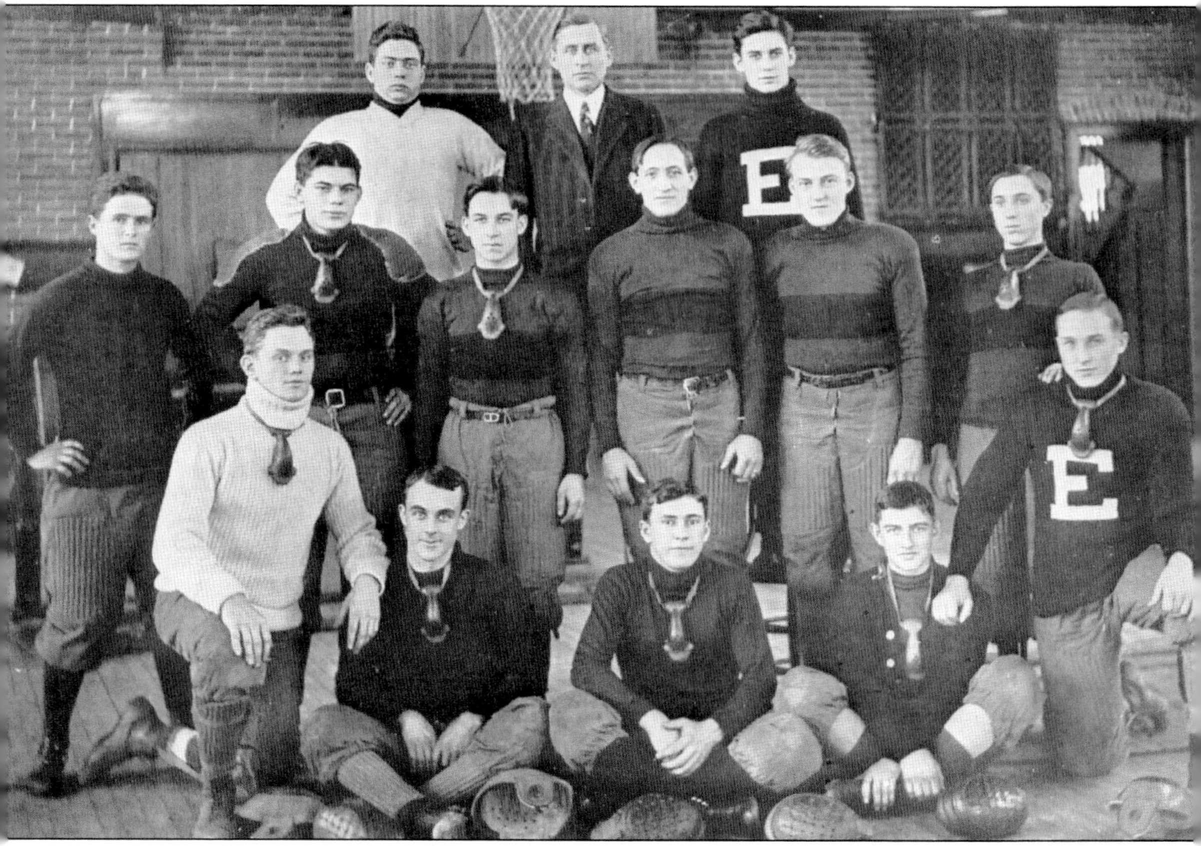

The 1910 yearbook labels this as the first official football team. The shoehorn-shaped objects hanging around their necks are noseguards. In 1910, they played local schools, including Meadville High School, North East (twice), Allegheny Reserve, and Alden Academy. It was not a successful season for the team; they managed to score only two points all year without one victory.

In their four games, the Edinboro ladies basketball team went undefeated against Meadville YMCA, Titusville, Cambridge Springs High School, and Cochranton High School.

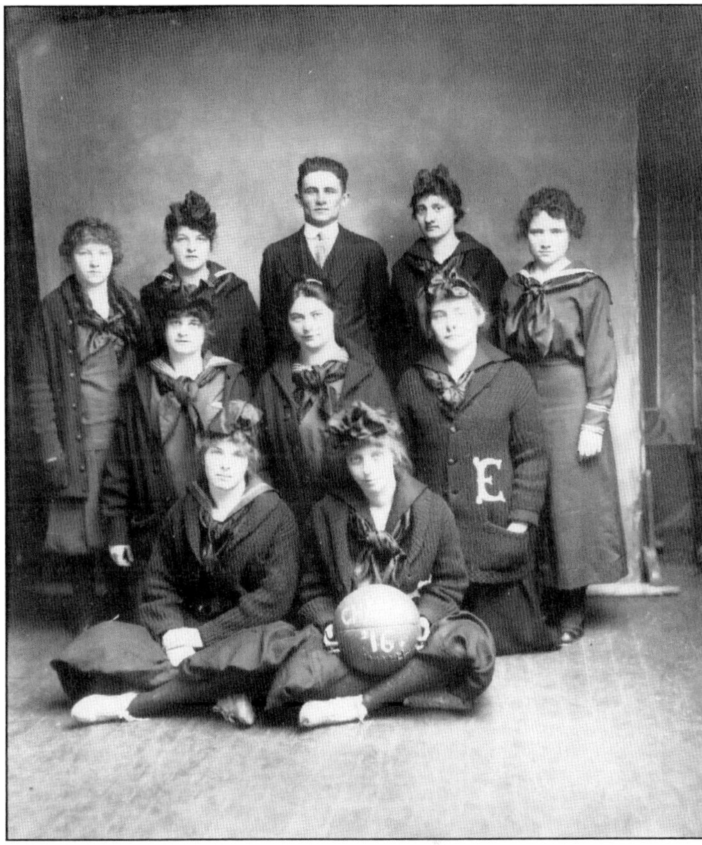

The 1911 basketball team had a rough start, as they did not have a coach for the first half of the season. Physics and chemistry professor Wallace Snyder stepped in as manager to get the season started before "Red" Phillips, a former guard at Allegheny, took over as coach. Phillips is in the center of the second row, and Snyder is to the right of him.

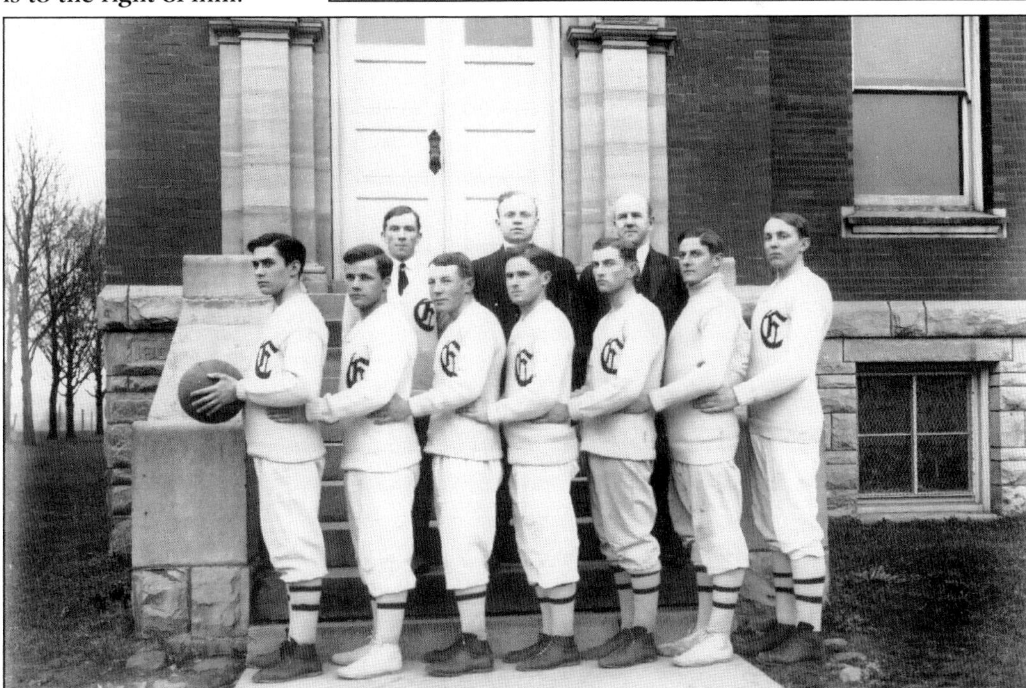

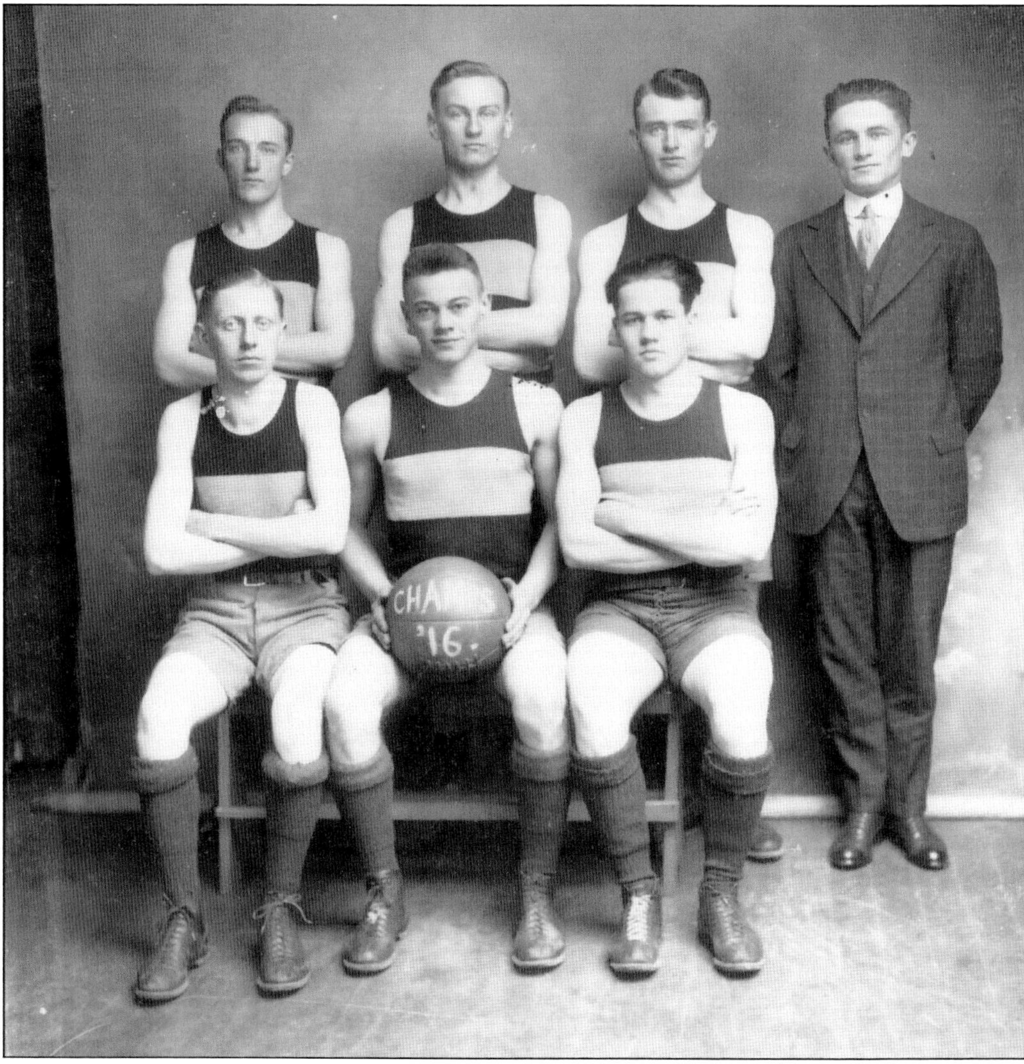

Stuart D. Graham attended Edinboro Normal School, the Springfield YMCA Training School, and Harvard Summer School. He returned to Edinboro to teach physical education, coach, and serve as director of athletics. He is seen here with the 1916 basketball team, who went undefeated in their nine games.

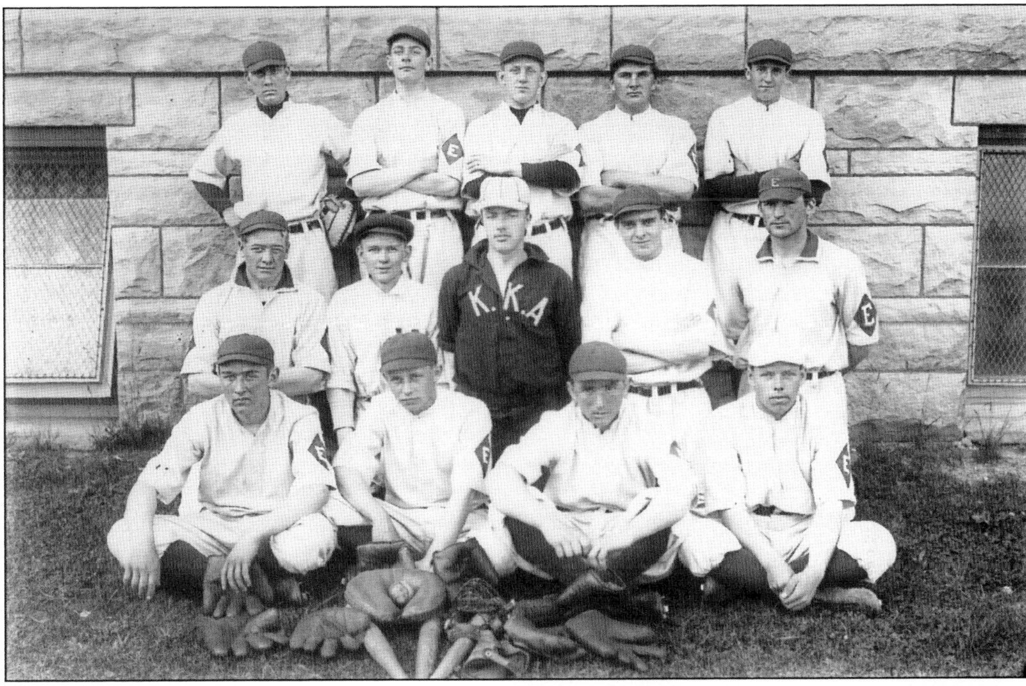

The 1913 baseball team poses for a team photograph with their equipment in front of them. Notice the flat catcher's mitt and the gloves with unconnected fingers and minimal webbing between the thumb and forefinger. With this glove, two-handed catching was a good idea. The catcher also had a mask and shin guards of padded material.

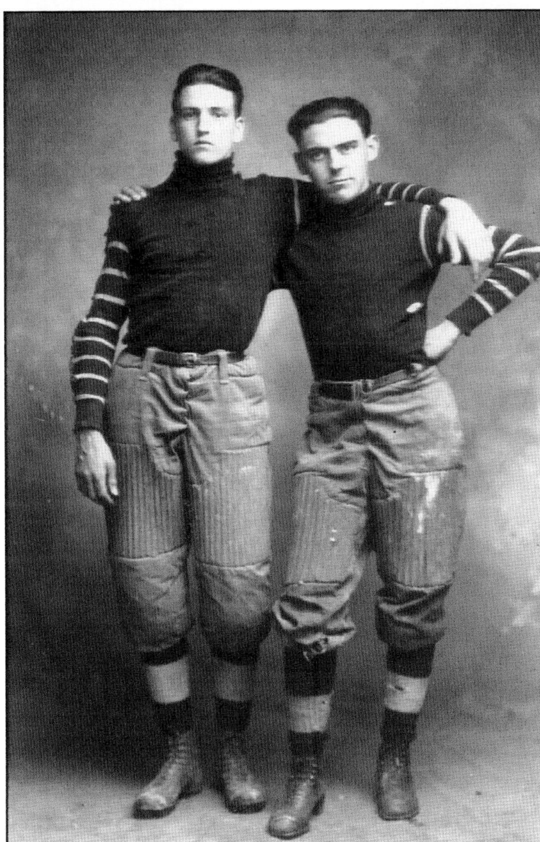

The closest the 1910 Edinboro football team came to winning was in a game against North East, which ended in a 0-0 tie. Regardless, they had fine-looking uniforms.

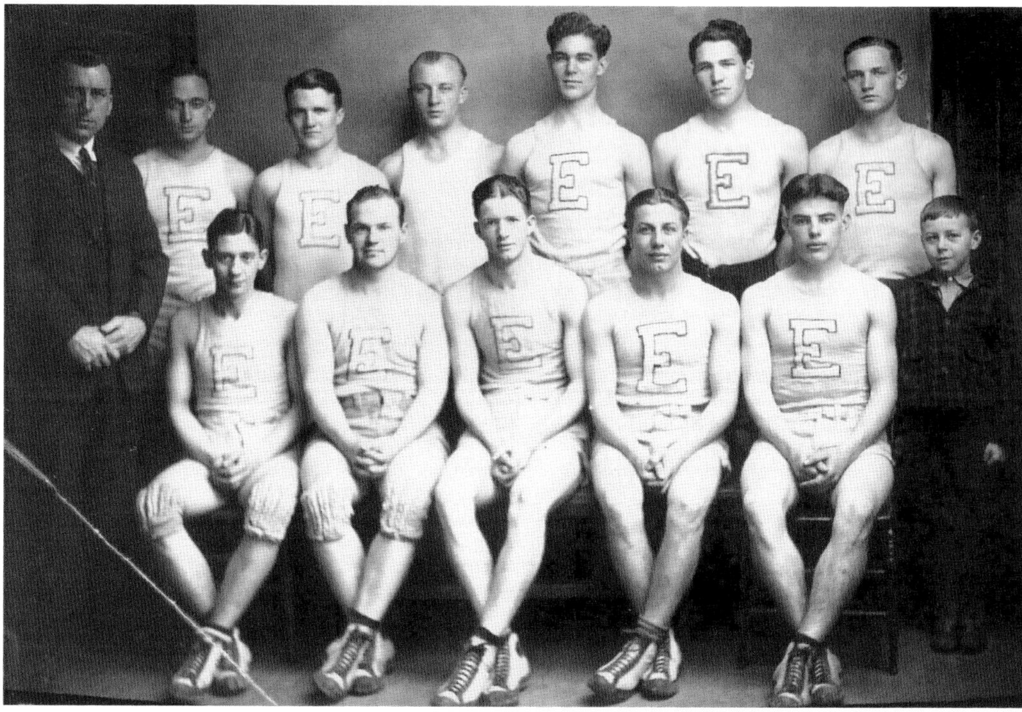

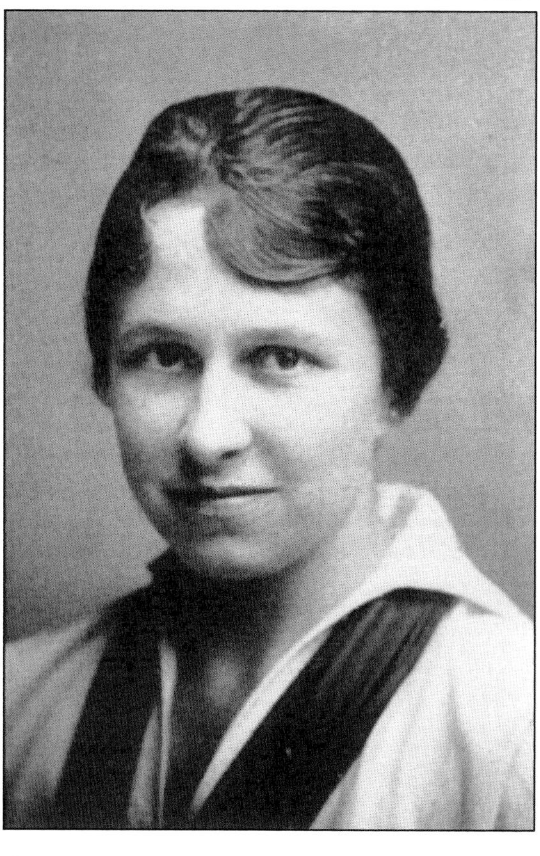

Edinboro has had its share of champions, including the 1925–1926 Western Pennsylvania champion basketball team coached by Sox Harrison. They won 11 of their 12 games and outscored their opponents 531-291. The young boy on the far right is Jim Harrison, who later became dean of students at Edinboro.

Throughout the 1800s and early 1900s, student athletic teams were coached by other students. In 1920, Catherine Avery was hired to teach the ladies' physical education classes and coach. Avery was succeeded by Nettie Mae Ruttle in 1925.

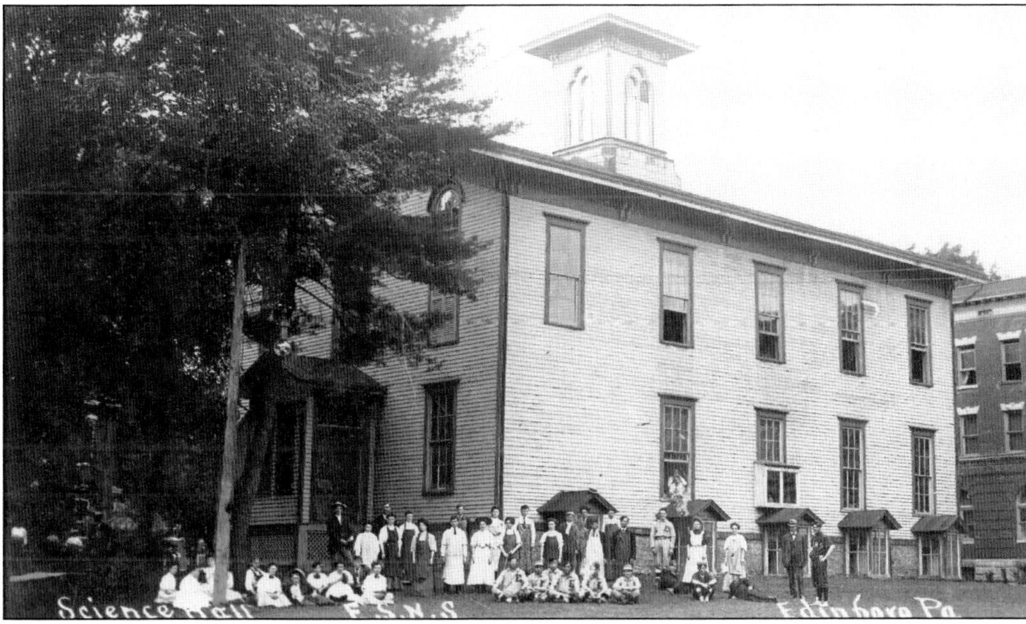

Assembly Hall has changed names over the years and was known as Science Hall in 1910. Wearing aprons in front of the building is what appears to be a science class. Behind the aproned ladies with the mustache is science teacher Ira Peavy. A student said of Peavy, "Everyone has to be happy in Professor Peavy's classes for the dry old sciences are taken apart and clothed again in an atmosphere of good cheer."

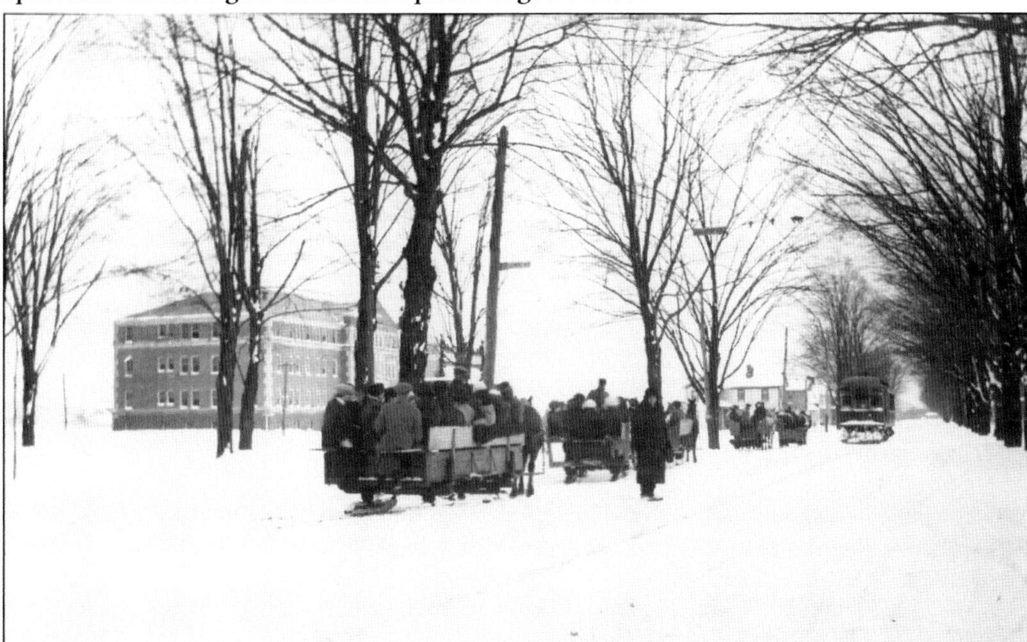

The senior sleigh ride to Cambridge Springs was an annual highlight for the students. Here, four sleighs full of excited (and probably cold) students head down to Cambridge Springs. In this image, a trolley arrives in Edinboro from Cambridge, dating the photograph between 1921 and 1928.

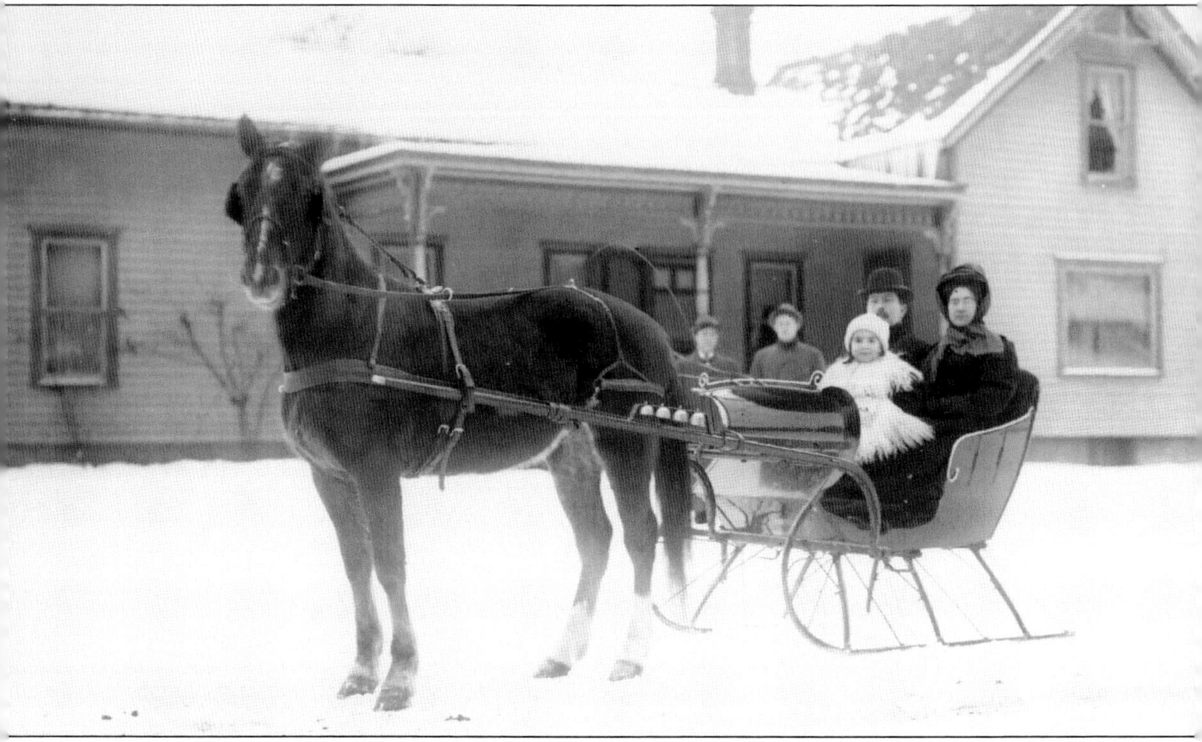

Professor Edgar Stover, a teacher of grammar, arithmetic, bookkeeping, and typewriting, takes his wife, Grace, out for a sleigh ride. For the hearty Edinboro citizen, the harsh winter was just another season to be enjoyed. Since Edinboro is in a snowbelt, it is common to get more than 100 inches of snow a year.

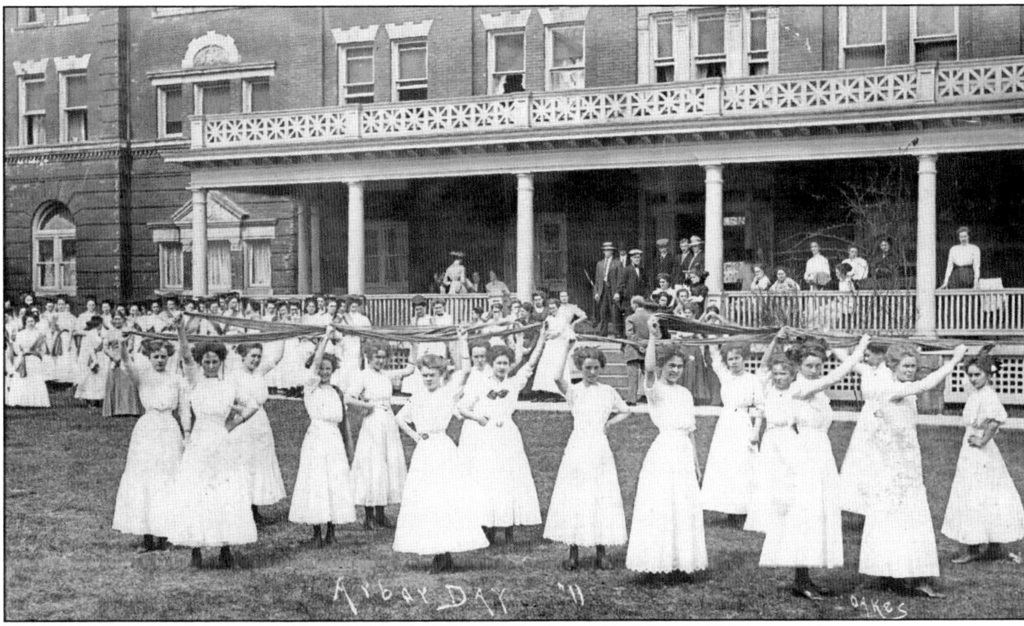

Arbor Day was quite the event in the early 1900s. This 1911 photograph shows the festivities in front of Haven Hall.

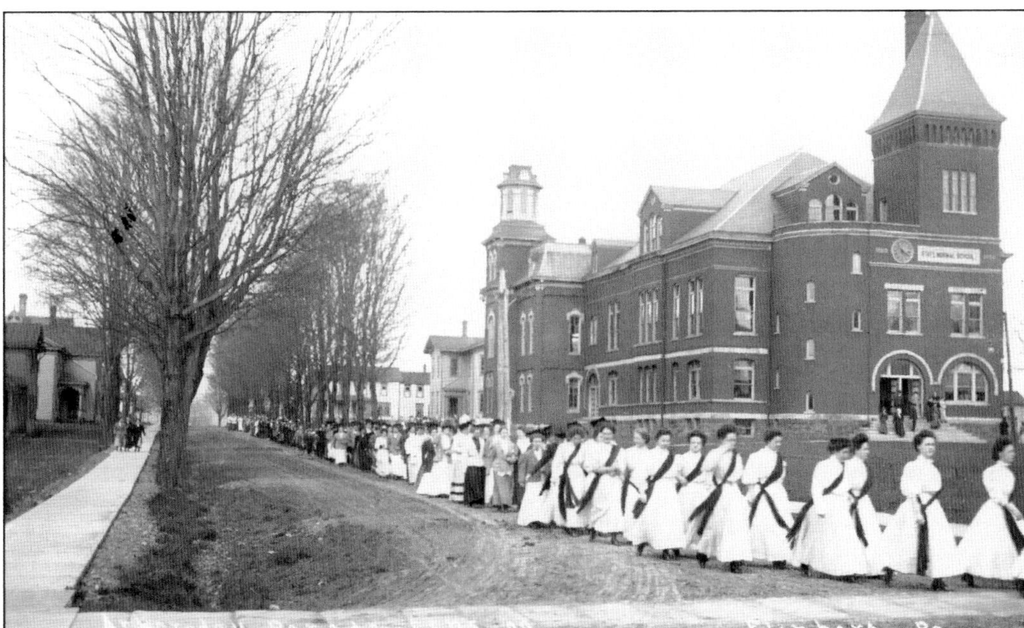

The crowds turned out to participate in the annual Arbor Day parade. This 1909 photograph shows the parade walking west on Normal Street, which was still a dirt road at the time.

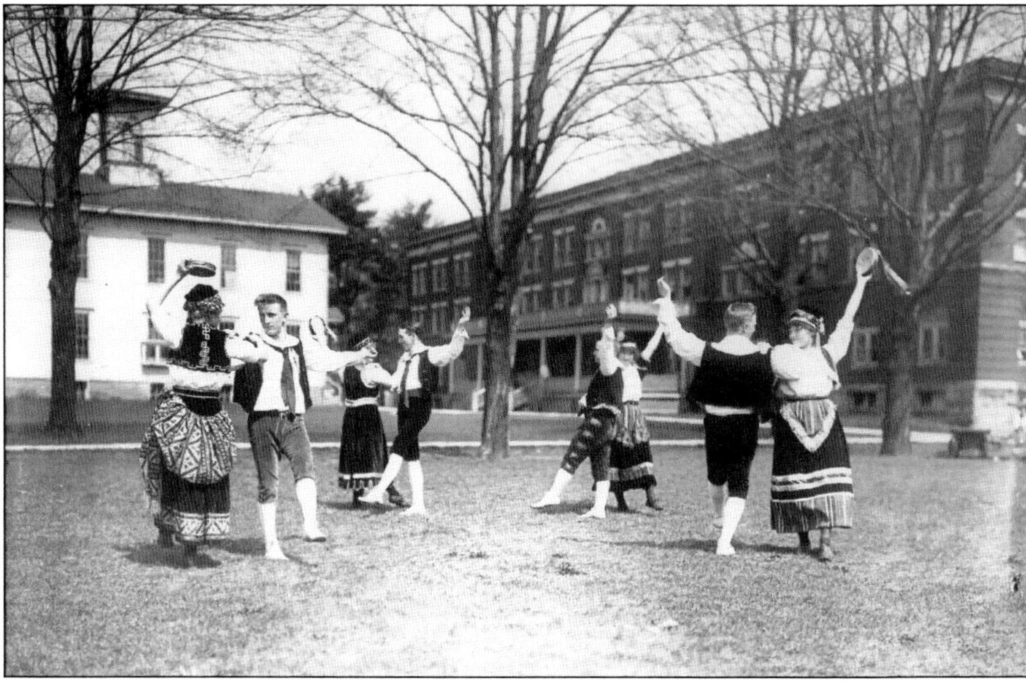

Traditionally on Arbor Day, the senior class would plant a tree, which the middle class (second-year students) would try to steal before it could be planted. Students, faculty, and townspeople all turned out for the festivities.

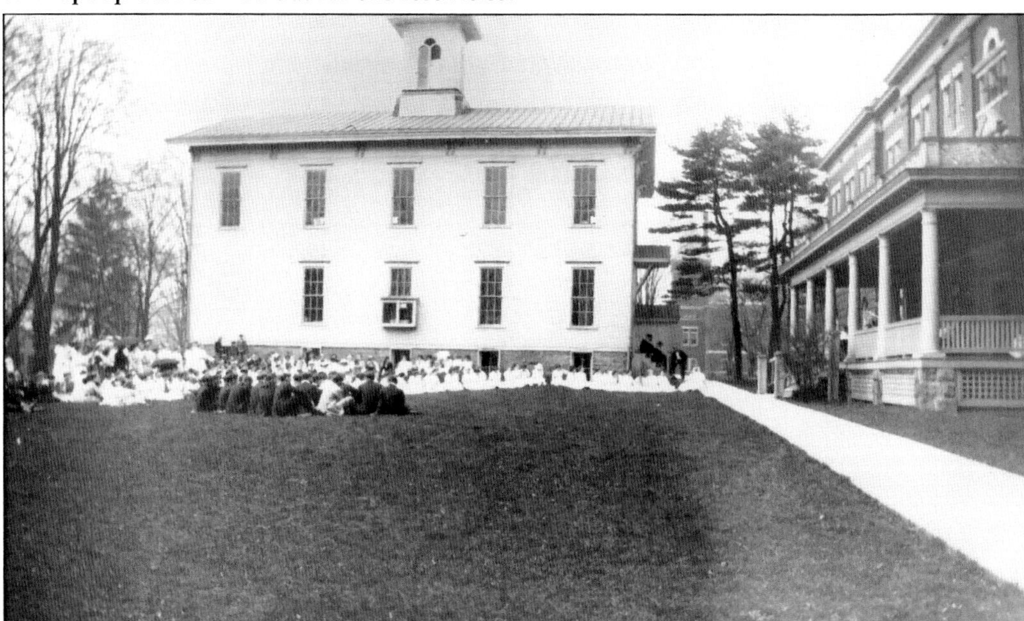

The May Day celebration took place on the lawn in front of Haven Hall. The white structure with the cupola is Science Hall, originally Assembly Hall, the second building erected on campus. Over the years, it housed science classes, the library, an armory, and of course, an assembly room.

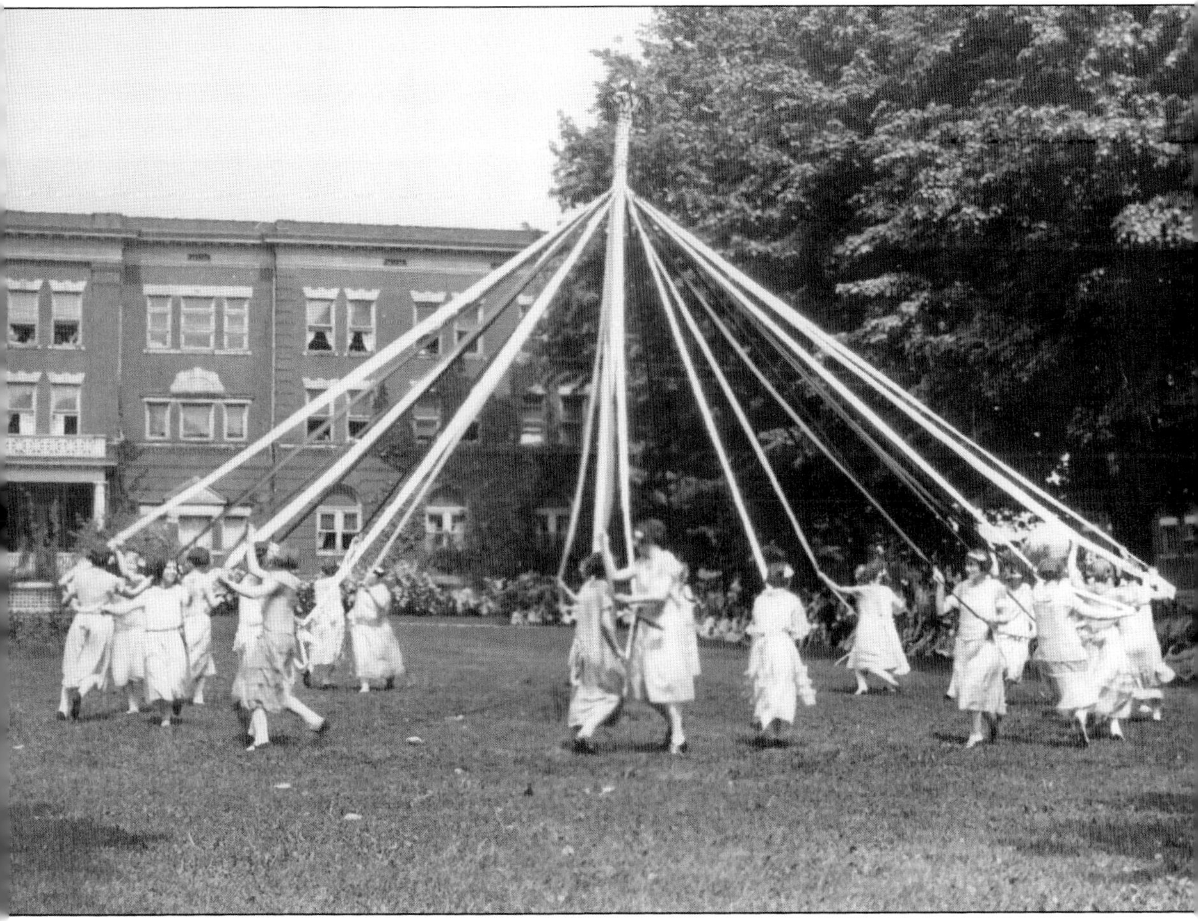

No doubt after Edinboro winters, spring celebrations, like this 1913 May Day, were welcome events. The ladies are all dressed in white and circle the maypole in the lawn in front of Haven Hall as spectators sit in the shade of the trees.

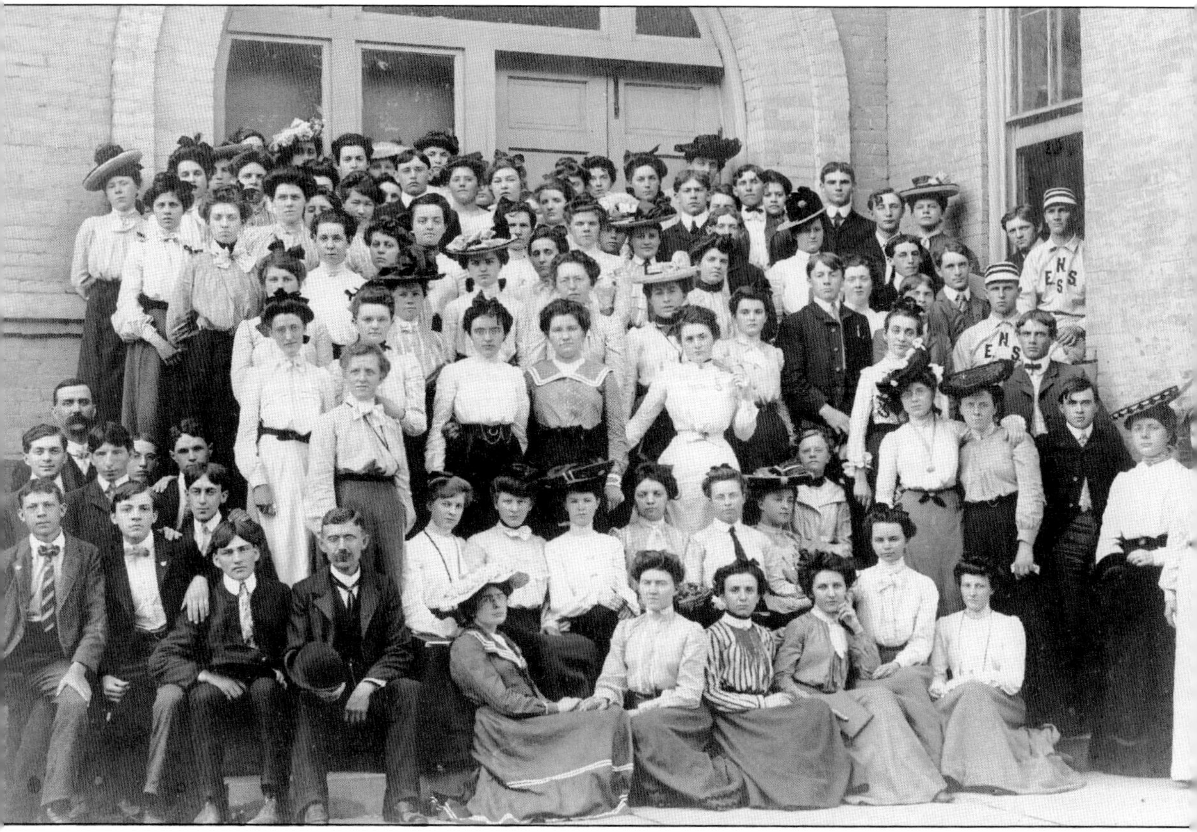

The class of 1908 had its share of attractive hats, as well as two baseball players. One of the popular activities of the day was bicycling. This new form of transportation would have provided the cyclist a bumpy ride on the dirt streets of Edinboro.

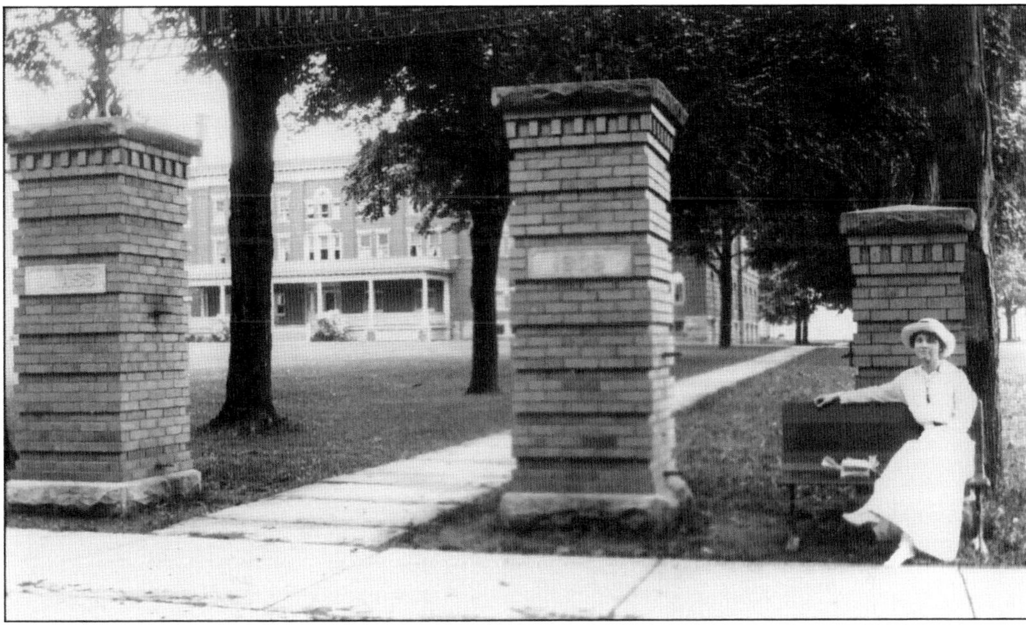

The entranceway pillars were donated by the class of 1908. Today, these pillars still stand but without the "State Normal School" ironworks at the top. In 1908, students paid $160.50 after state aid was subtracted for tuition, board, and a furnished room. Students who graduated and agreed to teach for two years in Pennsylvania schools were reimbursed all tuition costs.

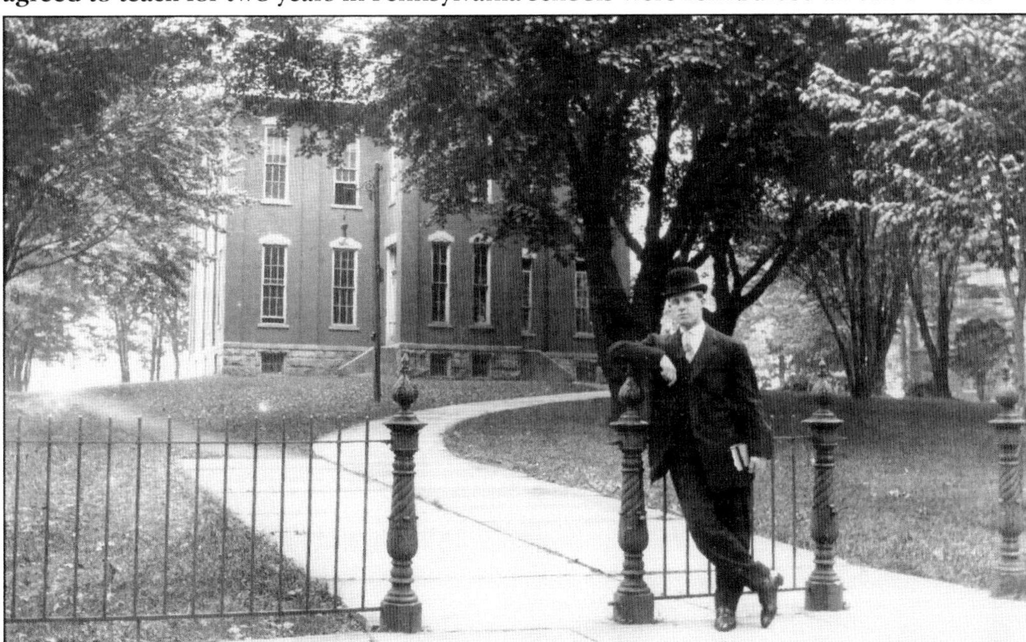

This 1910 photograph shows a typical student at Edinboro, wearing in his bowler hat, on the walkway leading to Recitation Hall. The building was designed by principal Joseph Cooper and dedicated in 1880. The first floor had no connecting hallways, so in order to change classrooms, students had to go outside and reenter the building. It was Cooper's philosophy that students should get a breath of fresh air between classes.

The Birch Rod

OF THE EDINBORO STATE NORMAL SCHOOL

Volume II | MONDAY, NOVEMBER 14, 1912 | No. 8

A CELEBRITY IN OUR MIDST

William Howard Taft Honors the Normal School With a Special Visit Saturday, Oct. 26.

David Grayson sets it down as a close secret regarding celebrities:

"They cannot survive without common people like you and me."

However that may be, Mr. Grayson's description of a visit of one clothed with great dignity is not amiss here:

"Not for many weeks have I had a more interesting, more illuminating, and when all is told, a more amusing, experience, than I had this afternoon. Since this afternoon the world has seemed a more satisfactory place to live in, and my own home here, the most satisfactory, the most central place in all the world. I have come to the conclusion that anything may happen here!

"We have had a celebrity in our small midst, and the hills, as the Psalmist might say, have lifted up their heads, and the trees have clapped their hands together."

In the bustle of the expectation of our entire community's journeying to Cambridge Springs to see the President on the occasion of his visit there on October 26, Principal Baker announced the possibility of the President's being persuaded to come to Edinboro to make a brief address to the Normal School. When the applause had subsided, he hastened to say that the matter was not yet settled but that he had every reason to expect the plan would materialize inasmuch as he had the approval of both Congressman Bates and The Birch Rod in the undertaking.

(Applause lasted thirty-four minutes at this point.)

Elsewhere every diplomatic move of the gentlemen who finally convinced the President's aides to make the journey to Edinboro has been published. It may here be said in entire propriety that the chief and final influence that won the signal distinction for the Normal School was the effect of the approval of The Birch Rod. Just because it is true, modesty need not forbid our saying that when the magic name of The Birch Rod was uttered in the face of any slight objection to the visit, everybody was all smiles; and even the President's aides were ready and eager to come.

A special car brought the President and his party to Edinboro at 5:20 on October 26. Passing from the train to Normal Hall, Mr. Taft was bombarded with flowers, the school children of Edinboro acting as an escort to the distinguished visitor. The students and citizens gave the President a hearty welcome on his entrance into the hall. His speech, which is here given verbatim, was as follows:

"I am glad to be here and to greet you. I thank the Auditor General for his kindly introduction, and I agree with what he has said about the importance of education, moral and secular, with the purpose of making good citizens, but what I would like to say tonight is something to encourage those who are going to embrace the profession of teaching.

"In many respects, the teacher's profession is the greatest in the world. It is the one which takes hold of the boy and girl at the formative period, when they can be made something of, or let go to be nothing. It is then that you in your profession of teaching will first develop his mind and then develop his character, and set him on the way to a higher ideal in life. Now if you embrace teaching as a profession, you have to be content to live in pretty moderate circumstances. You have got to be content to get along without luxuries and not become the rich of the earth. You have got to be content with living a life of usefulness. Your rewards are going to come from the contemplation of having done your duty, having worked out the problem that is before you and having done something to benefit the human race in making the boys and girls under your tutorage better men and women.

"I don't come here to sympathize with you. You don't need sympathy. The consciousness of having done your duty, the fact that you can look back over your life and see where your efforts have helped someone is going to make your life worth the living; that exceeds anything in the way of money. You think that is preaching, and it is; but I am fifty-one years old and have lived long enough to find out many things that you will learn as you grow older. The greatest asset you have is character and with character you will be able to play your part in a worthy manner. So standing shoulder to shoulder in the cause of education you can do wonders to help in the cause and can say when you are done, "I have done my little and for that I deserve credit."

"I like to speak to teachers because they do begin in the spirit of self-sacrifice. I realized this more than ever through my experience in the Philippines. In the Philippines we had to instruct half a million children. What language shall we teach them? Should it be English or Spanish? There were sixteen different dialects; none of them fit for civilized people. Seven per cent. spoke English, so we concluded to take up English. How were we going to get teachers? We had a thousand teachers, most of them young women, all from the United States. The destructive tendencies of matrimony carried away some of them, but we now have a trained body that has taught and has created a teaching body of from eight to nine hundred Philippine teachers who teach English to the boys and girls, so that there are now four hundred thousand children learning your language—English. It is the language through which these young Philipinos can learn modern civilization. The eight or nine hundred who contributed to that result have a right to say, "I have lived a life of usefulness to the community and have contributed that result which is an honor to the nation and an honor to those who have brought it about.

"You have embraced a profession that gives as great an opportunity for usefulness, and therefore, as great an opportunity for happiness as any profession we have in this society of ours.

"Young ladies and gentlemen, I honor, and you should honor, the profession you are about to enter. I congratulate you and I thank you."

Immediately upon the conclusion of this address, the President returned to Cambridge Springs, and by six o'clock was on board his special car for Washington.

Many things might be said of the visit of the President. Details eminently interesting at the time are less relevant now. The central fact of the President's having been with us is at this time the most important. Perhaps the best thing that has been said of the whole affair was Mr. Barnes' comment in the Edinboro Independent of October 31:

"Edinboro is justly proud of the honor accorded her in Mr. Taft's special visit. It is not an unusual thing for a small community on the main route of travel to secure, in campaign time, the visits of distinguished candidates, but for a town to obtain, as a personal favor largely, the honor of a purely social visit from the Nation's Chief Executive is exceedingly rare, and makes the experience of Saturday unique and memorable. It was an inspiration to us all, regardless of political bias, to have the great privilege of such an intimate view of the President of the United States—for it was as such that Mr. Taft was here—and no one who was in Edinboro on Saturday will ever forget the occasion."

Pres. William Howard Taft visited the school in 1912 and gave a short speech to the students before traveling back to Cambridge Springs, where he was taking part in the opening ceremony of Polish Alliance College.

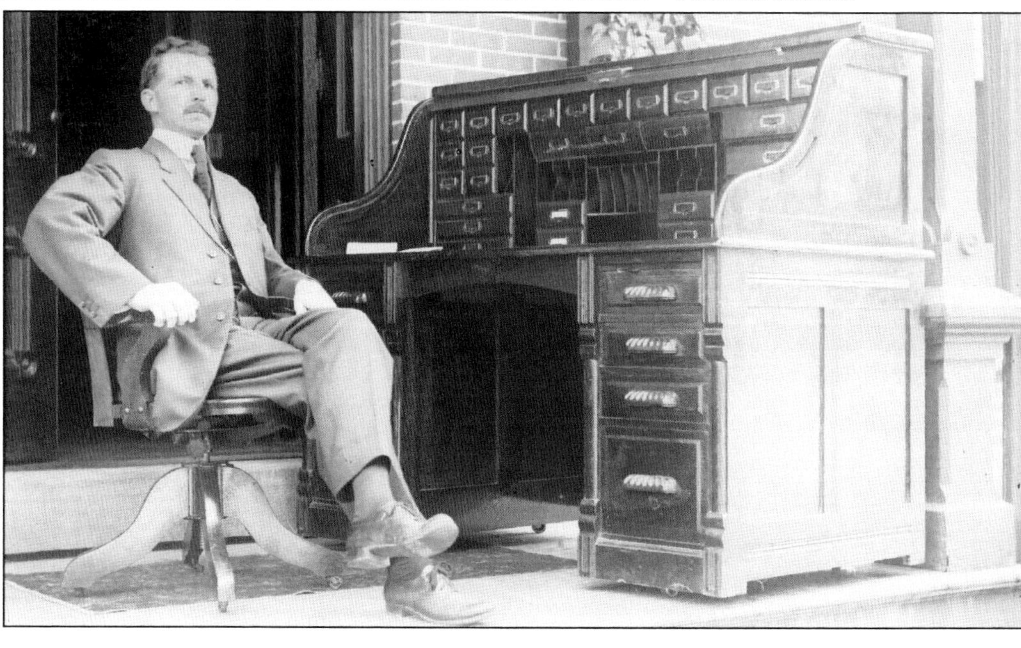

John Bigler, the principal from 1900 to 1911, seems to have moved his office outside. He was born in Barkeyville, Pennsylvania, in 1862 and attended Grove City College, where he earned his bachelor's degree. Afterward, Bigler taught at Barkeyville Academy before becoming superintendent of public instruction of Venango. In 1900, he became principal of the Edinboro State Normal School.

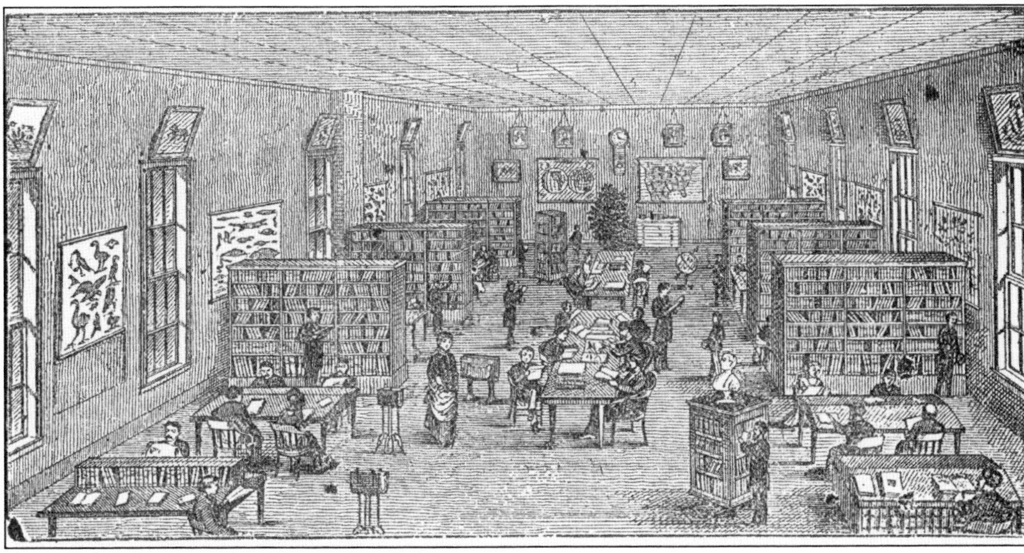

In 1889, the library had no electric lights and was lit entirely by five tall windows on either side of the building. Electricity arrived on campus in 1904. This engraving shows the library as it was on the second floor of Assembly Hall, which was known as Library Hall from 1880 to 1910.

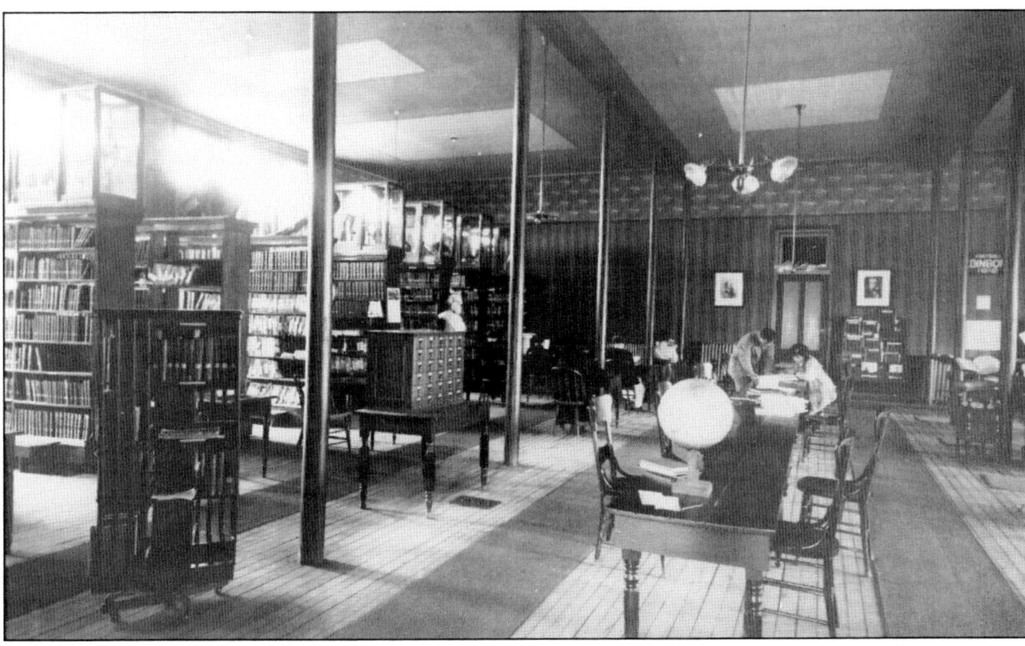

The library was eventually moved to the second floor of Normal Hall. By 1908, the Dewey system of organization had been implemented. The Enis Collection is in the cases above the bookshelves. The 1908 catalog describes the collection as consisting of "mounted animals, birds, alcoholic specimens of fishes, reptiles, etc; also a variety of coral shells, minerals and Indian relics."

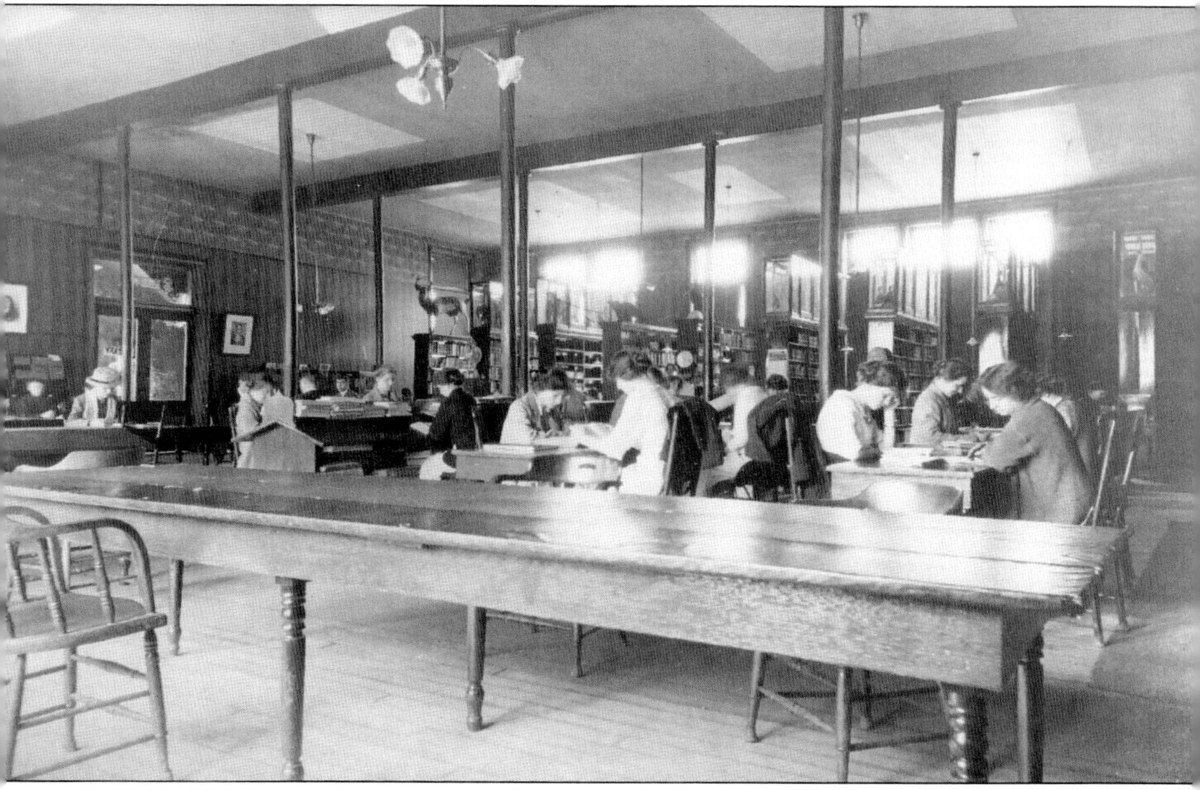

This 1912 photograph shows the library when it was on the second floor of Normal Hall. Long, tall windows supplemented the electric lighting.

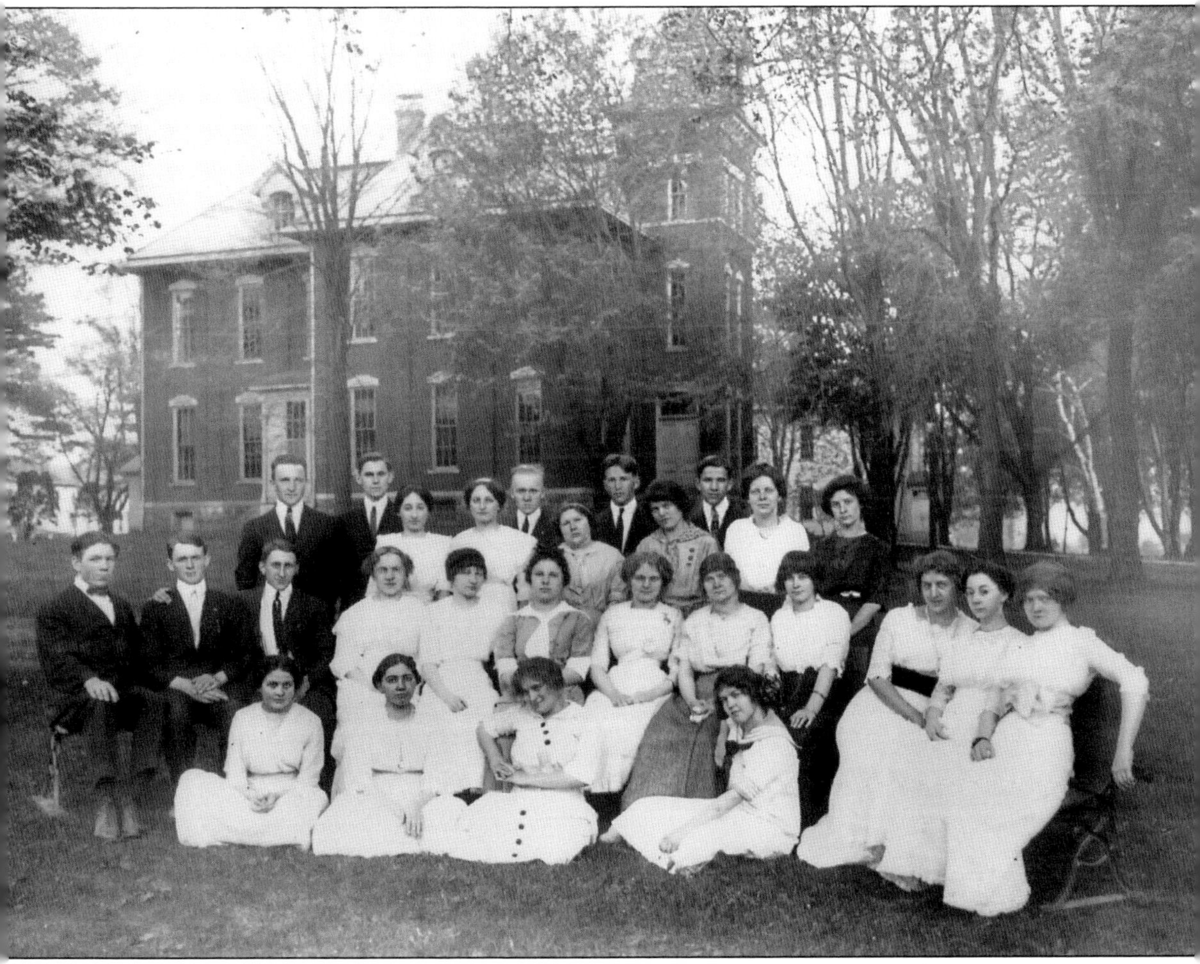

The 1916 class graduated in a period of low enrollment, with only 328 students attending classes. That same year, the mumps epidemic occurred, turning the entire first floor of Haven Hall into an infirmary. Another more serious epidemic followed two years later with the flu epidemic of 1918, and the school had to close twice in an effort to thwart the spread of the disease.

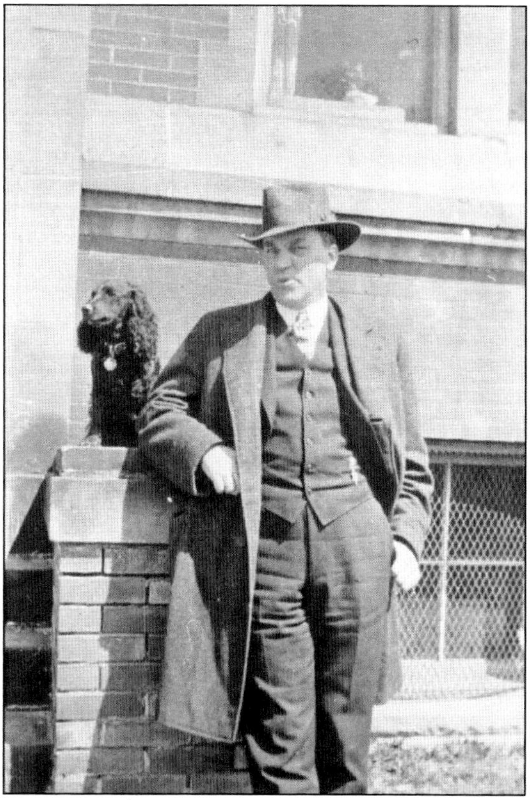

Frank Baker was the principal at Edinboro from 1911 to 1920. He graduated from Clarion State Normal School and went on to get an AB from Allegheny, an AM from Harvard, and a PhD from the University of Pennsylvania. His wife, a graduate of the Fannie Farmer School of Cooking, taught domestic science. Principal Baker was forced to resign in 1920 due to health concerns. He died in 1925.

Principal Frank Baker sits in the center of his faculty in 1913, a pivotal year for the school, as Pennsylvania purchased the property from the stockholders in December. The official program to transfer the title took place in April 1914.

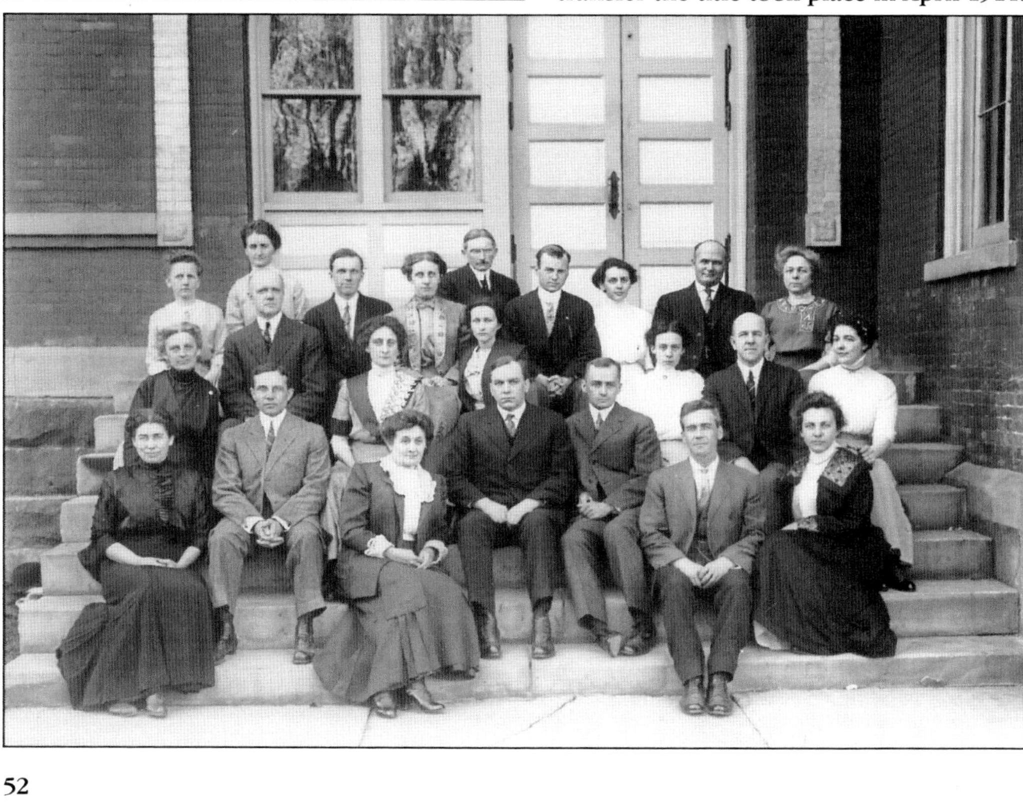

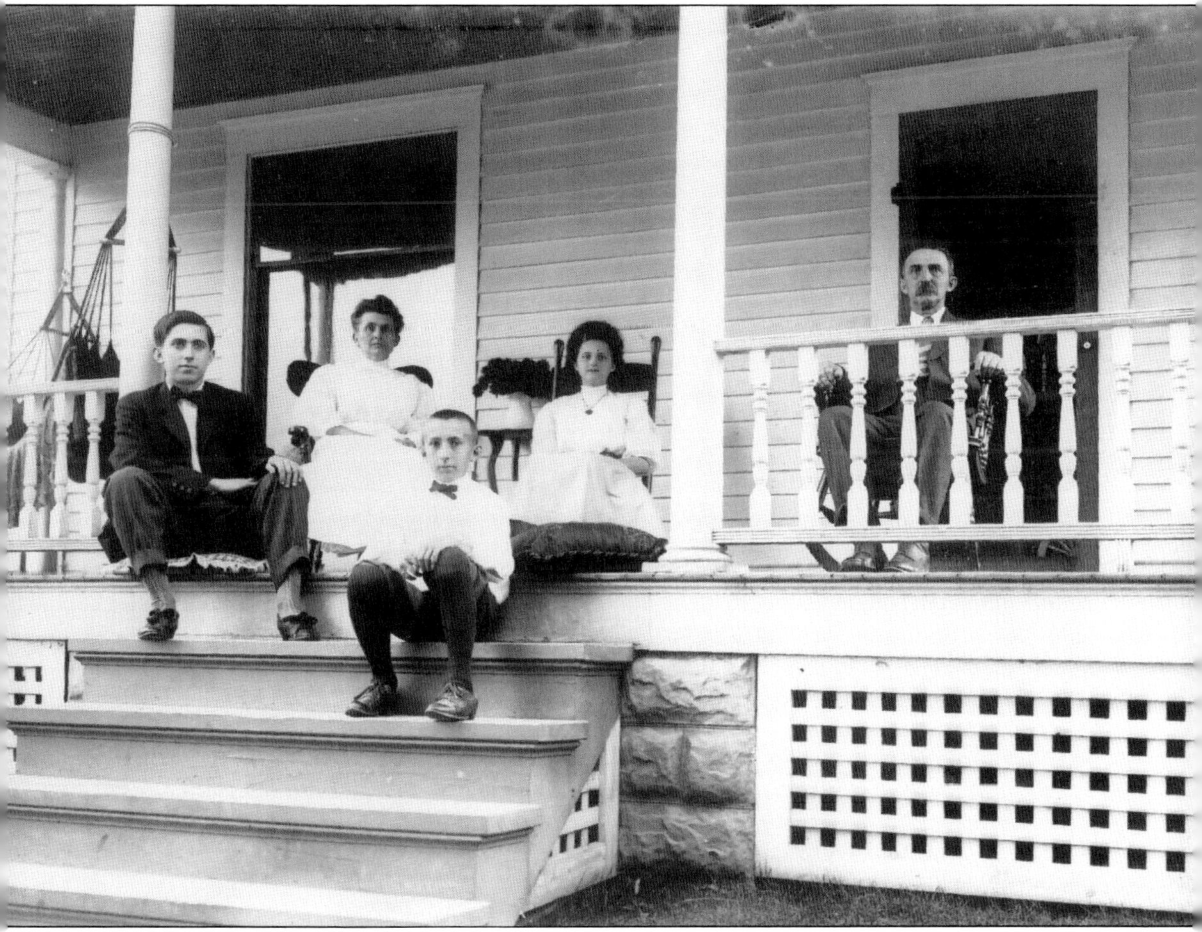

Prof. Jeremiah L. Ghering, far right in the rocking chair, taught from 1906 to 1910. He is shown here with his sons Harold and Boyd, his wife, and Mable Grandquist. Harold and Boyd both became physicians and were employed as college physicians at Edinboro. The Ghering Health Center was named in their honor.

FORM R-5

Edinboro State Normal School

STUDENT'S TICKET

The Bearer Harold Hopkins
has paid the Term Registration Fee and is entitled to admission to all numbers of the Lecture Course and to all Athletic Games given under the control of the Board of Trustees until Dec. 18, 1919.

NOT TRANSFERABLE

LECTURE COURSE—ATHLETICS

Student identification cards have come a long way since 1919. This card permitted admittance to lectures and athletic events. In that year, a student could enjoy baseball games, football games, and men's and women's basketball games. There were also plenty of intramural sports.

EDINBORO'S CREED

¶ We believe in our community, in youth, in the nobility of labor, in every enterprise that makes life more worth while or adds to civic pride.

¶ We believe in fields and brooks, in birds and song, in schools that fit for life, in all that helps us work and live and laugh, and love both God and men.

¶ We believe in training for our work; that he who trains has double chance to win.

¶ We believe that teaching is a work worth while; that he who trains and does his best, may stand unblushing with the host that have made the world worth while. —C. C. CRAWFORD

EDINBORO STATE NORMAL SCHOOL
Arthur G. Crane, Principal

EDINBORO TRAINS TEACHERS

"Edinboro's Creed" was written by Clarence Crawford between 1920 and 1922 while Arthur Crane was principal. Crane's two-year tenure was shortest for a principal or president of the school.

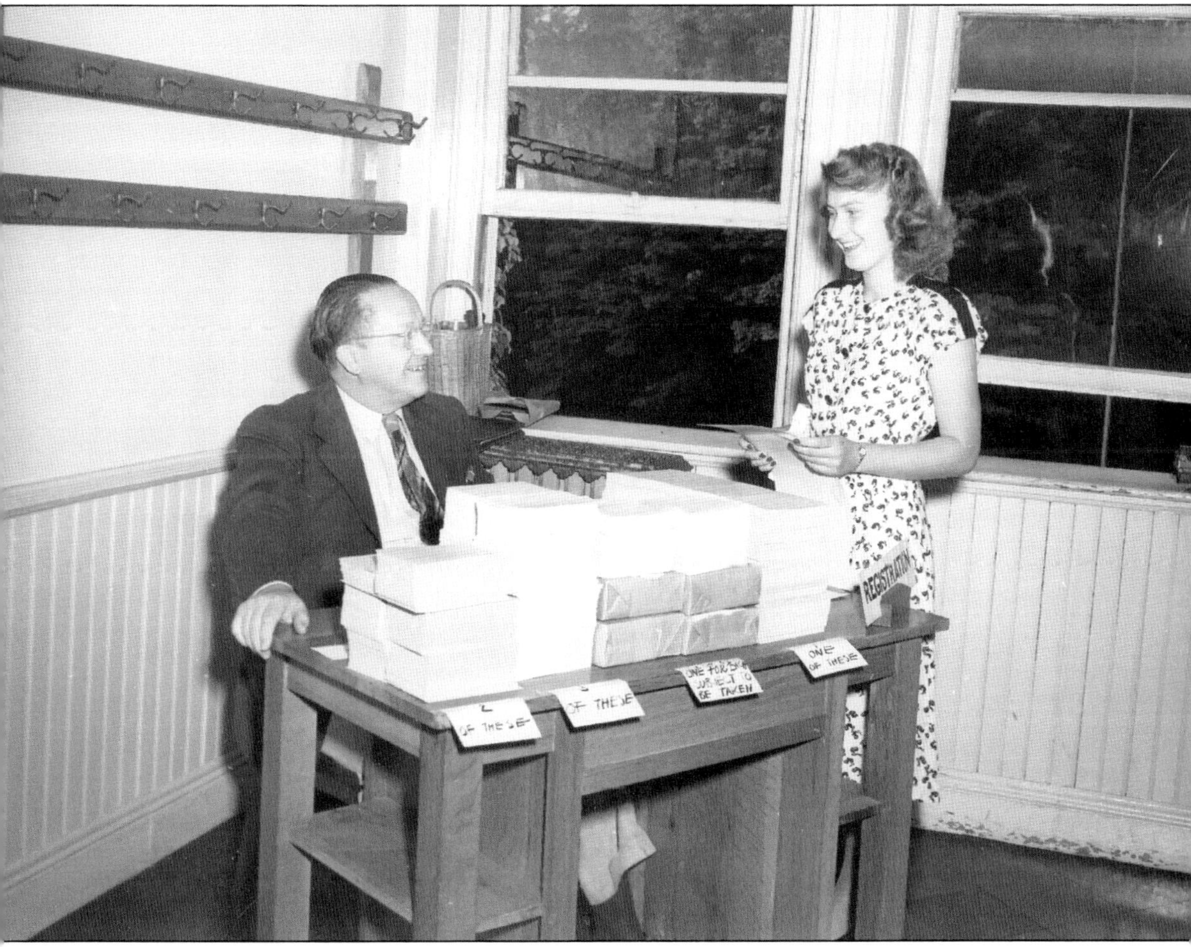

The art department was established in 1920 with Waldo F. Bates Jr. as the department head. That same year, the board of principals divided the state normal schools into specialized service areas. Edinboro was designated in the elementary education and art area.

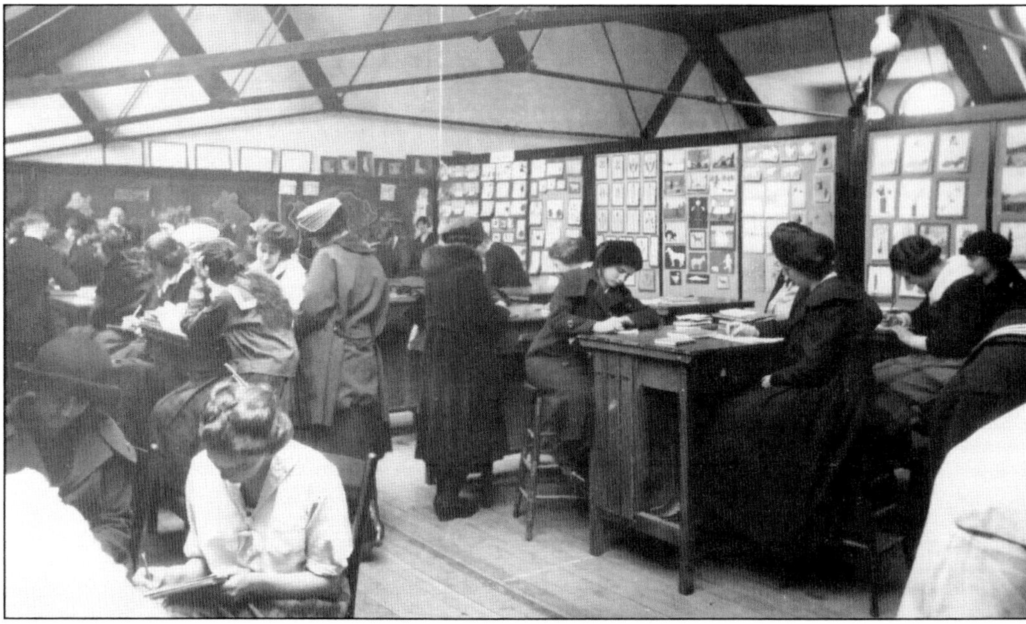

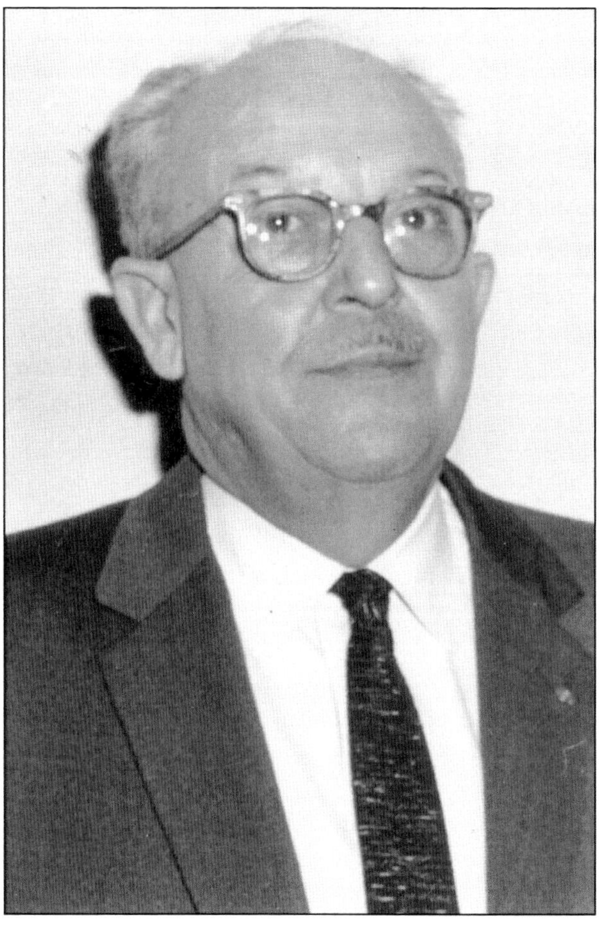

The art department had been on the ground floor of Normal Hall, but in 1920, it moved to its third floor attic home, shown here. It was not a favorite location for the students, and they were pleased to hear it would be moving to a new building in 1931, when the student newspaper, the *Plaid*, wrote, "Those of us who have climbed the three flights of stairs together for a decade or more are filled with mingled emotions as we transfer our affections and muscular development to a more level plane. We will have no more holes in the floor to fall through and please heaven the ceilings and skylights will never descent on our heads in the new situation."

The art department is the largest department at Edinboro. Along with Waldo Bates, Amie Doucette deserves credit for building the foundation of the well-respected program. Doucette came to Edinboro as the second art instructor in 1923 and stayed until 1960. A building is named in his honor.

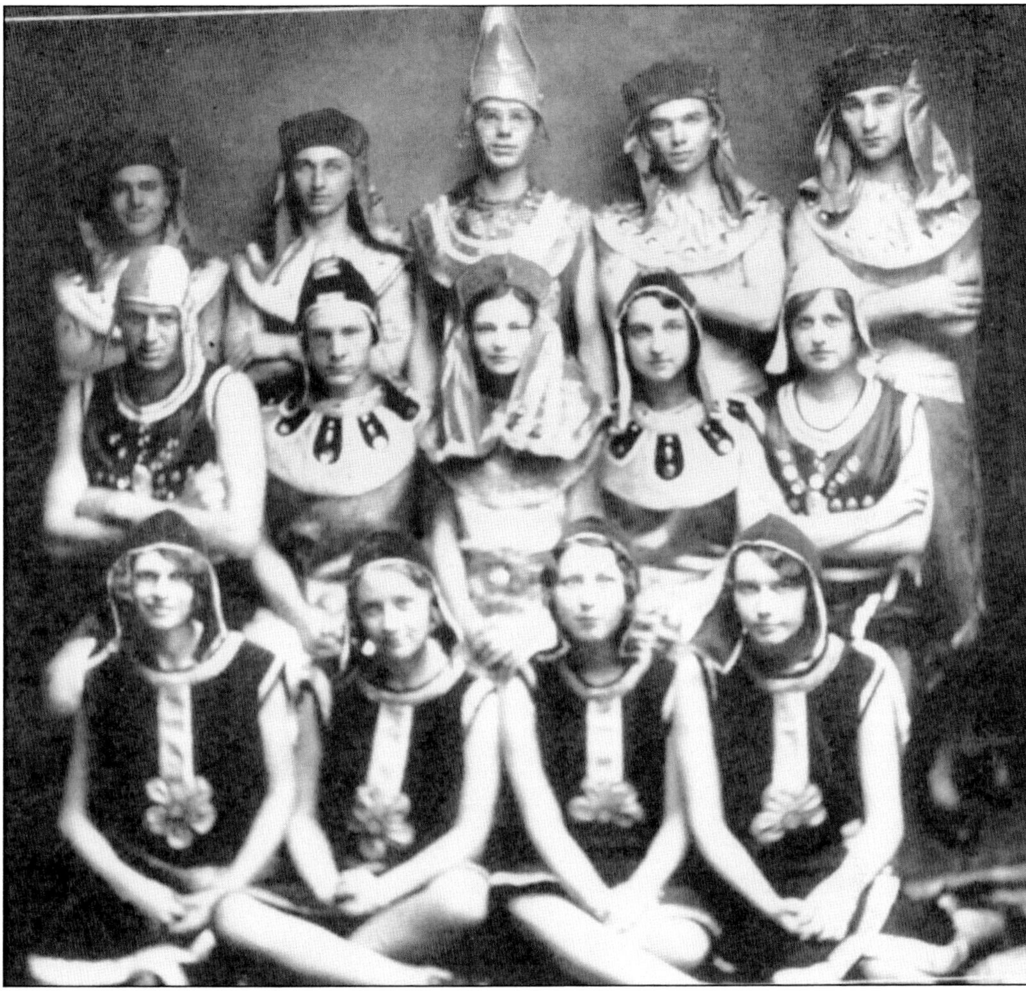

The ScaRab Club was an unusual group formed by art professor Waldo Bates in 1923. The group, comprised of art students, dressed in Egyptian costumes and maintained an Egyptian theme to their activities. The brother and sister bugs, as they called themselves, had different color outfits to match their class standing.

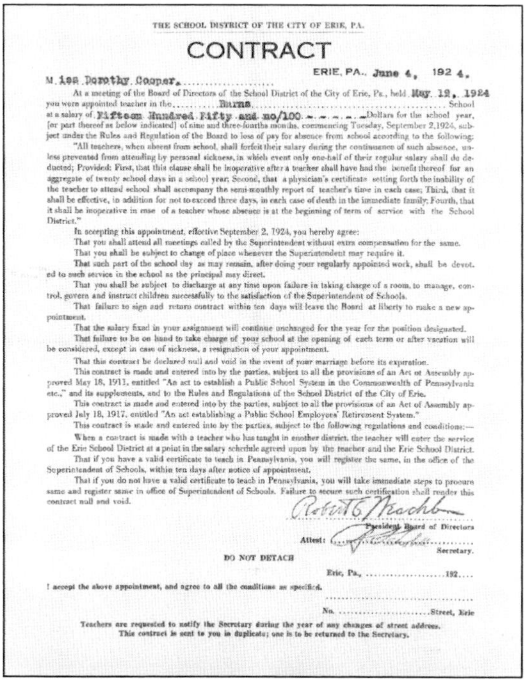

THE SCHOOL DISTRICT OF THE CITY OF ERIE, PA.

CONTRACT

ERIE, PA., June 4, 1924.

Miss Dorothy Cooper.

At a meeting of the Board of Directors of the School District of the City of Erie, Pa., held May 12, 1924 you were appointed teacher in the Burns School at a salary of Fifteen Hundred Fifty and no/100 Dollars for the school year, [or part thereof as below indicated] of nine and three-fourths months, commencing Tuesday, September 2, 1924, subject under the Rules and Regulation of the Board to loss of pay for absence from school according to the following:

"All teachers, when absent from school, shall forfeit their salary during the continuance of such absence, unless prevented from attending by personal sickness, in which event only one-half of their regular salary shall be deducted; Provided: First, that this clause shall be inoperative after a teacher shall have had the benefit thereof for an aggregate of twenty school days in a school year; Second, that a physician's certificate setting forth the inability of the teacher to attend school shall accompany the semi-monthly report of teacher's time in each case; Third, that it shall be effective, in addition for not to exceed three days, in each case of death in the immediate family; Fourth, that it shall be inoperative in case of a teacher whose absence is at the beginning of term of service with the School District."

In accepting this appointment, effective September 2, 1924, you hereby agree:

That you shall attend all meetings called by the Superintendent without extra compensation for the same.

That you shall be subject to change of place whenever the Superintendent may require it.

That such part of the school day as may remain, after doing your regularly appointed work, shall be devoted to such service in the school as the principal may direct.

That you shall be subject to discharge at any time upon failure in taking charge of a room, to manage, control, govern and instruct children successfully to the satisfaction of the Superintendent of Schools.

That failure to sign and return contract within ten days will leave the Board at liberty to make a new appointment.

That the salary fixed in your assignment will continue unchanged for the year for the position designated.

That failure to be on hand to take charge of your school at the opening of each term or after vacation will be considered, except in case of sickness, a resignation of your appointment.

That this contract be declared null and void in the event of your marriage before its expiration.

This contract is made and entered into by the parties, subject to all the provisions of an Act of Assembly approved May 18, 1911, entitled "An act to establish a Public School System in the Commonwealth of Pennsylvania etc.," and its supplements, and to the Rules and Regulations of the School District of the City of Erie.

This contract is made and entered into by the parties, subject to all the provisions of an Act of Assembly approved July 18, 1917, entitled "An act establishing a Public School Employees' Retirement System."

This contract is made and entered into by the parties, subject to the following regulations and conditions:—

When a contract is made with a teacher who has taught in another district, the teacher will enter the service of the Erie School District at a point in the salary schedule agreed upon by the teacher and the Erie School District.

That if you have a valid certificate to teach in Pennsylvania, you will register the same, in the office of the Superintendent of Schools, within ten days after notice of appointment.

That if you do not have a valid certificate to teach in Pennsylvania, you will take immediate steps to procure same and register same in office of Superintendent of Schools. Failure to secure such certification shall render this contract null and void.

Robert C. Nachb[illegible]
President Board of Directors

Attest: [illegible]
Secretary.

DO NOT DETACH

Erie, Pa., ...192....

I accept the above appointment, and agree to all the conditions as specified.

....

No. ....Street, Erie

Teachers are requested to notify the Secretary during the year of any changes of street address.
This contract is sent to you in duplicate; one is to be returned to the Secretary.

This contract is between the City of Erie and schoolteacher Dorothy Cooper, the granddaughter of principal Joseph Cooper. As was typical in contracts for ladies in 1924, there is the stipulation that said, "This contract shall be declared null and void in the event of your marriage before its expiration."

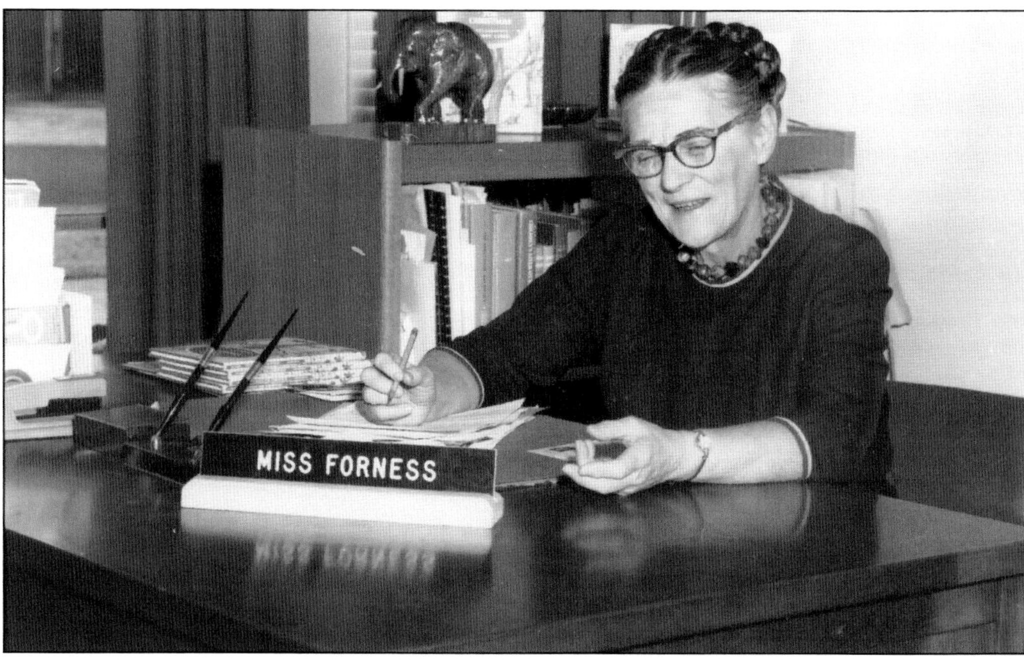

Mildred Forness was introduced to the Edinboro campus as a youth when she and her mother lived in Reeder Hall. At the time, her mother was serving as a housemother. Mildred began working at Edinboro as an assistant librarian in 1922, becoming head librarian in 1925. At the time, the library was on the second floor of Normal Hall. "We had 25,000 volumes, I remember well," Forness said. In 1960, she organized the library science department while remaining the head librarian. She moved into the library science department full time in 1966 and retired in 1969. The library is named in her honor.

Two

State Teachers College Years 1927–1960

This period brought serious challenges to the school. In 1927, enrollment stood at 602, and by 1960, there were 1,147 students, but these figures hide the problems confronted in the intervening years. During this time, the school endured the Great Depression and World War II, both resulting serious downturns.

Carmon Ross was president during the Depression years. As the student body shrank closer to 200, Ross was able to partner with the Works Progress Administration (WPA) to initiate a building plan in 1938, which brought four new structures to campus, all of which are still in use.

Private colleges felt the effects of the Depression as well, banding together to craft a legislative agenda that aimed to close eight of the state-owned schools. Instead of operating all those schools, a scholarship fund was proposed, which would allow students to take their college money anywhere they chose. Those efforts fell short as more dire issues took priority.

World War II affected everyone in America, including the Edinboro State Teachers College. Still reeling from the effects of the Depression, enrollment dipped to only 106 students. Since male students were rare, football was canceled, and the military honor roll grew. The school contributed to the war effort with programs for cadet nurses and an aviation ground school.

The end of the war brought great relief to everyone. Veterans flocked to campuses, taking advantage of the GI Bill. Enrollment at Edinboro doubled in one year, as overenrolled Penn State sent students to Edinboro for their first year of study.

In 1954, Dr. Tom Miller arrived as president, and his tenure spanned the state teachers college years and the state college years. His was a time of unmatched growth in enrollment, faculty, and the campus footprint.

During this period, Edinboro seesawed from poverty to prosperity. With competent leadership and a dedicated faculty, Edinboro was able to end the state teachers college years with stable footing.

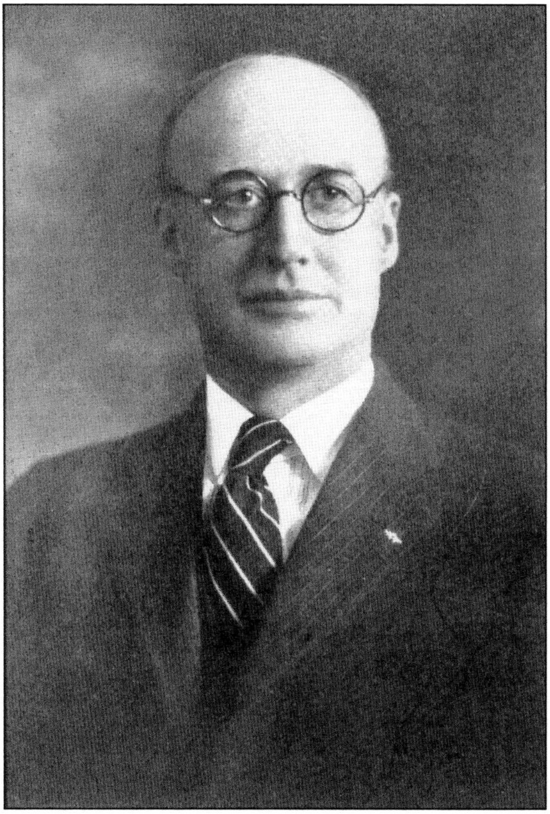

Clarence Crawford has the distinction of being both principal and president of Edinboro. He was elected principal in 1922 but resigned from that office in 1934 for health reasons. During his tenure as chief officer of the school, Edinboro changed from a normal school to a state teachers college, thus the change in his title. After he resigned as president, he stayed on to teach social studies until his retirement in 1940. The Crawford Center for Health and Physical Education and Disability Resource is named in his honor.

Justina Baron was a librarian at the school from 1925 to 1966, working in Edinboro's Erie branch for two of those years. The current library opened in 1976 and is named in her honor.

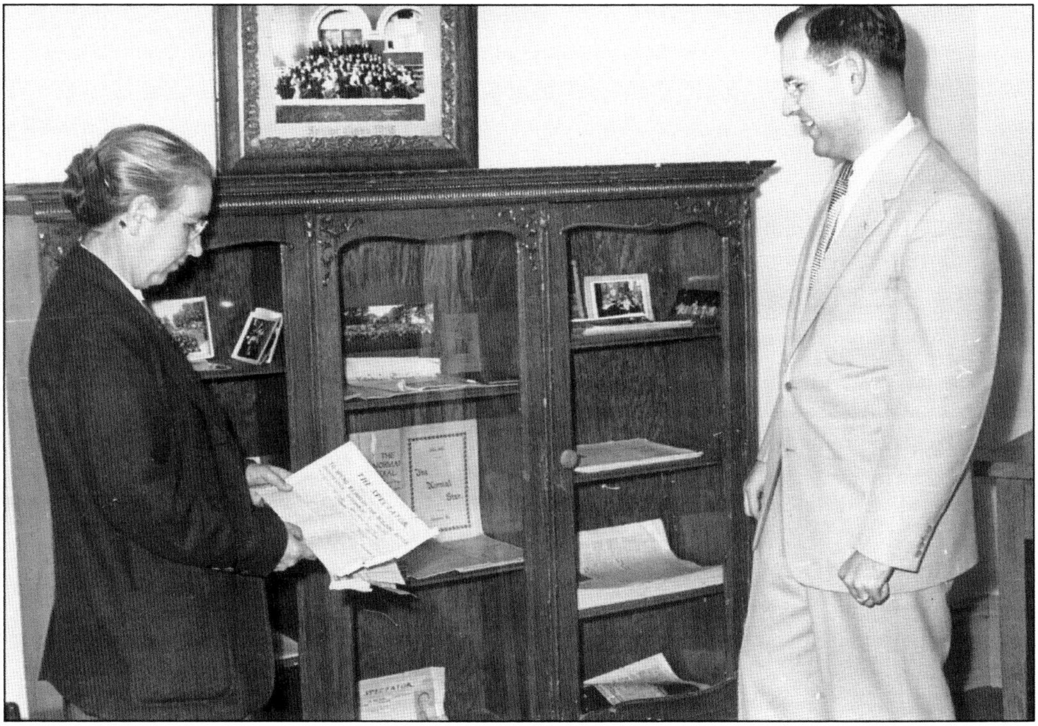

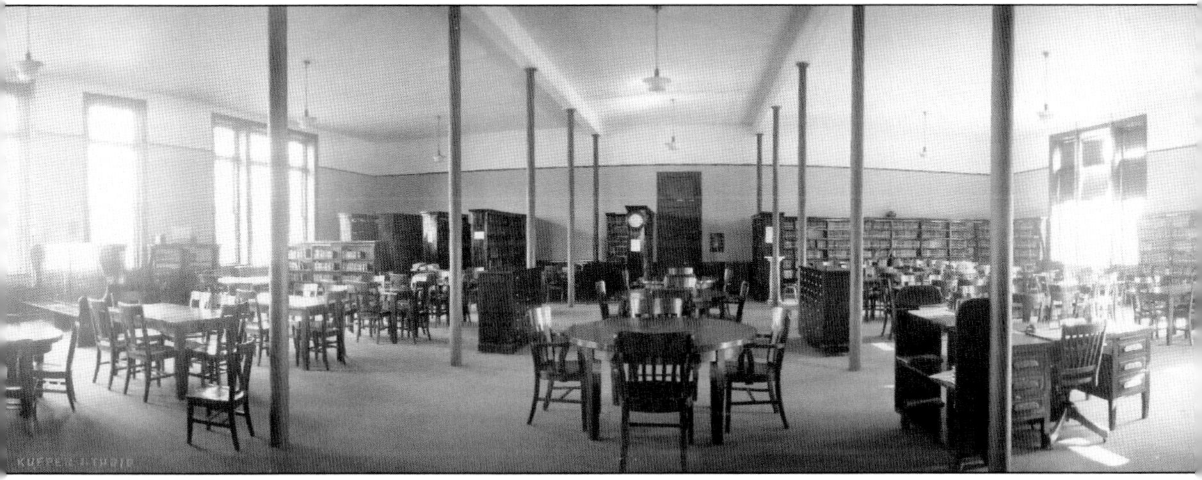

In 1927, the library was on the second floor of Normal Hall. During this period, Edinboro operated what was known as a Rural School Circulating Library. Boxes of books were packed neatly and loaned to local schools. At the time, northwest Pennsylvania was largely an agricultural area spotted with one-room schoolhouses. Schools participating in the program were appreciative of the books and always anxious for the next shipment.

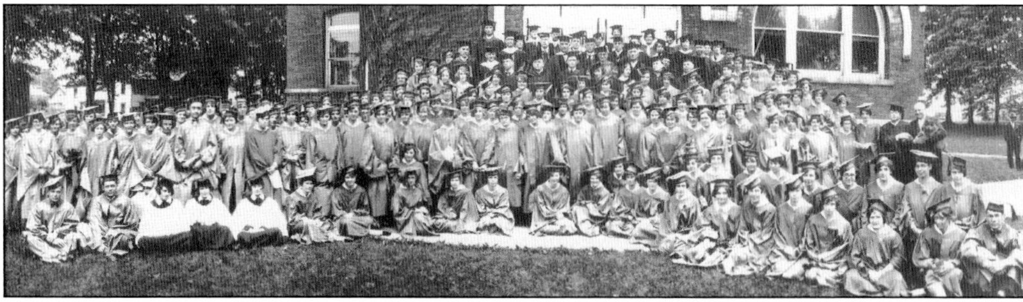

The class of 1927, seen here, witnessed the school's change from Edinboro State Normal School to Edinboro State Teachers College, which officially occurred on May 31, 1927. Three years later, Edinboro was accredited by the American Association of Teachers Colleges with a Class-A rating. That year, students paid $288 for board, home, and laundry; a $25 registration fee; and up to $24 in lab fees. There were no additional tuition fees.

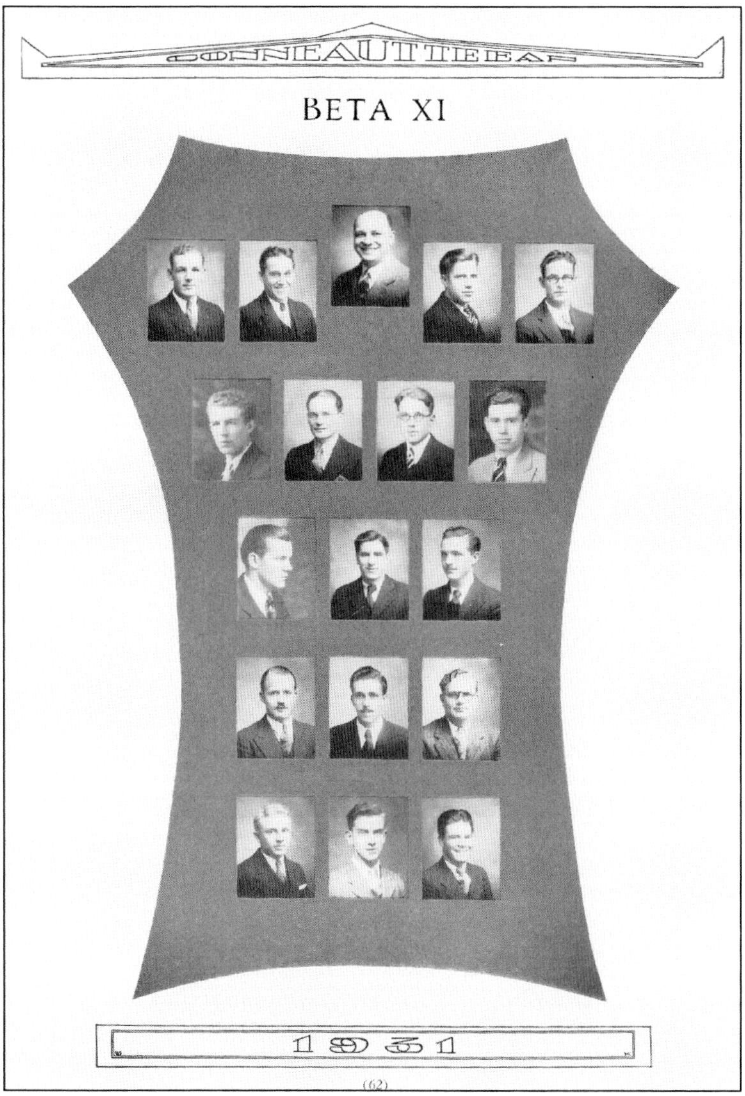

The Board of State Normal School principals, comprised of the principals of the state normal schools, originally ruled that fraternities and sororities were not permitted on campuses, but in 1926, the board decided that each campus could make its own rules regarding Greek societies. Beta Xi was around the campus informally since 1925, sponsoring dances and banquets. In 1928, it became the first Greek organization recognized at Edinboro. It was followed soon afterward by Chi Delta Sigma. The first sorority was Alpha Delta, also founded in 1928.

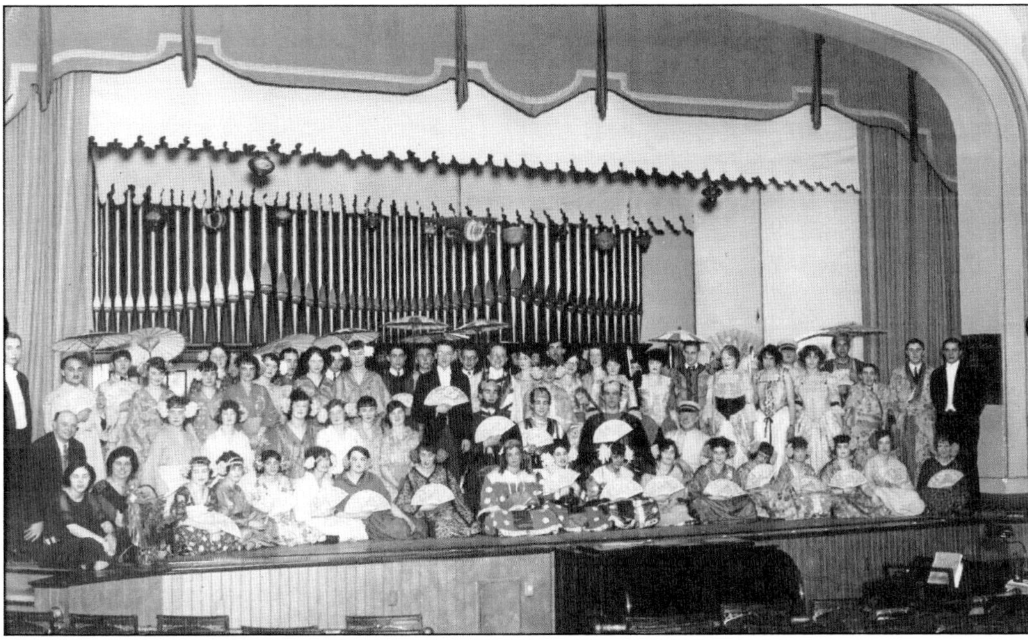

A Mikado, or comic opera, was performed in Normal Hall around 1930. In this image, the pipe organ is plainly seen behind the cast. The organ, installed in 1921, was in use until 1940. From the time the literary societies produced plays through today, the arts have been a big part of campus life.

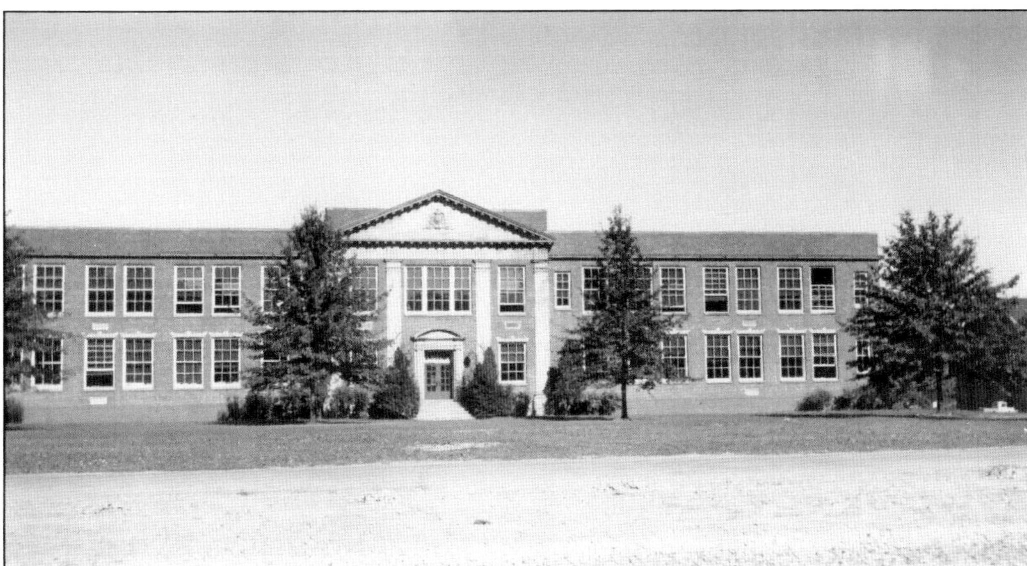

Francis A. Loveland was vice president and treasurer of the J.W. & A.P. Howard Leather Company, located in Corry, Pennsylvania. He served on the board of trustees for eight years, beginning in 1917. Loveland Hall was built in 1931 to house the art and science departments. Since 1965, it has been occupied solely by the art department.

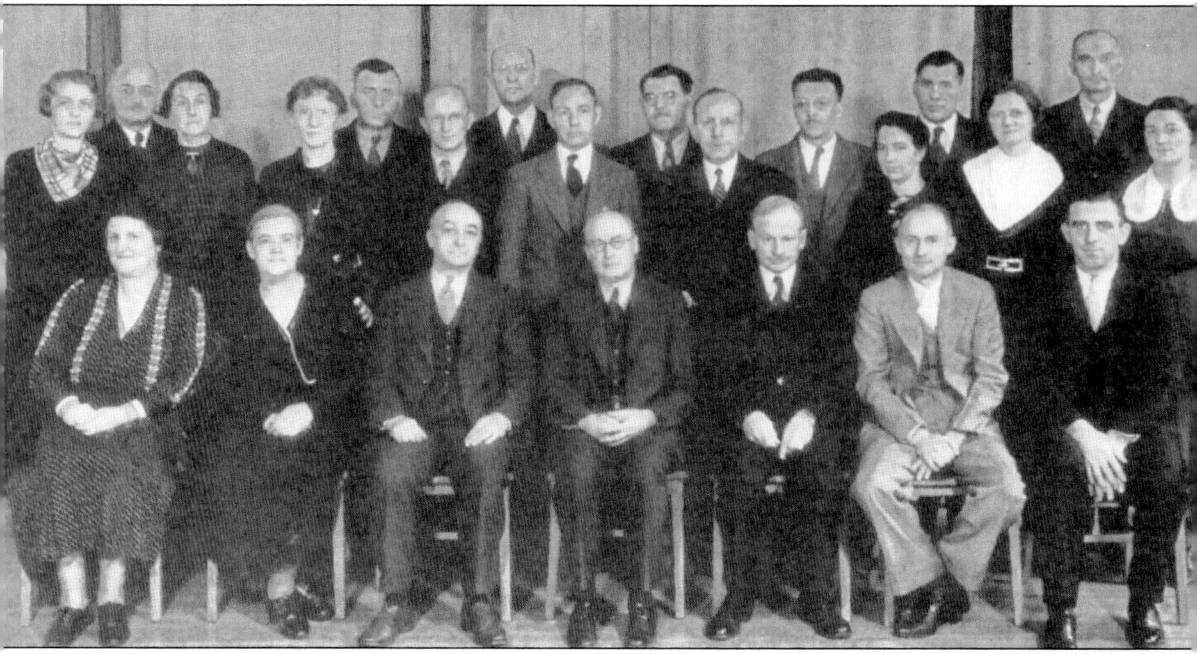

The Great Depression deeply affected the school. Enrollment dropped from 602 in 1929–1930 to 240 in 1937–1938. In 1931, the faculty salary schedule was canceled, and in 1933, salaries were cut 10 percent, a reduction that was not restored until 1937. This is a picture of the faculty in 1935.

Carmon Ross accepted the presidency of Edinboro in the thick of the Depression. The state was cutting back significantly on the state teachers colleges while simultaneously increasing funding for state-related schools. Ross said, "It is this unjustifiable reduction which give the friends of the People's Colleges much cause for alarm." Despite the funding shortage, Ross was able to grow the campus with the 1938 building plan. That year, a ground-breaking ceremony was held for four buildings later named Compton Hall, Crawford Center for Health for Health and Physical Education and Disability Resource, Memorial Auditorium, and the powerhouse.

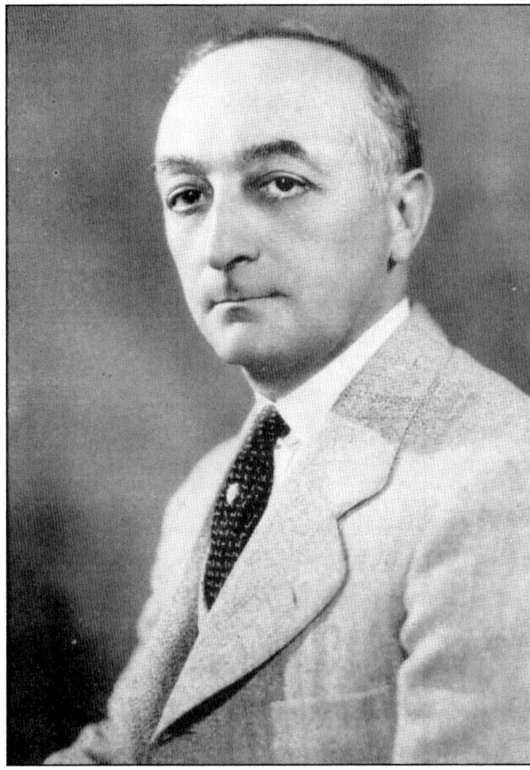

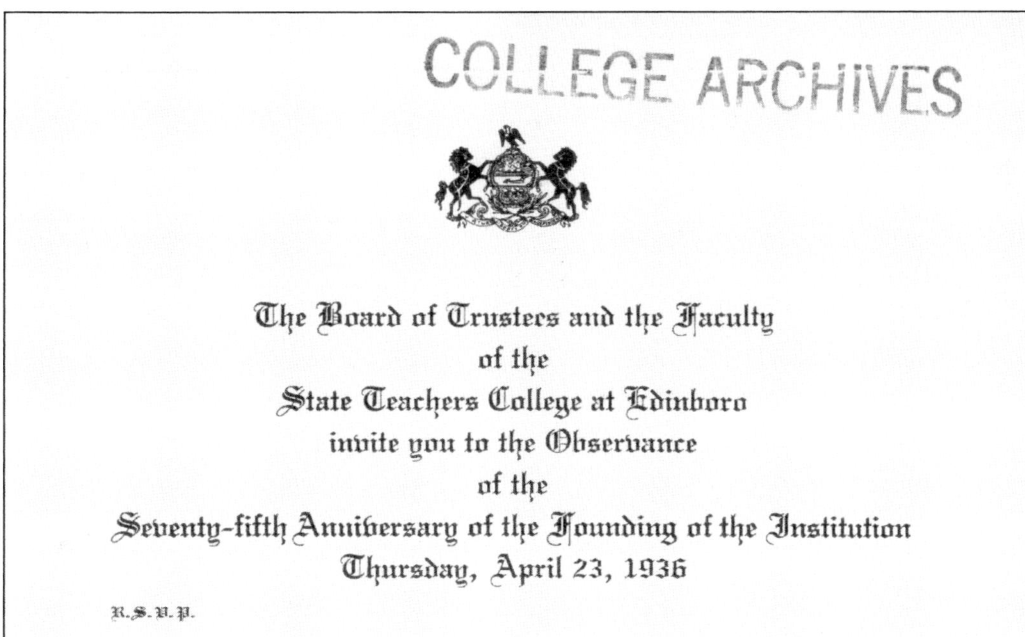

The Board of Trustees and the Faculty
of the
State Teachers College at Edinboro
invite you to the Observance
of the
Seventy-fifth Anniversary of the Founding of the Institution
Thursday, April 23, 1936

R.S.V.P.

The 75th anniversary of the school was celebrated in 1936. Even in the midst of hard times, it was a grand celebration with dignitaries from across the state taking part, including Ned Dearborn, an Edinboro alum and the dean of general education at New York University for whom a dormitory is named, and Pennsylvania governor George Earle.

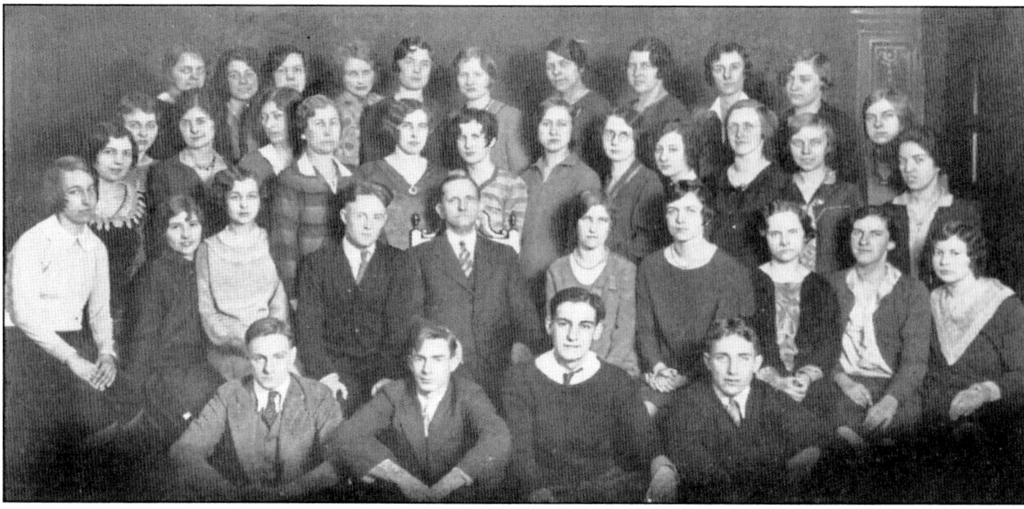

Gertrude Barber was president of her senior class at Edinboro's Erie Branch in 1930 and went on to open what has become the Dr. Gertrude A. Barber Center National Institute in Erie. While at Edinboro's Erie branch, she participated in the Brush and Palette Club, as well as the Forum Club, a current events discussion group. This is a photograph of the Forum Club during the year Barber was involved.

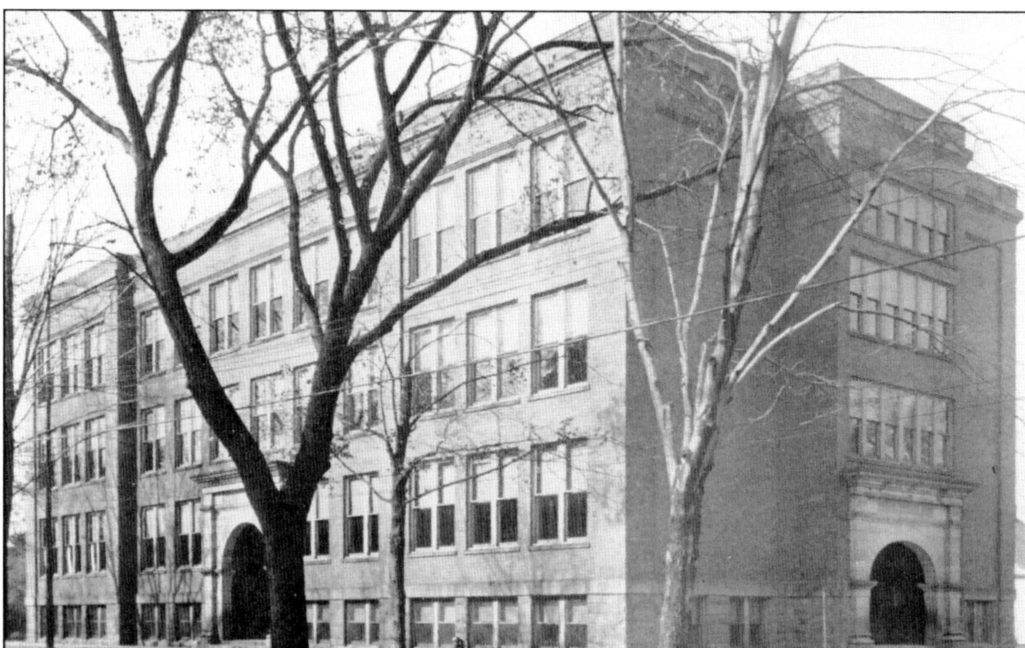

Edinboro's Erie branch campus was located on the third floor of Washington School at Twenty-first and Sassafras Streets in Erie. The Erie School Board had operated its own normal school, but the certification they conferred was not accepted outside of Erie County; thus, they entered into an agreement with Edinboro to operate the Erie school. The school was vibrant with activity. Clubs, athletic teams, a yearbook, and all the affairs usually seen on a main campus were available at the Erie campus.

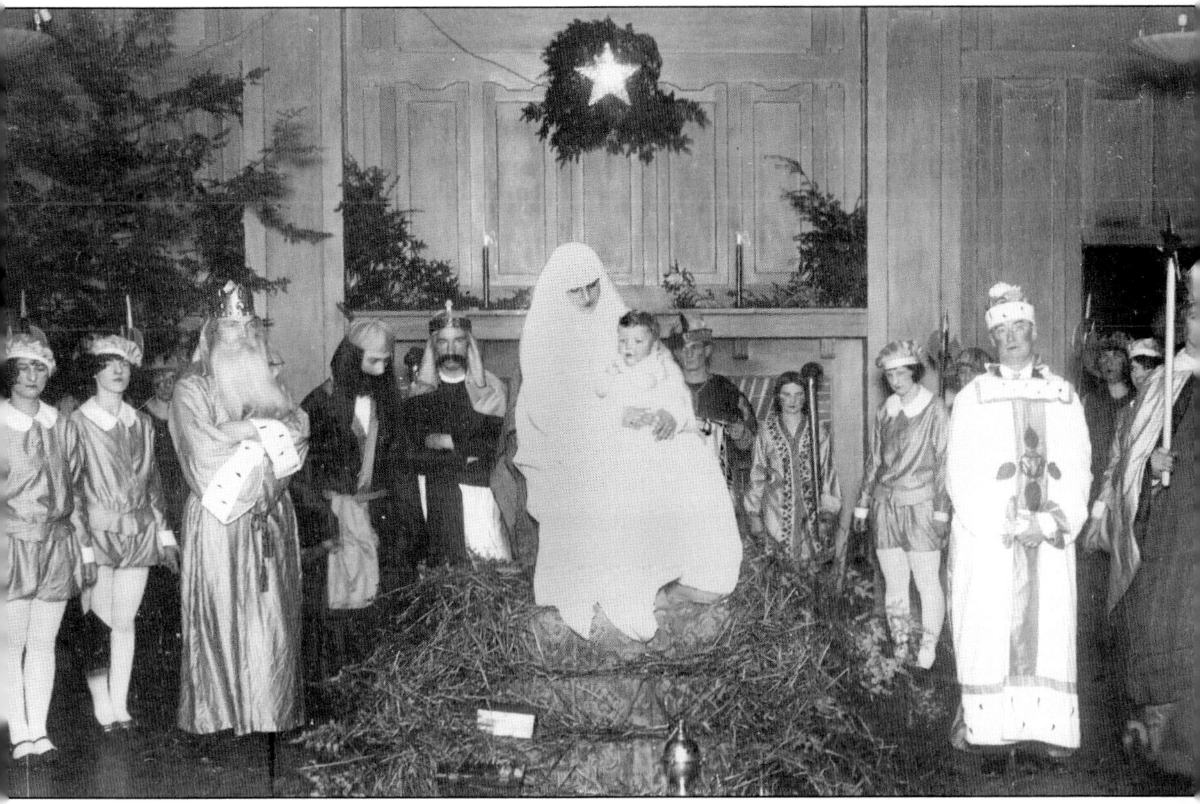

Ye Old English Yuletide Ceremonial was an established and much-anticipated event in 1935. There was no pretense of trying to maintain a secular stance. The baby Jesus, Mary, and the three kings were all present. In 1935, school president Carmon Ross played the part of the spirit of Christmas. The event was accompanied by a banquet in the Haven Hall dining room.

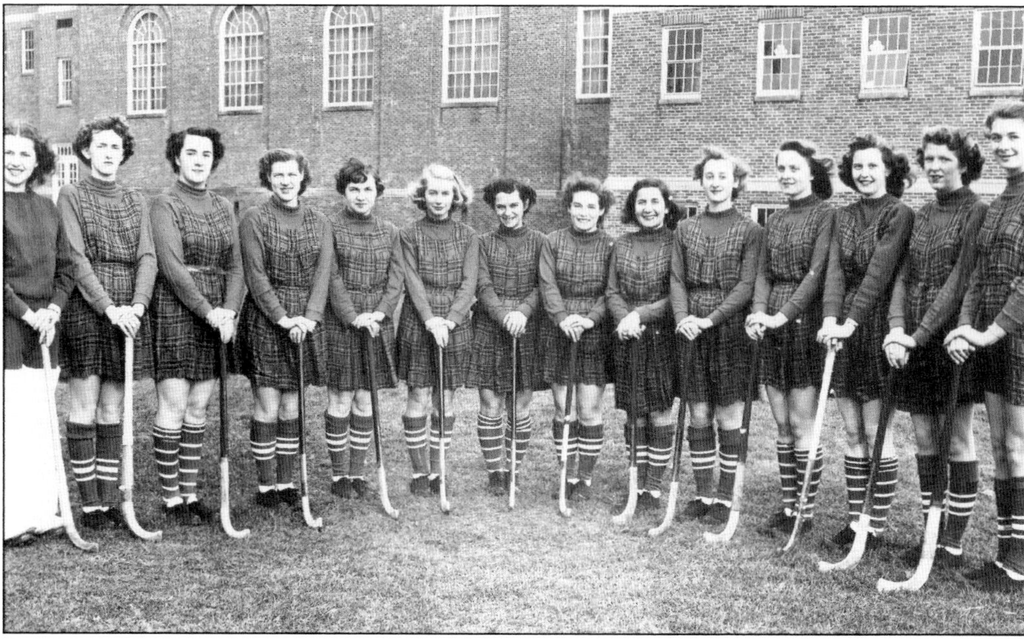

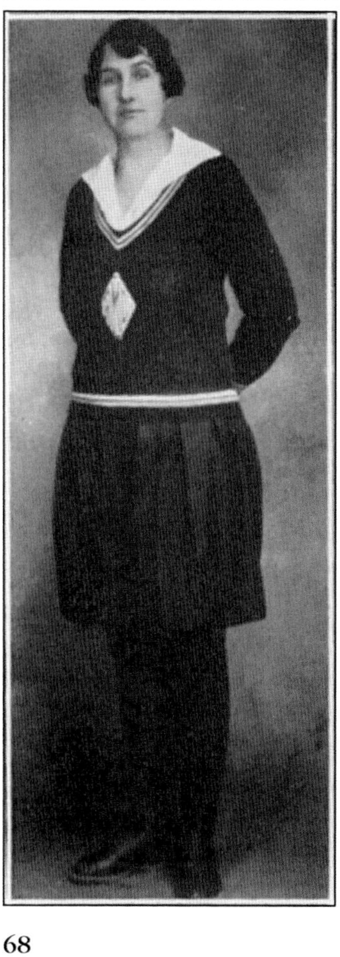

Edinboro had field hockey teams at the main campus and the Erie campus. Many of the games were played as an intramural sport with limited intercollegiate play. In 1936, the team joined the US Field Hockey Association. Also that year, Edinboro joined the women's division of the National Amateur Athletic Federation.

Nettie Mae Ruttle arrived at Edinboro in 1925 and stayed until 1953. Under her direction, women's athletics blossomed. In 1928, over 80 ladies turned out for the first basketball practice. Out of this, several teams were formed for intramural games, and 14 student athletes were selected for the varsity team.

Student handbooks were easily carried in a back pocket. All the clubs, activities, and rules were in one convenient place. Lights out, curfew, permission to go off campus, visiting hours, dining times, and physical education activities were all spelled out in the small book. Beginning in 1937, all students statewide were required to participate (without credit) in one physical education activity each semester.

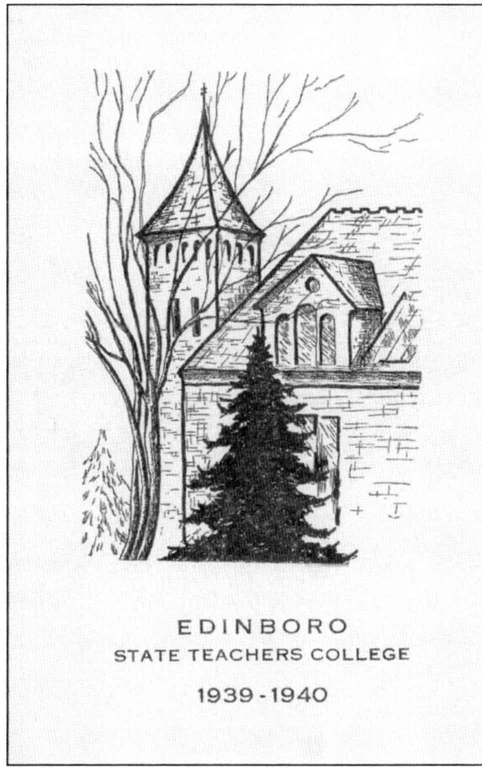

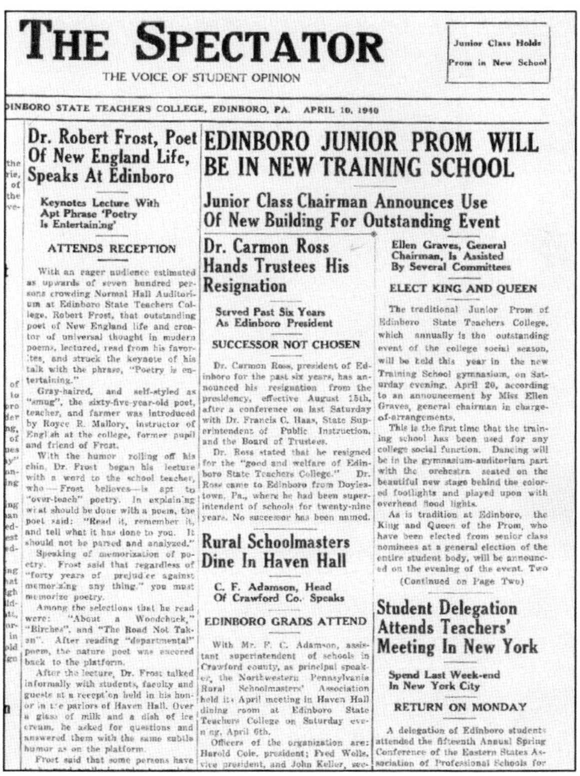

THE SPECTATOR

THE VOICE OF STUDENT OPINION

Junior Class Holds Prom in New School

EDINBORO STATE TEACHERS COLLEGE, EDINBORO, PA. APRIL 10, 1940

Dr. Robert Frost, Poet Of New England Life, Speaks At Edinboro

Keynotes Lecture With Apt Phrase 'Poetry Is Entertaining'

ATTENDS RECEPTION

With an eager audience estimated as upwards of seven hundred persons crowding Normal Hall Auditorium at Edinboro State Teachers College, Robert Frost, that outstanding poet of New England life and creator of universal thought in modern poems, lectured, read from his favorites, and struck the keynote of his talk with the phrase, "Poetry is entertaining."

Gray-haired, and self-styled as "smug", the sixty-five-year-old poet, teacher, and farmer was introduced by Royce R. Mallory, instructor of English at the college, former pupil and friend of Frost.

With the humor rolling off his chin, Dr. Frost began his lecture with a word to the school teacher, who — Frost believes — is apt to "over-teach" poetry. In explaining what should be done with a poem, the poet said: "Read it, remember it, and tell what it has done to you. It should not be parsed and analyzed."

Speaking of memorization of poetry, Frost said that regardless of "forty years of prejudice against memorizing any thing," you must memorize poetry.

Among the selections that he read were: "About a Woodchuck," "Birches", and "The Road Not Taken". After reading "departmental" poem, the nature poet was encored back to the platform.

After the lecture, Dr. Frost talked informally with students, faculty and guests at a reception held in his honor in the parlors of Haven Hall. Over a glass of milk and a dish of ice cream, he asked for questions and answered them with the same subtle humor as on the platform.

Frost said that some persons have

EDINBORO JUNIOR PROM WILL BE IN NEW TRAINING SCHOOL

Junior Class Chairman Announces Use Of New Building For Outstanding Event

Ellen Graves, General Chairman, Is Assisted By Several Committees

ELECT KING AND QUEEN

The traditional Junior Prom of Edinboro State Teachers College, which annually is the outstanding event of the college social season, will be held this year in the new Training School gymnasium, on Saturday evening, April 20, according to an announcement by Miss Ellen Graves, general chairman in charge-of-arrangements.

This is the first time that the training school has been used for any college social function. Dancing will be in the gymnasium-auditorium part with the orchestra seated on the beautiful new stage behind the colored footlights and played upon with overhead flood lights.

As is tradition at Edinboro, the King and Queen of the Prom, who have been elected from senior class nominees at a general election of the entire student body, will be announced on the evening of the event. Two

(Continued on Page Two)

Dr. Carmon Ross Hands Trustees His Resignation

Served Past Six Years As Edinboro President

SUCCESSOR NOT CHOSEN

Dr. Carmon Ross, president of Edinboro for the past six years, has announced his resignation from the presidency, effective August 15th, after a conference on last Saturday with Dr. Francis C. Haas, State Superintendent of Public Instruction, and the Board of Trustees.

Dr. Ross stated that he resigned for the "good and welfare of Edinboro State Teachers College." Dr. Ross came to Edinboro from Doylestown, Pa., where he had been superintendent of schools for twenty-nine years. No successor has been named.

Rural Schoolmasters Dine In Haven Hall

C. F. Adamson, Head Of Crawford Co. Speaks

EDINBORO GRADS ATTEND

With Mr. F. C. Adamson, assistant superintendent of schools in Crawford county, as principal speaker, the Northwestern Pennsylvania Rural Schoolmasters' Association held its April meeting in Haven Hall dining room at Edinboro State Teachers College on Saturday evening, April 6th.

Officers of the organization are: Harold Cole, president; Fred Wells, vice president, and John Keller, sec-

Student Delegation Attends Teachers' Meeting In New York

Spend Last Week-end In New York City

RETURN ON MONDAY

A delegation of Edinboro students attended the fifteenth Annual Spring Conference of the Eastern States Association of Professional Schools for

In April 1940, poet Robert Frost spoke to the students at Edinboro. Royce Mallory, an education and English professor at Edinboro and former student of Frost's, introduced him. While at Edinboro, Frost read some of his most famous poems, including "Birches" and "The Road Not Taken." After his talk, he met informally with students and faculty at a reception in the Haven Hall dining room.

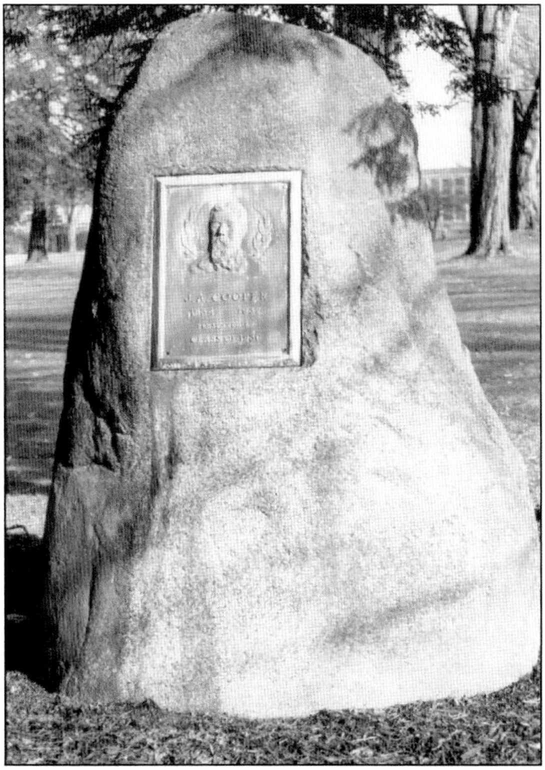

Cooper's Rock still stands facing Meadville Street in the front of campus. The plaque commemorates former principal Joseph Cooper and his contributions to the school. The memorial was donated by the class of 1936.

Dr. Lyman H. VanHouten served as president of Edinboro from 1941 to 1954. His first appointment was as director of the branch campus in Erie. He moved to the Edinboro campus in 1928 to teach education and psychology and became president 13 years later. After leaving Edinboro, he taught psychology at Westminster College.

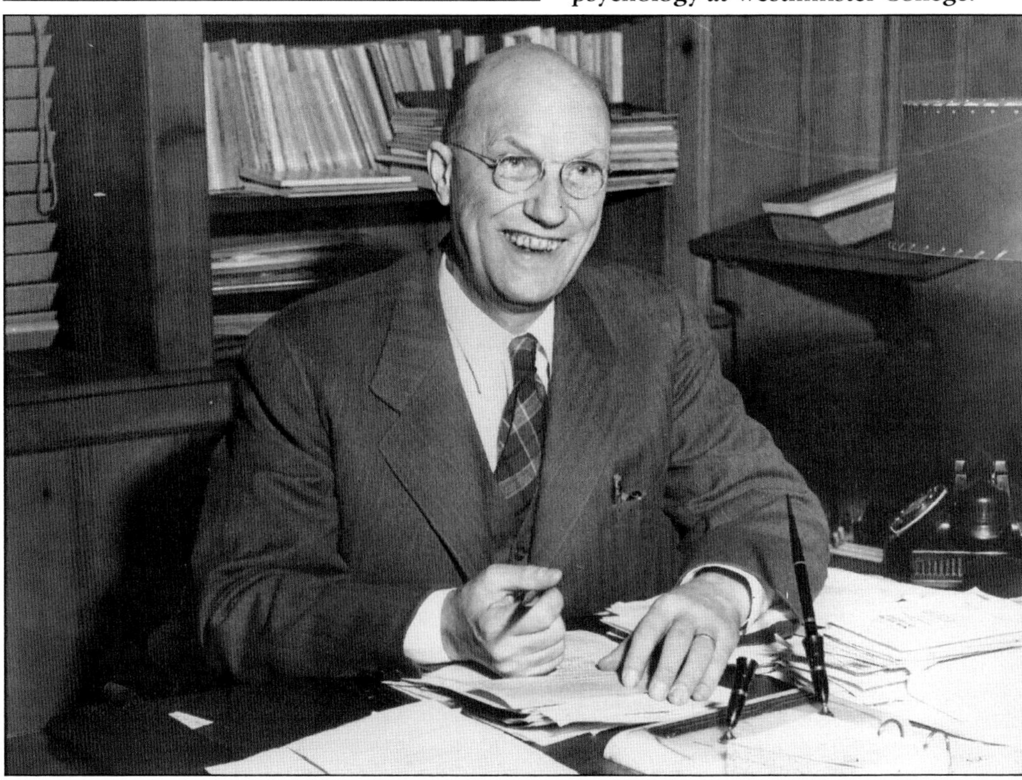

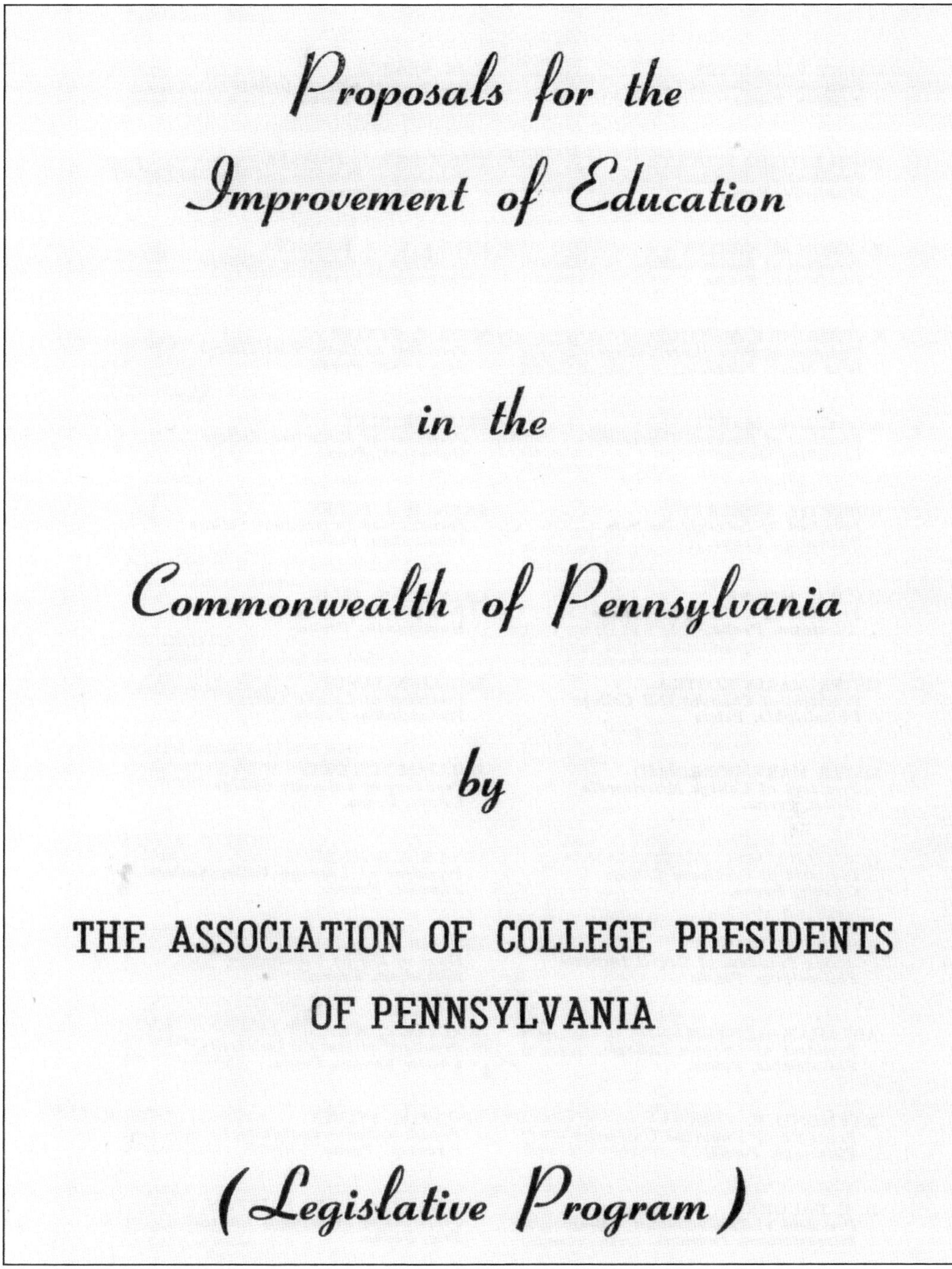

Proposals for the Improvement of Education

in the

Commonwealth of Pennsylvania

by

THE ASSOCIATION OF COLLEGE PRESIDENTS OF PENNSYLVANIA

(Legislative Program)

The Association of College Presidents of Pennsylvania was composed of the presidents of 56 private colleges in Pennsylvania. This 1941 legislative program questioned the need for Pennsylvania to operate 14 public colleges and suggested they only needed six. The eight that would close would be used for "the vocational, welfare, and other public needs not now adequately provided for in the state." Instead of funding schools, their plan was for the state to operate a scholarship fund and let the students pick among the existing private schools.

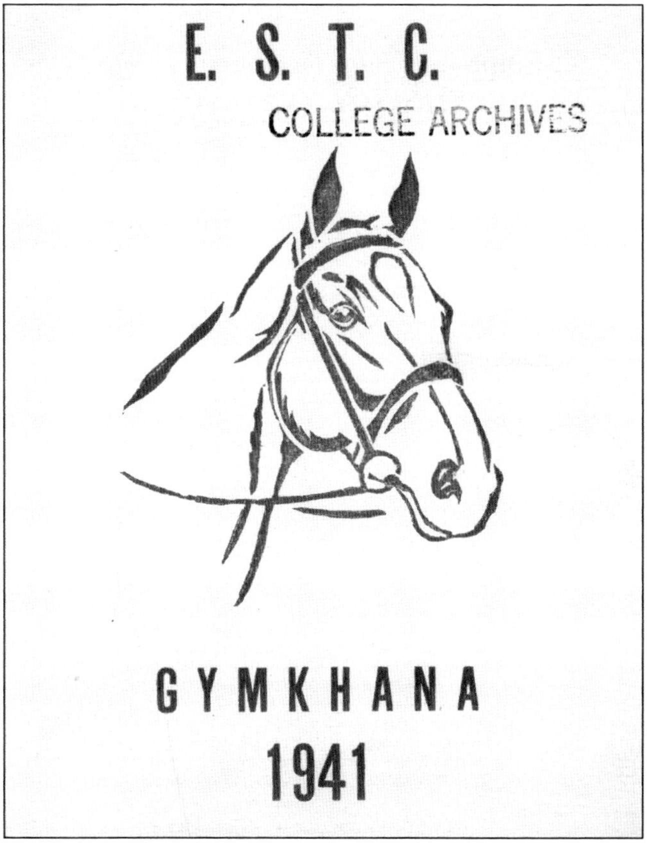

The Edinboro State Teachers College Horse Show, a gymkhana event, had dozens of participants competing in equitation, jumping, and more. With all the land Edinboro owns, having an equestrian team seems a natural fit. For years, the students enjoyed horseback riding at Culbertson Hills, now a golf course.

President Lyman VanHouten sits behind the table on the right with the 1946 faculty. After Carmon Ross resigned in 1940, the board of trustees nominated two different people to the position of president. Both times, the governor refused to appoint them. The board then appointed VanHouten as acting president. In January 1941, the state approved his appointment as president. He served in this position until 1954.

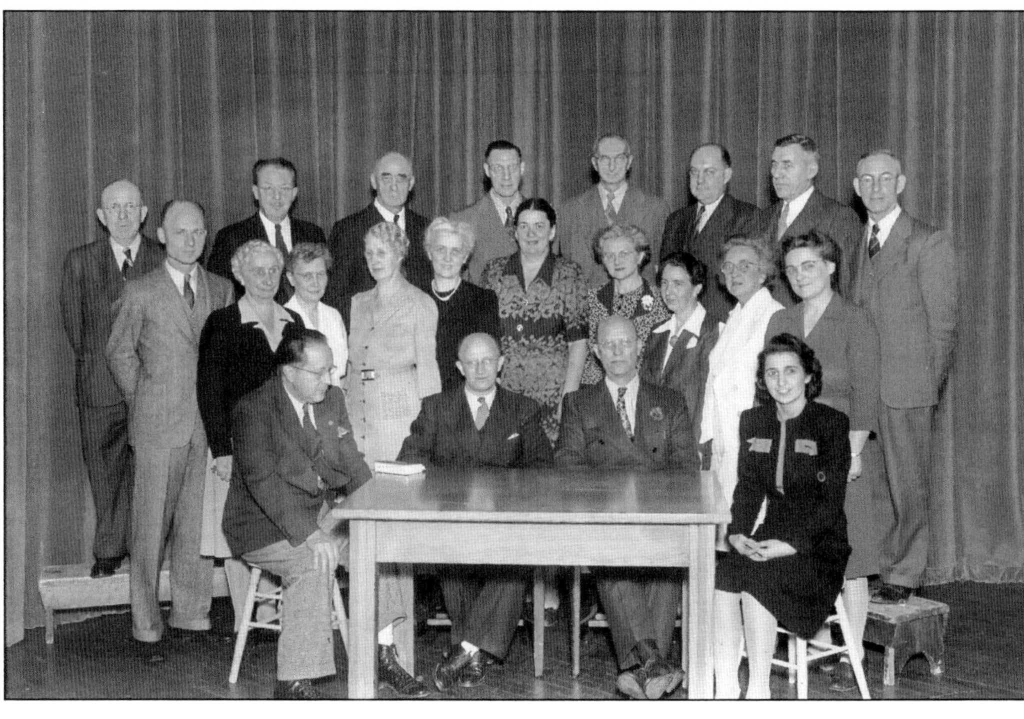

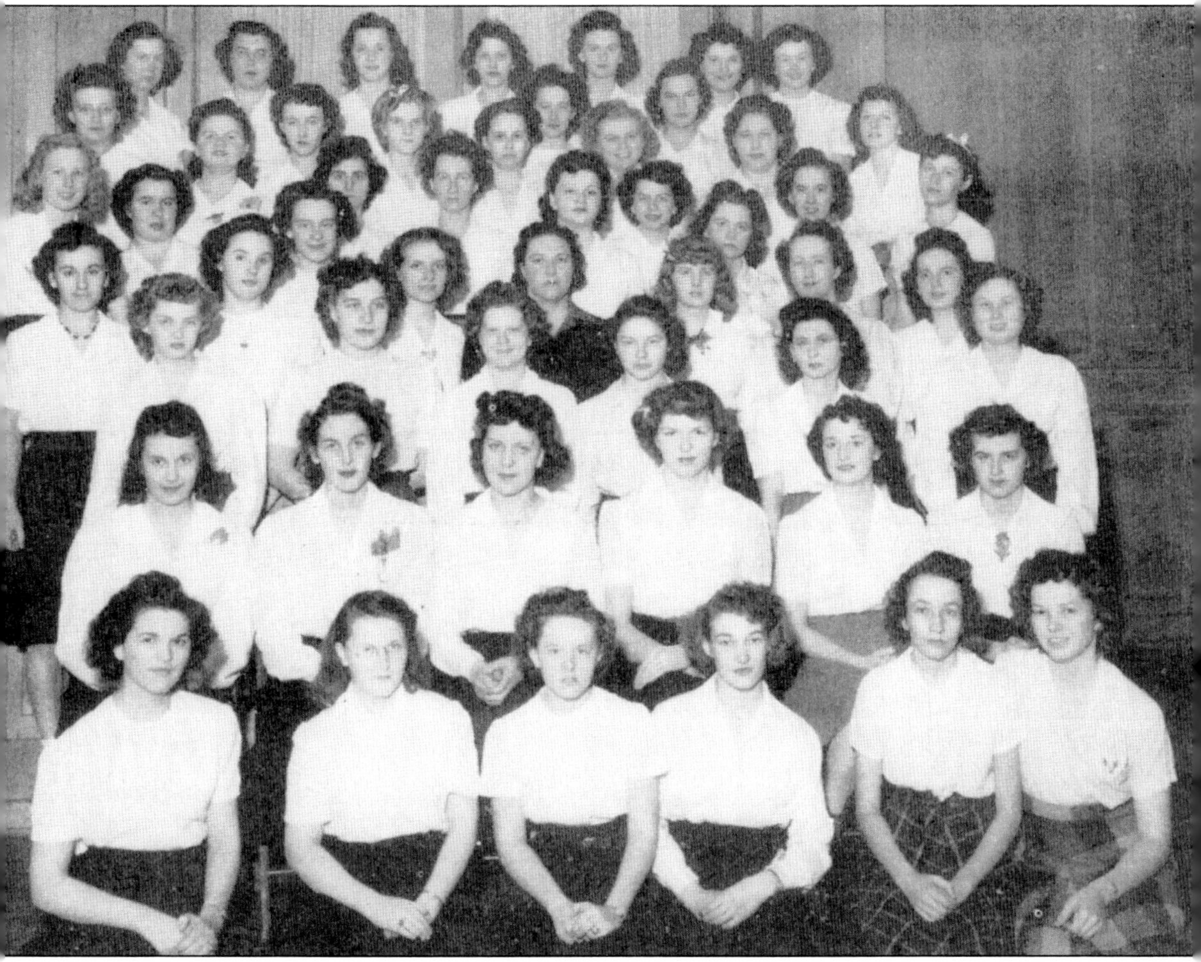

Edinboro did its part during World War II. The curriculum was expanded to include the nurse cadet program and the war training service link instrument course, which had 40 students enrolled. At that time, signs outside of Reeder Hall read, "Military Reservation." Both programs were canceled soon after the war.

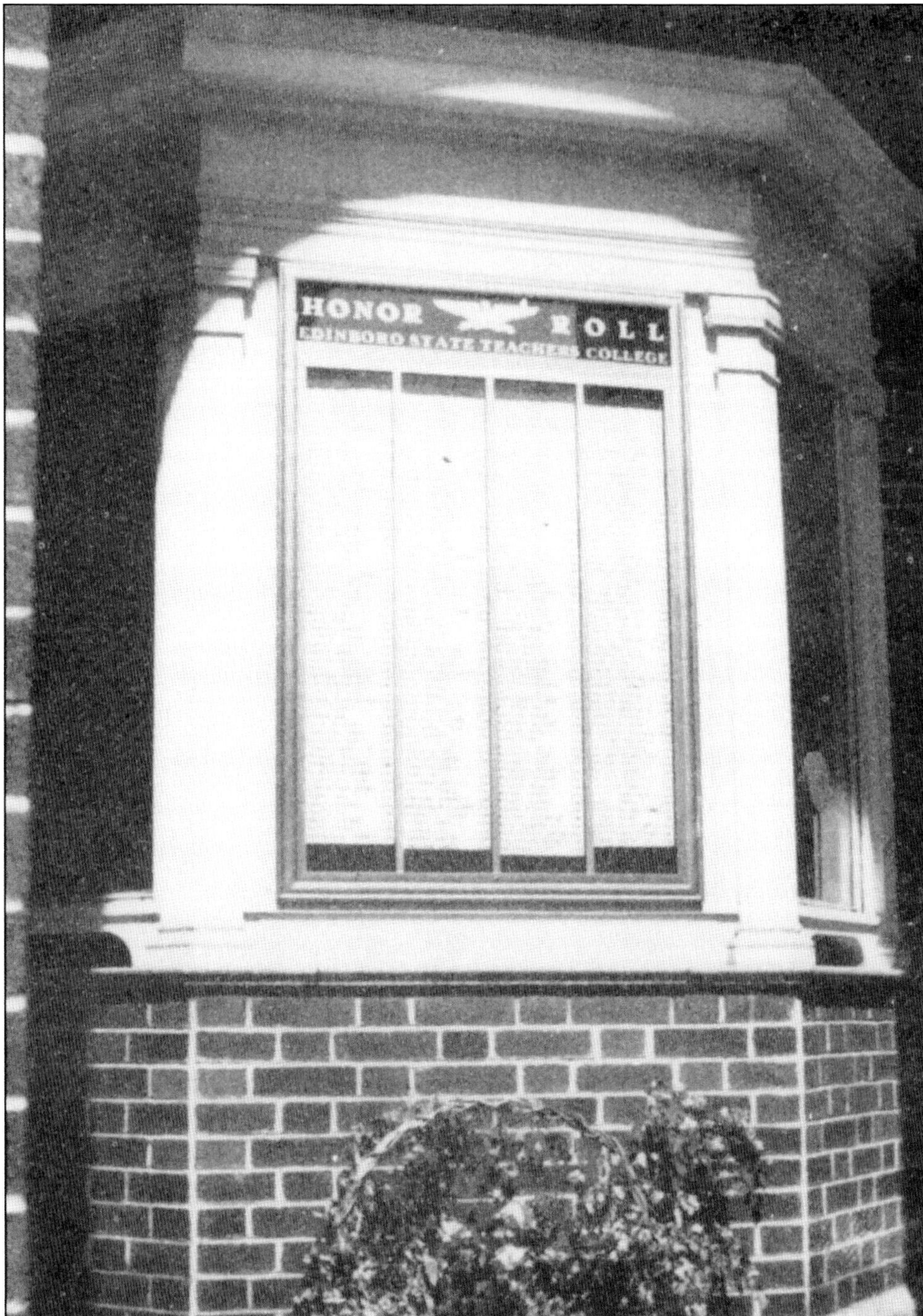

Outside of Memorial Auditorium was an honor roll listing the names of those who left school and entered the service. Enrollment during the war swiftly declined, and by 1943, the school had only 103 students, nearly all of them women. Football was canceled from 1944 to 1946, and men's sports were all but gone. During the war, the student newspaper ran a column titled "News of E.S.T.C. Men in the Service." Too often, the students read the phrases "missing in action" or "wounded."

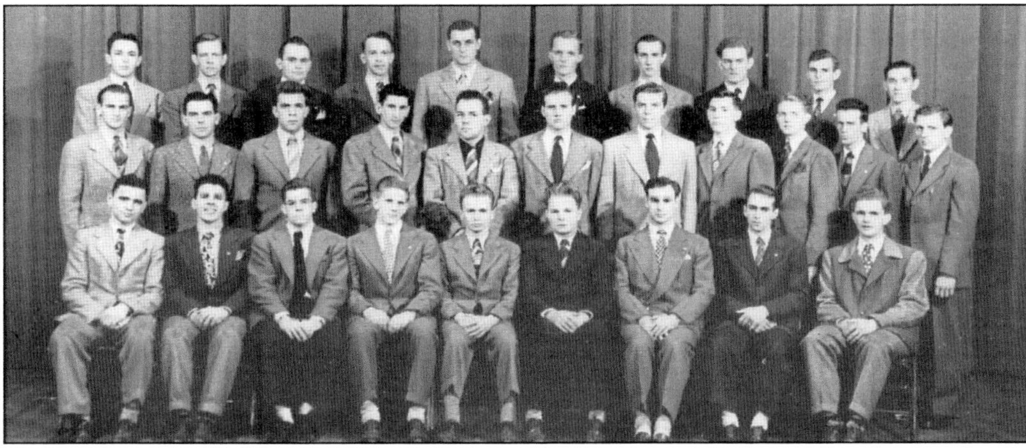

The 1947 men's glee club was a sign of the return of men to campus. After the war, thanks to the GI Bill, soldiers flocked to colleges. Edinboro's enrollment jumped 400 percent, thanks in part to the Penn State assignees, which were the students that Penn State could not accommodate. Men's sports were revived, but the first football team back lost all six of its games and was outscored 154-7.

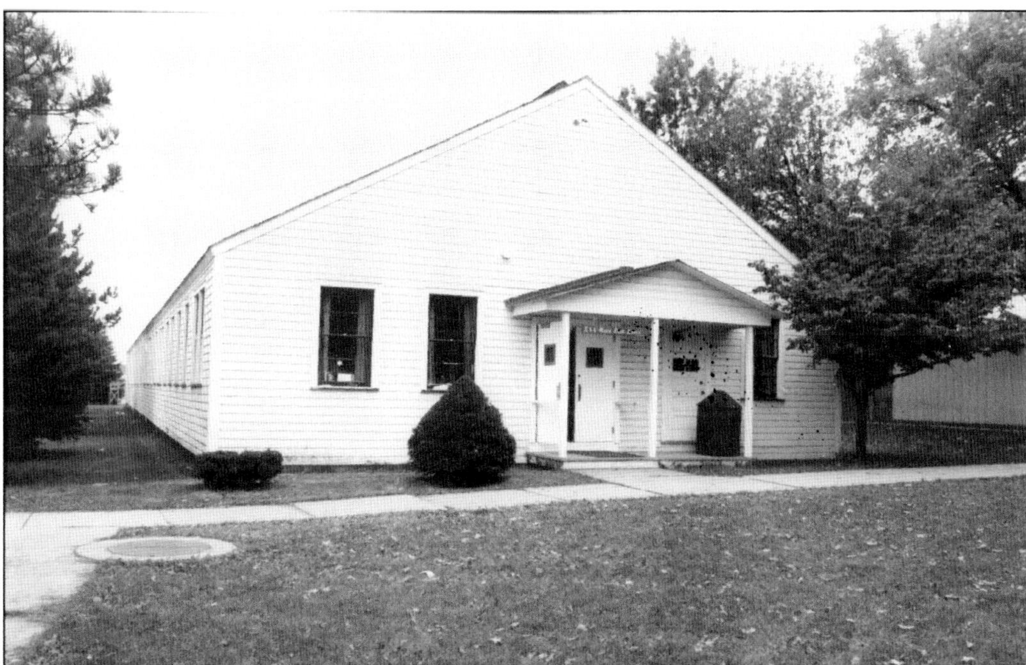

The original East Hall was a barracks purchased from the Keystone Ordinance Works near Meadville in 1947. It burned down in 1991, and a new East Hall was erected in 1995, which houses workspace for ceramics and sculpture students.

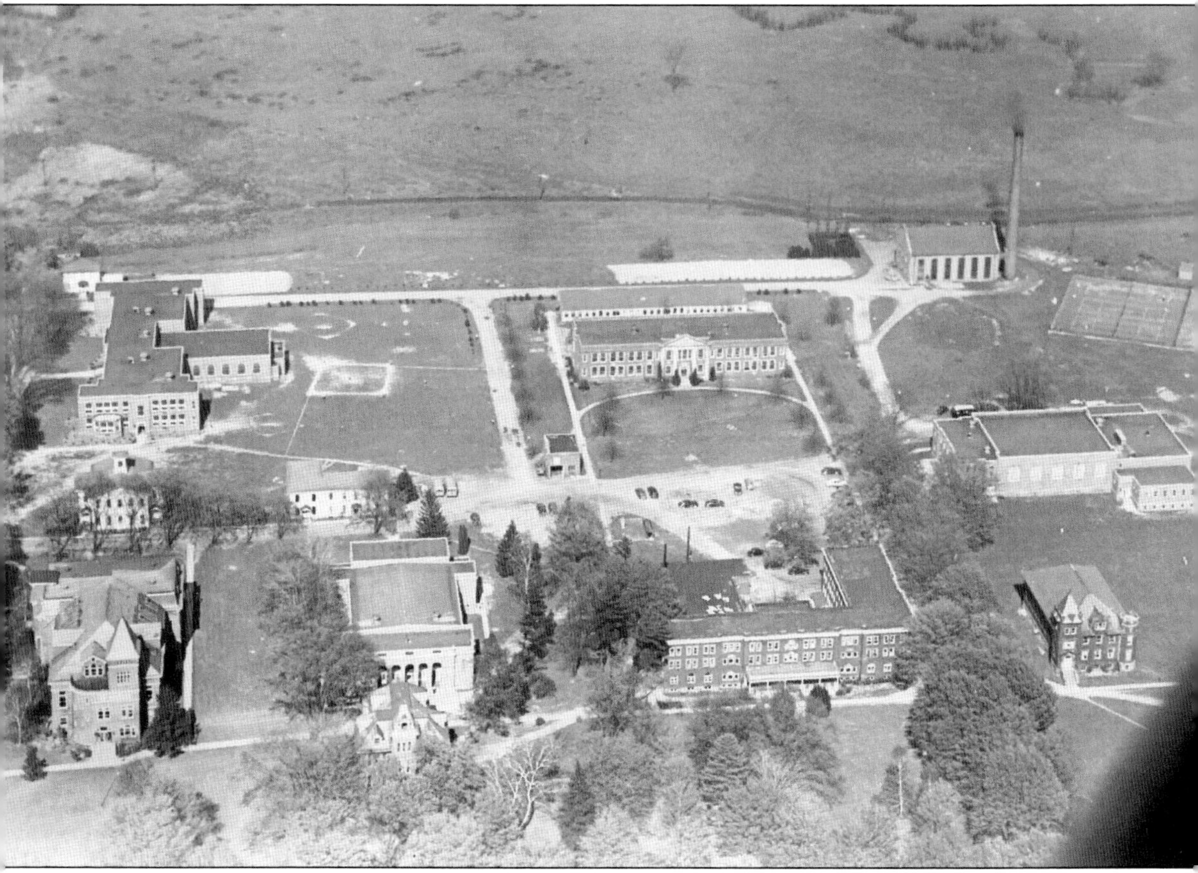

In 1949, the campus occupied 35 acres and had 669 students with 44 faculty members. The sudden influx of students created a housing problem. All students were required to live on campus unless they had the permission of the housing committee. These off-campus housing assignments were either accepted as issued or the students' application for admission would be withdrawn.

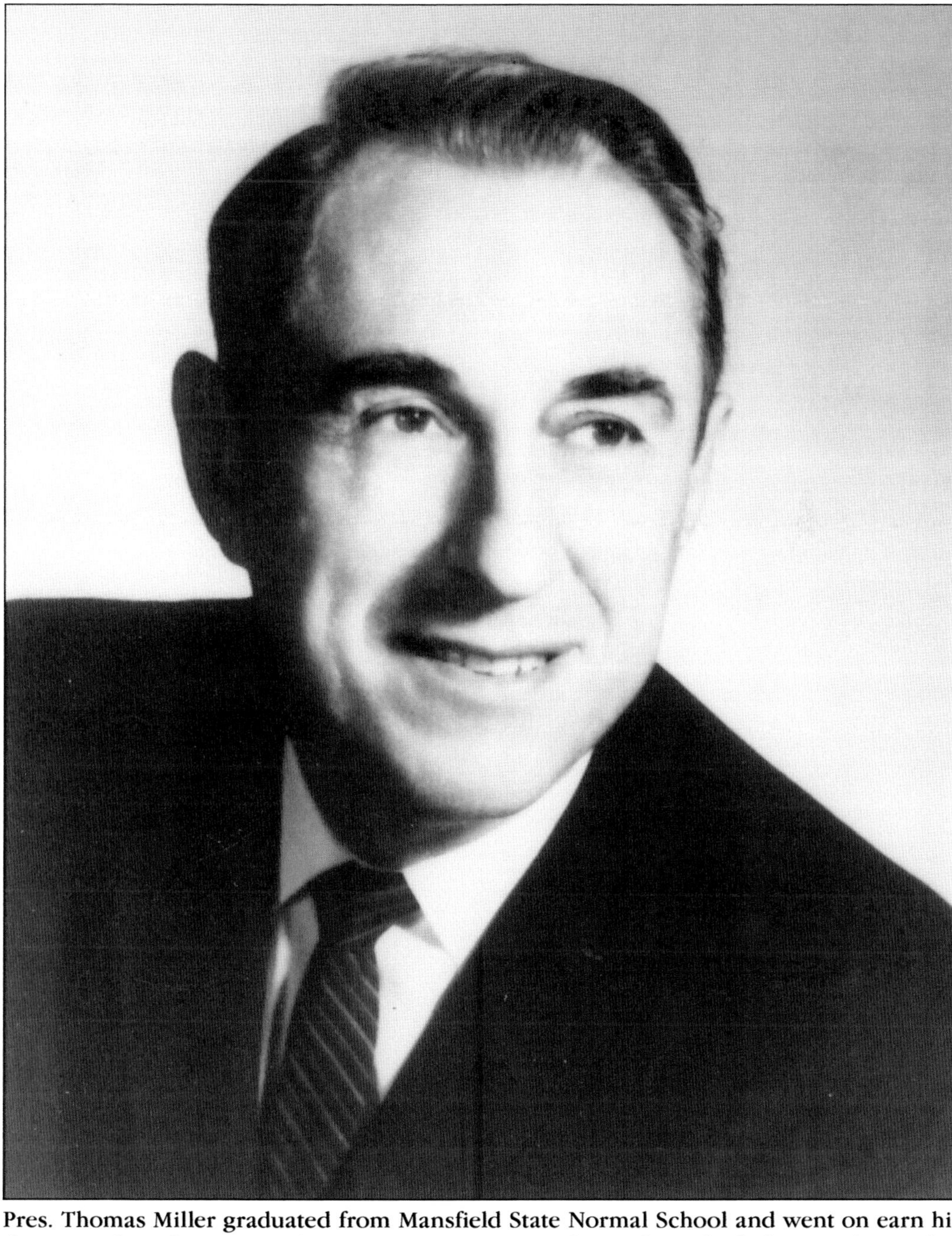

Pres. Thomas Miller graduated from Mansfield State Normal School and went on earn his doctorate from Syracuse University. He was appointed president of Edinboro in September 1954. Under his presidency, the campus grew more than during any other period. Enrollment grew from 400 to over 3,500, and the faculty increased from 14 to 182. He added 10 buildings and grew the campus footprint from 40 acres to 535 acres. Dr. Miller died at his desk in February 1966.

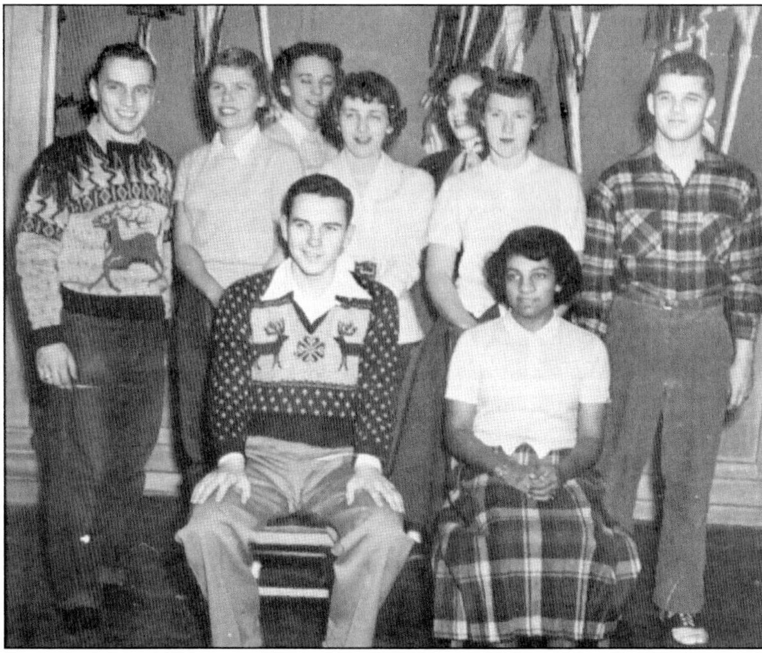

Edinboro had several religious clubs. The Canterbury Club, an Episcopalian organization, is seen here in 1953. In the earliest years, the school required students to attend a religious service on Sunday. Since then, state schools have made a steady retreat from connections with religion.

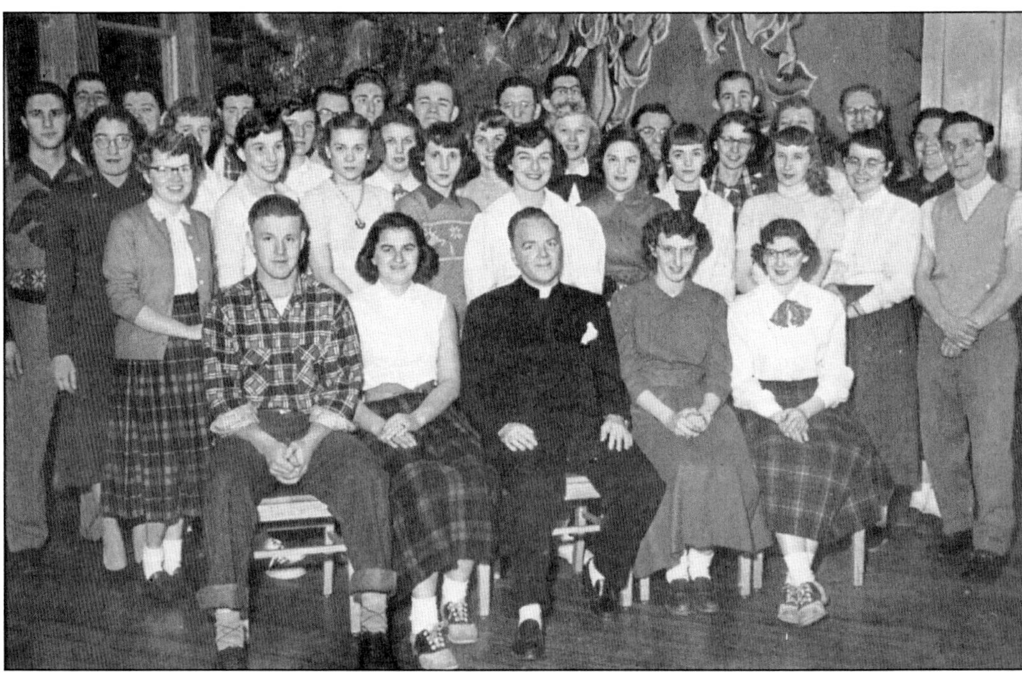

The Newman Club, associated with the Catholic faith, is shown here with Father Dwyer. Catholics had nowhere to worship on Sunday until Loveland Hall was made available to them in the 1930s. The first Catholic church in Edinboro was Our Lady of the Lake, which opened in 1950. Edinboro art professor Aime Doucette and William "Pat" Flynn were instrumental in getting it built.

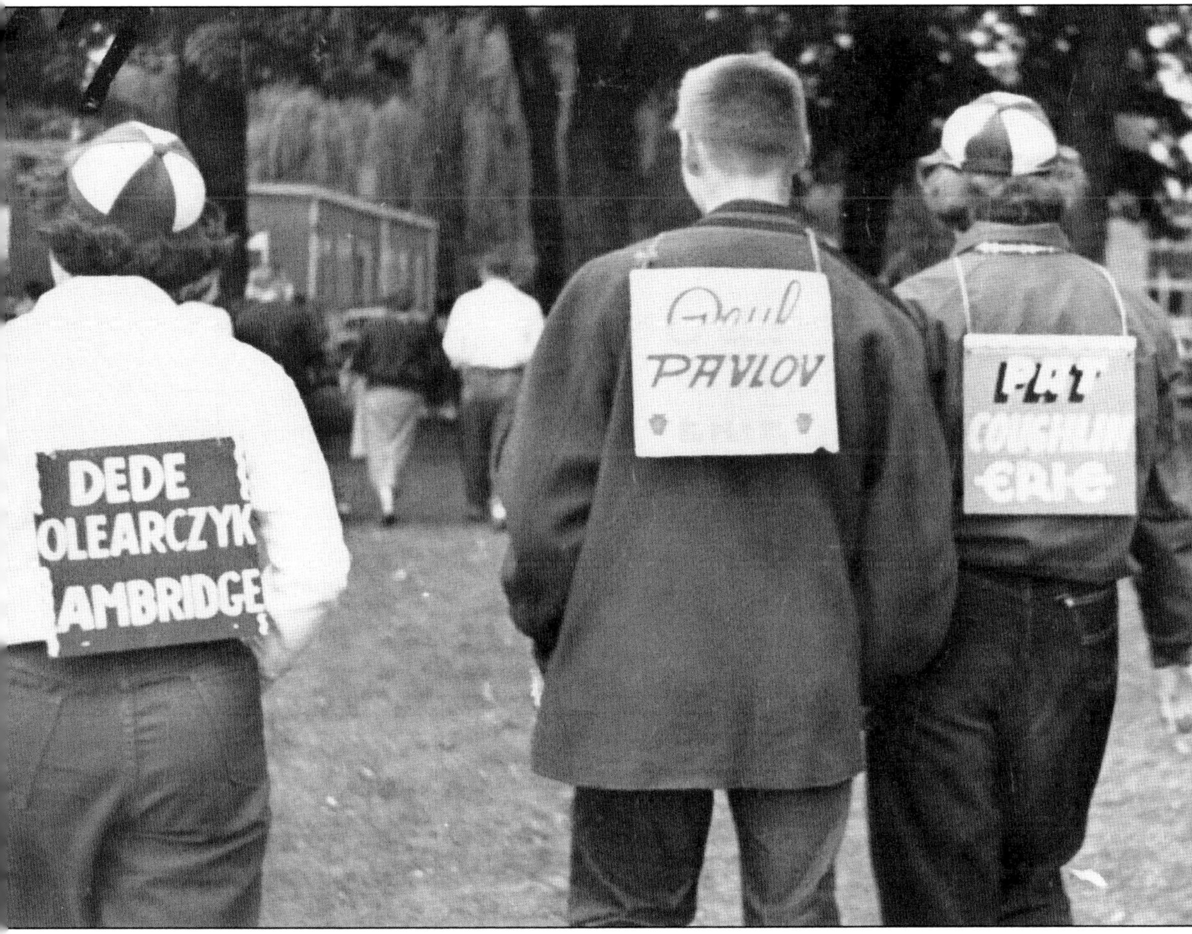

Freshman at Edinboro were required to wear a "dink" and a nameplate. According to tradition, the nameplate was worn until the homecoming bonfire, where it was tossed into the flames. The tradition was prevalent in the 1950s and 1960s.

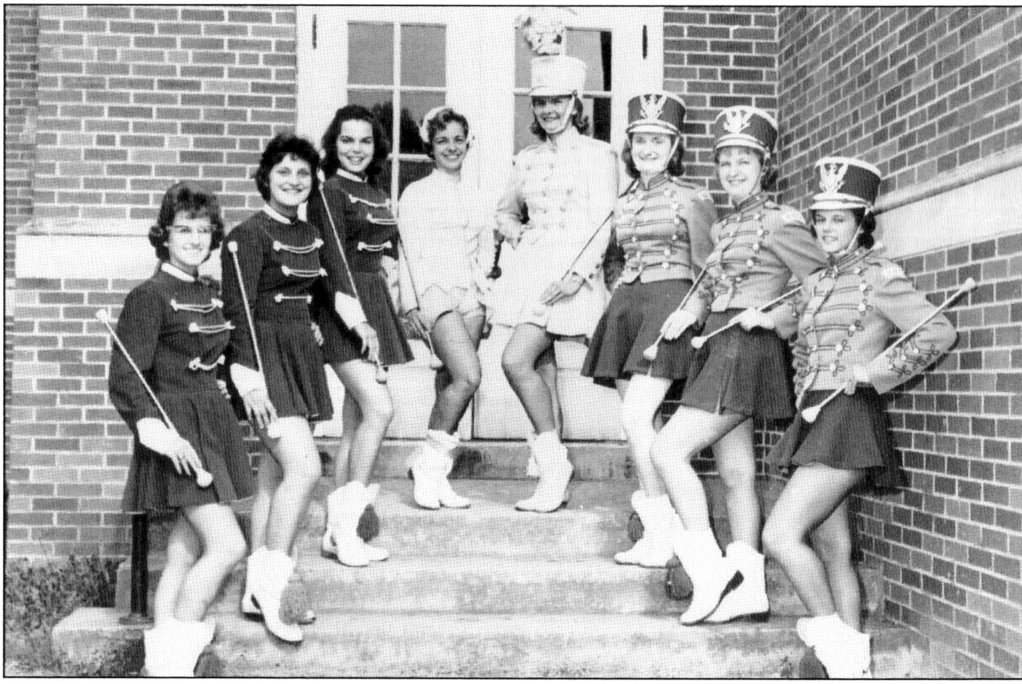

The band did not go on the field unaccompanied; these charming majorettes helped entertain the fans. Dr. William Alexander formed the first marching band in 1962 with 17 members. By the early 1970s, there were 160 members.

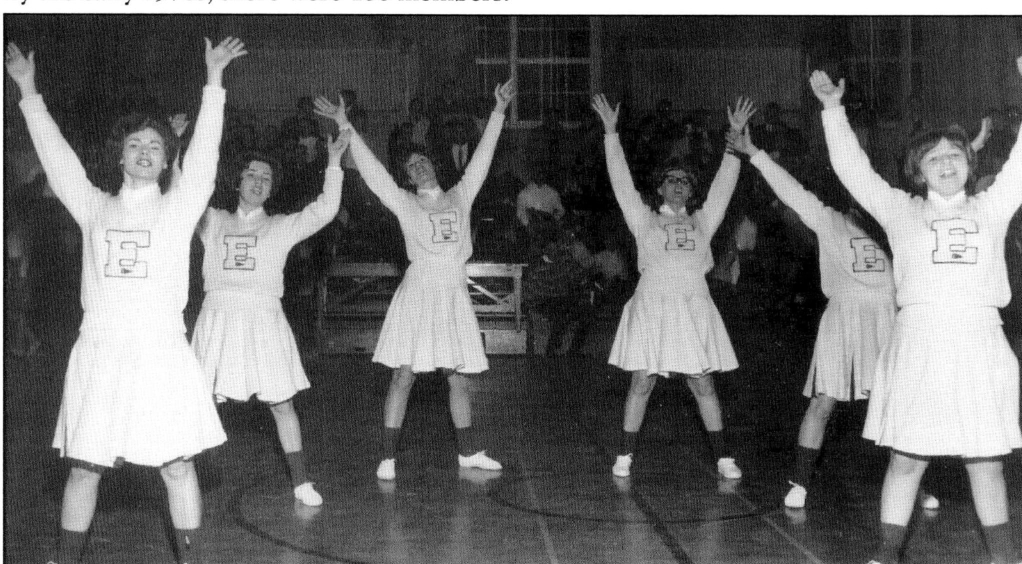

Cheerleaders root for the basketball team in Crawford Gymnasium around 1960. The gymnasium, built in 1940, was used for basketball games until the McComb Field House was completed in 1971. Remembering his time coaching in Crawford Gymnasium, Jim McDonald said, "People would be there by 5:00 o'clock for a 6:00 o'clock JV game. By 5:15 you couldn't get a seat . . . You couldn't even find the out of bounds lines, then we got to the point where we had closed-circuit television."

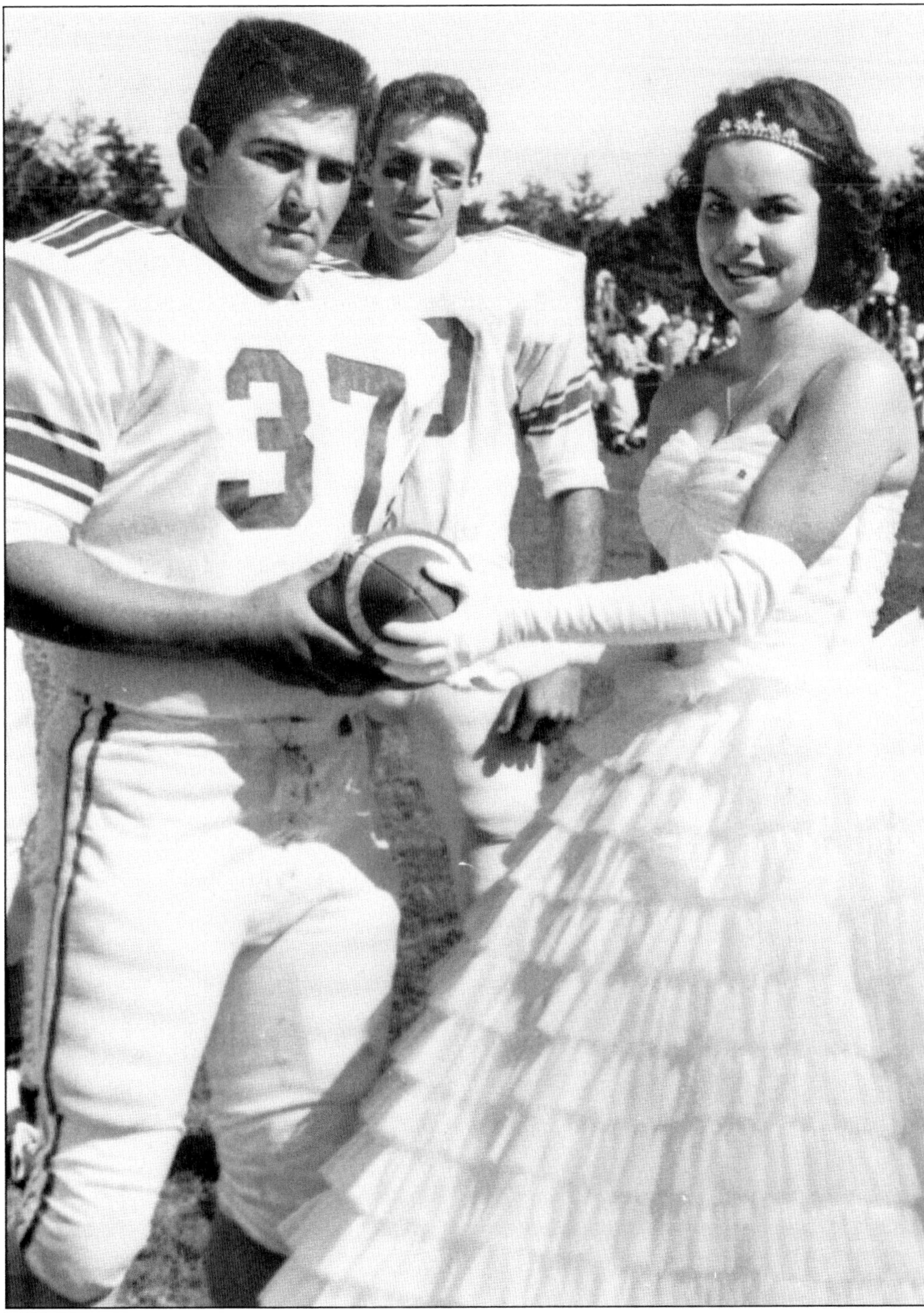

In the 1950s and 1960s, the homecoming queen presented the game ball to the team captain. Here, queen Dianne Elliott presents the ball to Dave O'Dessa, who was nicknamed "Three-ton." When asked why he had acquired the nickname, he said the team already had a "Four-ton." Homecoming also included an "E" Ball, a formal dance named after the letter given to those who earned a letter in sports, which was often sewn onto sweaters or jackets.

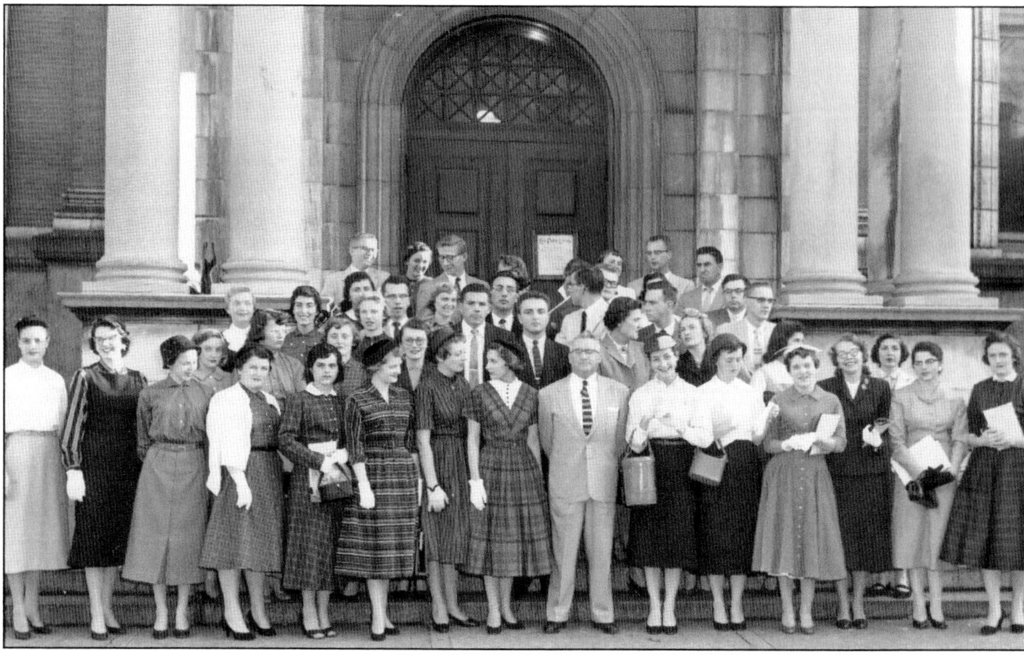

Student teaching has always been a large part of the school's curriculum. Until 1960, when the school was transformed into a state college instead of a state teacher's college, all the degrees awarded were education degrees. In the early years before transportation improved, most student teaching was done in the laboratory school on campus. This 1956 photograph shows Edinboro student teachers in Erie. These students paid for the entire school year with $90 in contingent fees; $216 for room, board, and laundry; and an activity fee of $17. There were no tuition costs.

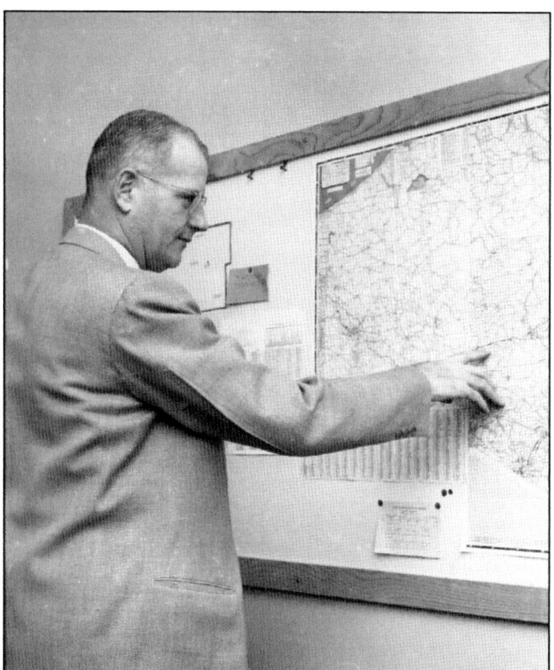

The auditorium in Butterfield Hall is named after Leeland W. VanLaningham, who came to Edinboro in 1949 and served as the director of student teaching until his unexpected death in 1967. He was president of the Northwest Pennsylvania State Educational Association and was on the executive council of the Pennsylvania State Educational Association.

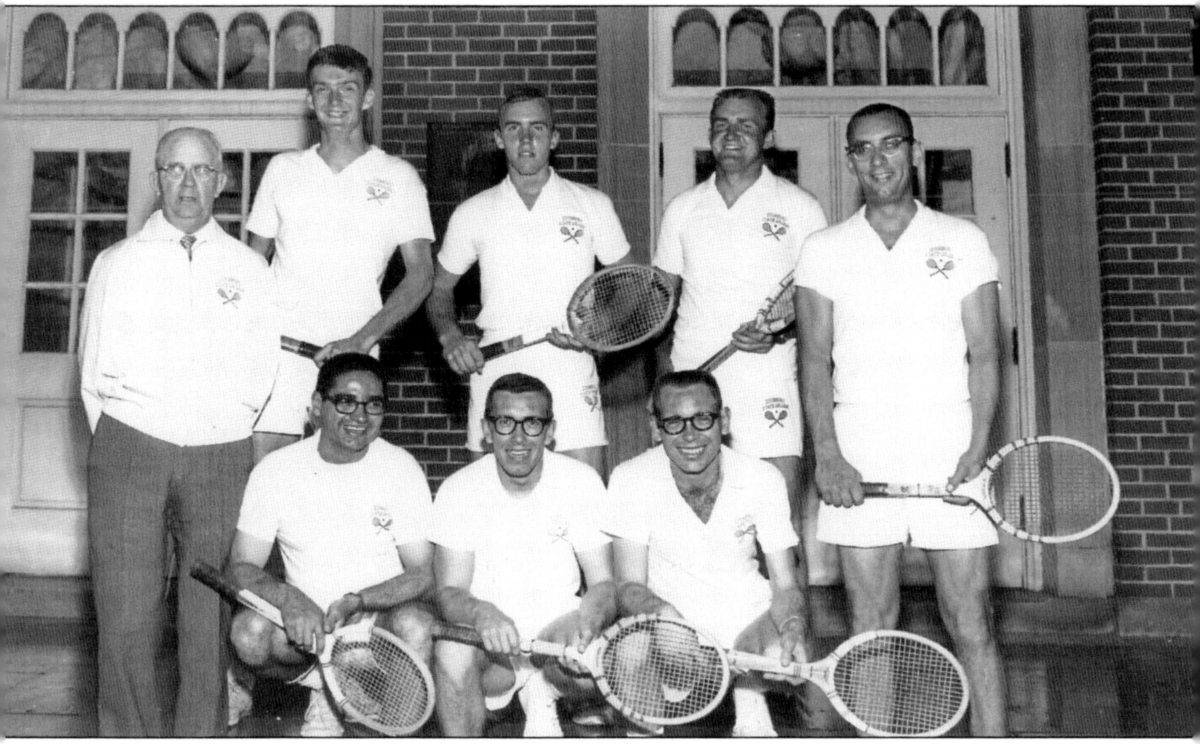

Coach Art McComb, standing here with his tennis team around 1960, was a graduate of Slippery Rock State Normal School in 1920. He went on to get a BS and master's degree in education from the University of Pittsburgh. After his long and fruitful career at Edinboro, the current field house was named in his honor.

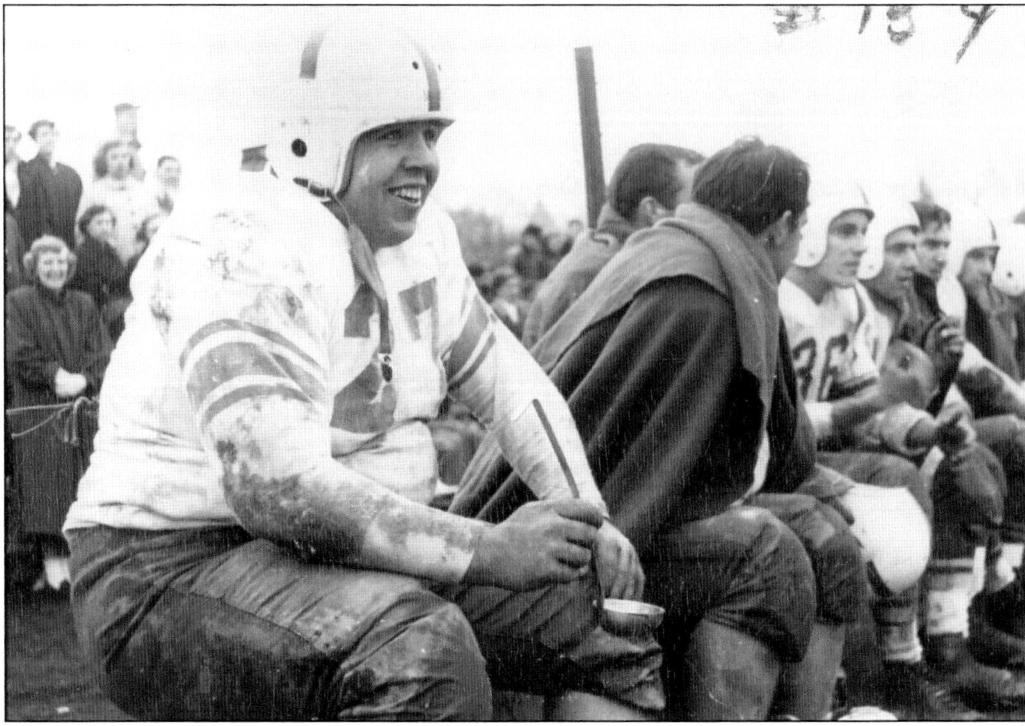

In 1953, the games were played behind Crawford Gymnasium, where the current Arts and Sciences Building is today. The grandstands were limited and only a few feet from the bench, but it did not deter fans from coming to cheer their team.

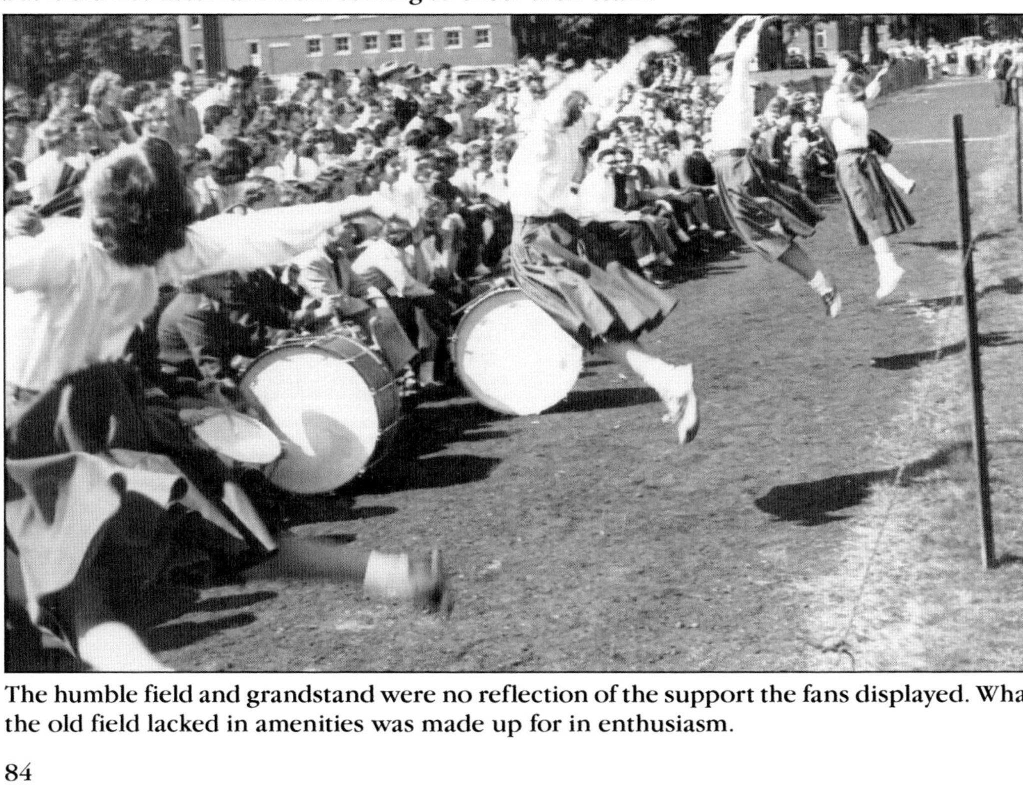

The humble field and grandstand were no reflection of the support the fans displayed. What the old field lacked in amenities was made up for in enthusiasm.

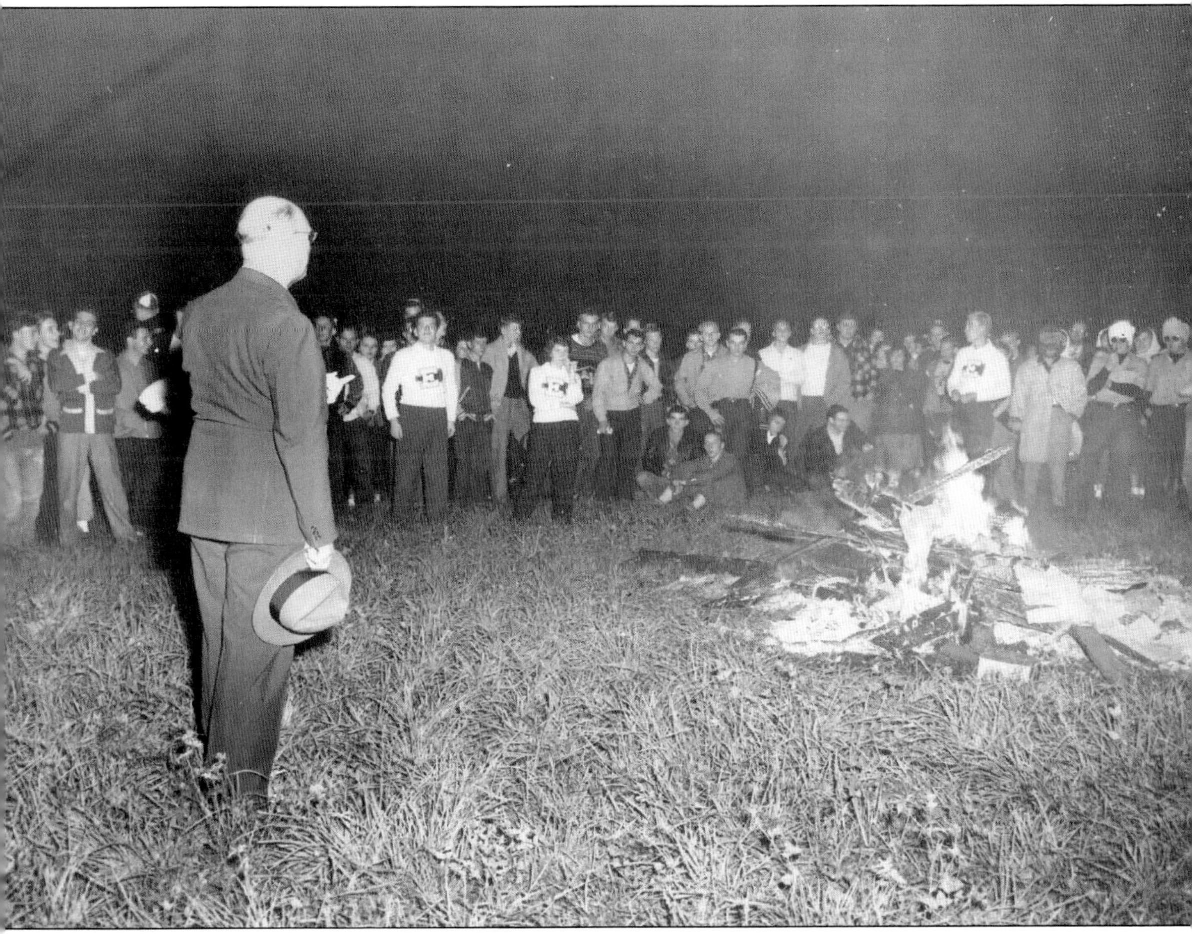

The tradition of a bonfire the night before homecoming included the burning of the name placards freshman wore as part of their first-year experience. In this photograph from around 1950, school president Dr. Lyman VanHouten addresses the students at the bonfire.

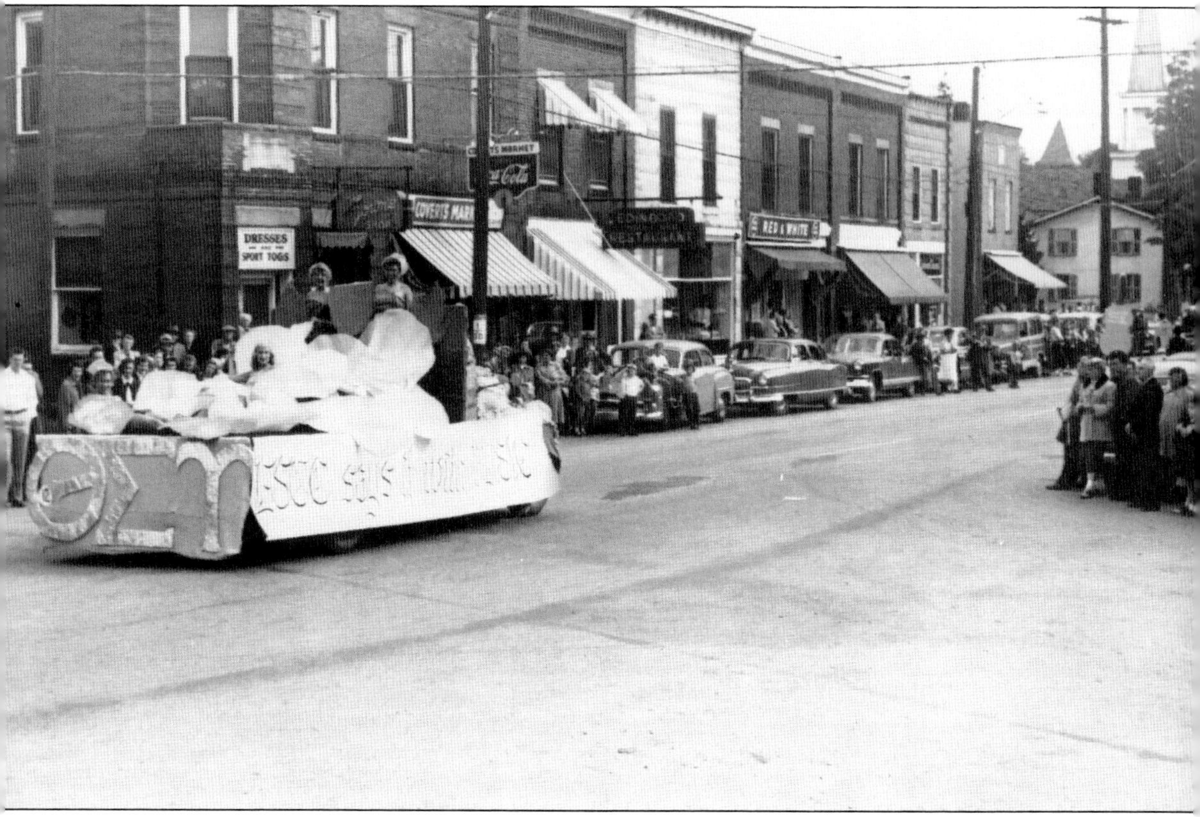

The 1953 homecoming parade travels along Meadville Street in downtown Edinboro. Except for a brief few years under school president Jeremy Brown, homecoming has always traveled through town and provided a bond between the school and the town.

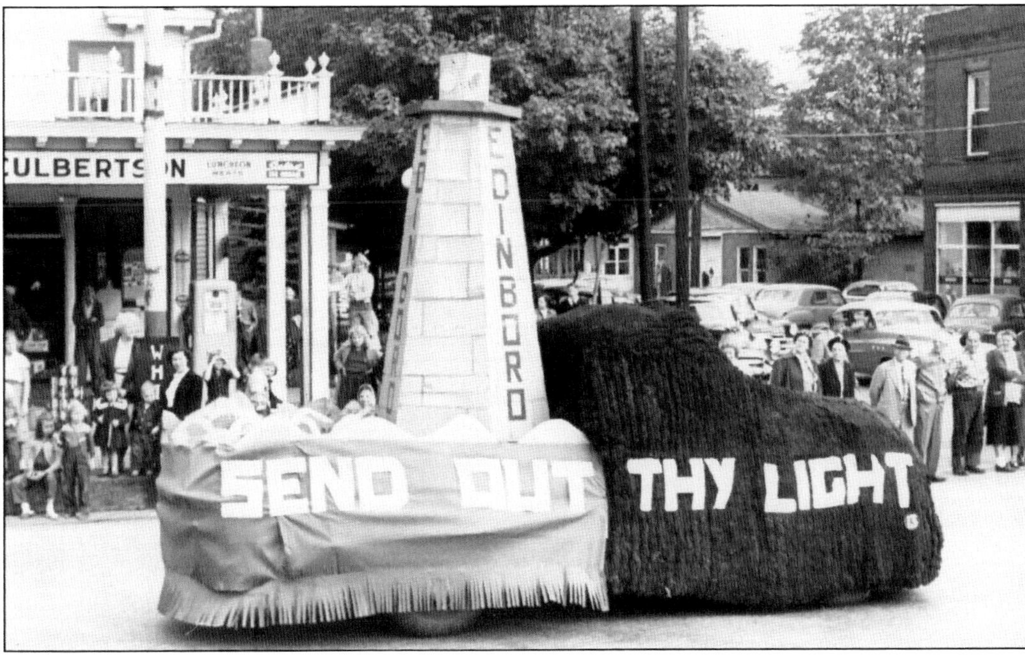

This 1953 homecoming float drives though downtown Edinboro in front of Culbertson's store. It is a wonder how the driver could see where they were going. Noticc thc gas pump sitting close enough to the road to fill the gas tanks of cars on the street.

BACCALAUREATE SERVICE

NINETY-NINTH

ANNUAL COMMENCEMENT

EDINBORO STATE COLLEGE

AT EDINBORO

PROGRAM

PROCESSIONAL: *"God of Our Fathers"* . . . . . . WARREN

INVOCATION . . . . THE REV. S. JAMES SCHMITTLE
Pastor, Methodist Church, Edinboro, Pa.

"Cante Domino" . . . . PITONI
Collegiate Singers

SCRIPTURE . . . . THE REV. RALPH BLAIR
Pastor, St. Paul's Lutheran Church
Drakes Mills, Cambridge Springs, Pa.

Baccalaureate Sermon . . . . . . THE REV. FRANKLIN JENSEN
Pastor, Luther Memorial Church, Erie, Pa.

"Gladsome Radiance" . . . . GRETCHANINOFF
Collegiate Singers

Benediction . . . . THE REV. LINFORD WILCOX
Pastor, Baptist Church, Edinboro, Pa.

RECESSIONAL: *"O God, Beneath Thy Guiding Hand"* . . HATTON
Collegiate Singers

SUNDAY, MAY TWENTY-NINTH,
NINETEEN HUNDRED SIXTY
At 3:00 P.M.—Daylight Saving Time

Immediately at the close of the service, graduates, their parents, and friends, and the faculty, are invited to attend a reception at the home of the President.

As late as 1960, public colleges were still sponsors of religious programs. This baccalaureate program shows four different reverends offering prayers and a scripture reading.

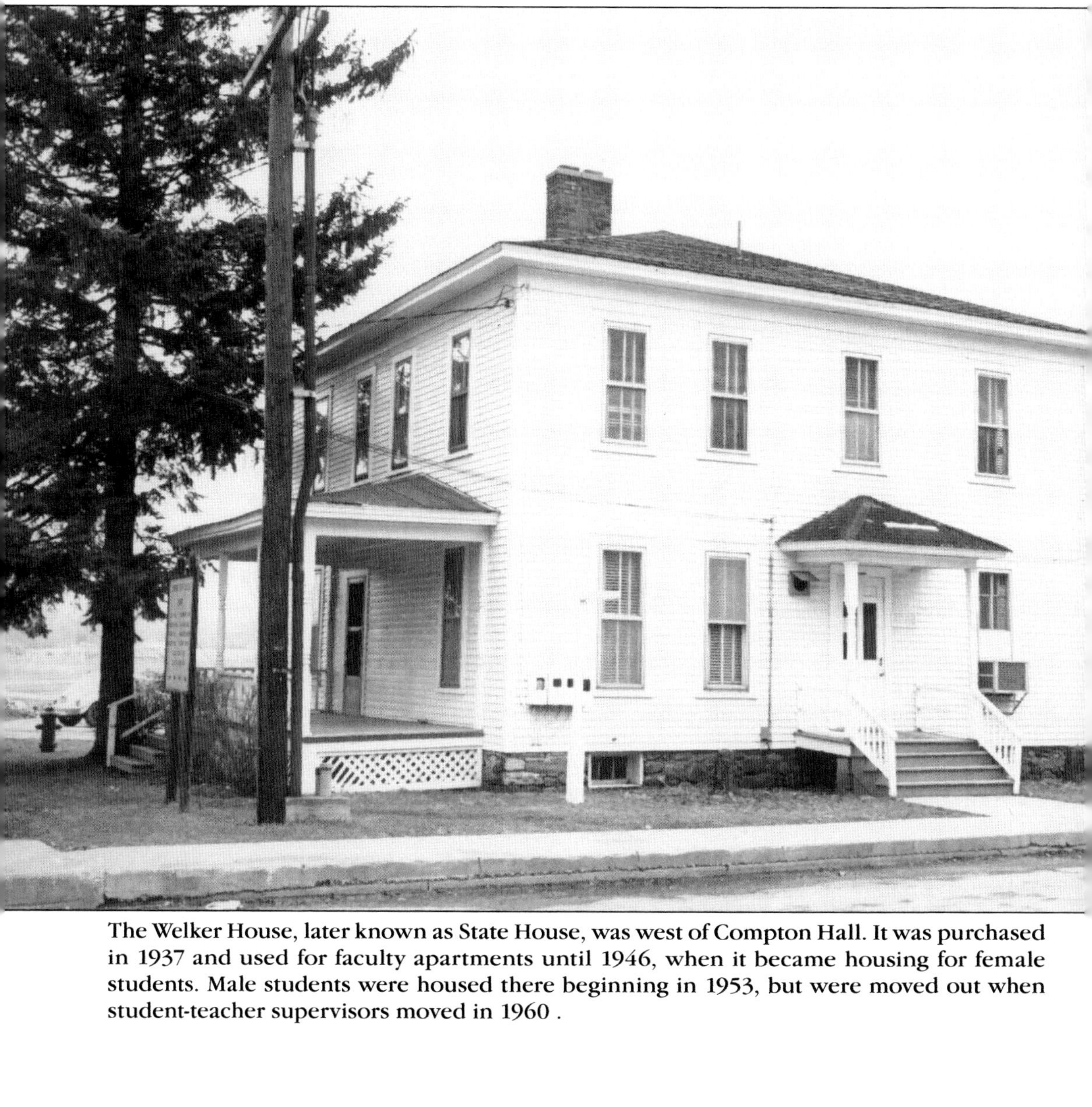

The Welker House, later known as State House, was west of Compton Hall. It was purchased in 1937 and used for faculty apartments until 1946, when it became housing for female students. Male students were housed there beginning in 1953, but were moved out when student-teacher supervisors moved in 1960 .

Three

State College Years 1960–1983

The state college years provided Edinboro with some of its brightest moments. The era opened with Dr. Tom Miller still at the helm. During his 12 years in office, enrollments quadrupled, faculty numbers increased, and the campus grew to over 500 acres. It was a painful tragedy for Edinboro when Dr. Miller died working at his desk, but the school moved forward.

In the 1960s and 1970s, most popular performers played college venues, and Edinboro hosted its share of top artists, many of whom are now enshrined in the Rock and Roll Hall of Fame. Other equally famous personalities performed or spoke on campus including Henry Kissinger, Gerald Ford, F. Lee Bailey, and Julian Bond.

Civil rights and the Vietnam War were on everyone's mind during this period. While protests and violence erupted on campuses across the country, the issues at Edinboro were the same, but the tenor was not violent. Women's rights advocates protested for the right to have birth control dispensed at the health center, and African American students protested their treatment with a sit-in at the president's office. There were also teach-ins to discuss the war.

These issues were all put aside when an electrical fire in the attic of Normal Hall spread through the old building and could not be contained. While the structure burned, students, faculty, administrators, and bystanders formed a bucket brigade to get records out of the building before it was too late. They worked fast and hard until the fireman insisted that they leave the building.

A plethora of sports emerged at this time, many of which are no longer played at Edinboro, including men's soccer, trap shooting, men's and women's golf, bowling, and others. Greek societies also grew in popularity and participation.

The era ended on a down note as the economy went into a recession, and the school found itself in another financially challenging position. Foster Diebold was hired to lead the school through the difficulties, and his tenure extended into the university era.

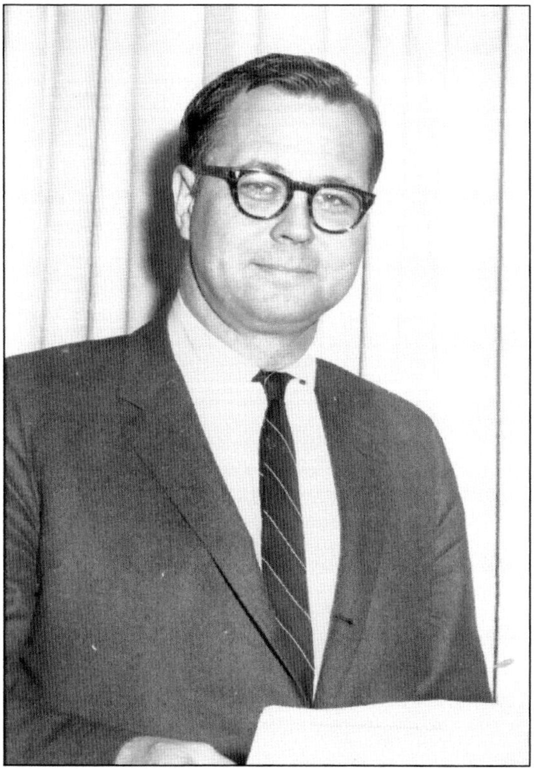

Irving Murphy was a member of the board of trustees from 1961 to 1971. As an attorney, he was instrumental in working with dean of men Jim Harrison in developing a policy on search and seizure.

The Haven Hall dining room was reputed to be one of the best in the state. Students and faculty dined together in assigned seats. Through the 1960s, students were expected to dress for dinner, with men in sport coats and ties and women in dresses. Waiters, who were also dressed appropriately, served the meal.

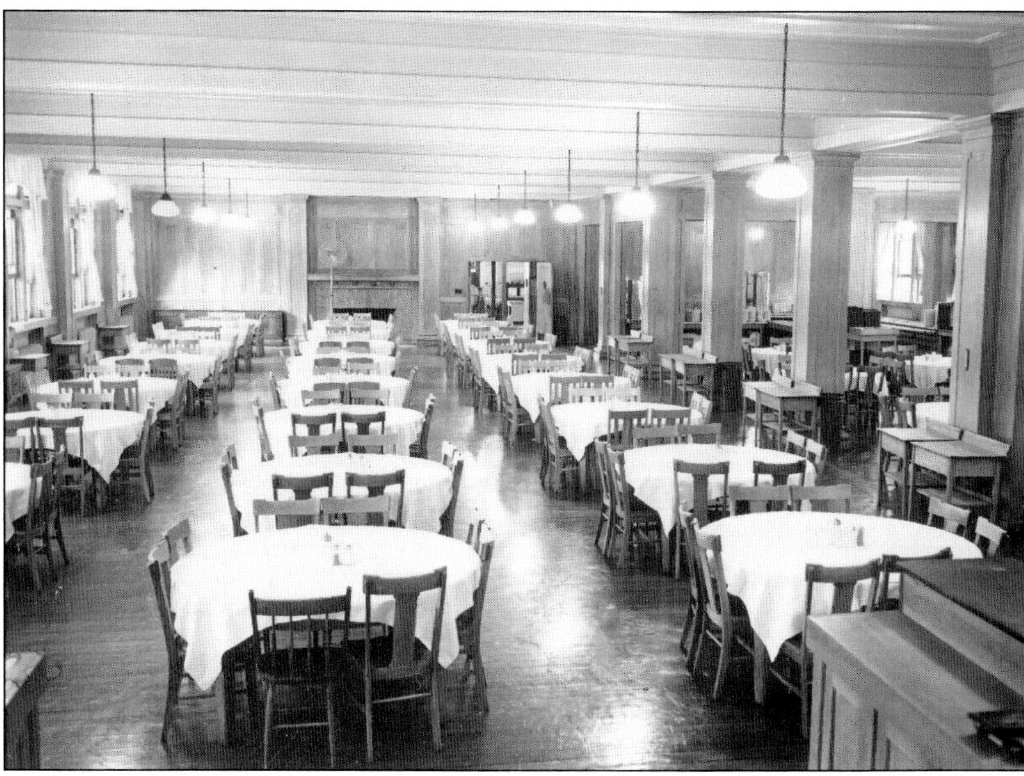

Edinboro radio station WJKB was first broadcast in 1964 by closed circuit over telephone lines. It was originally housed in Centennial Hall and funded by student government. It expanded in 1970, broadcasting on local cable television. In 1978, the FCC licensed the radio station to broadcast over the air. The original hope was that the station would be called WHRE for Highland Radio Edinboro. As it turned out, the call letters are now WFSE.

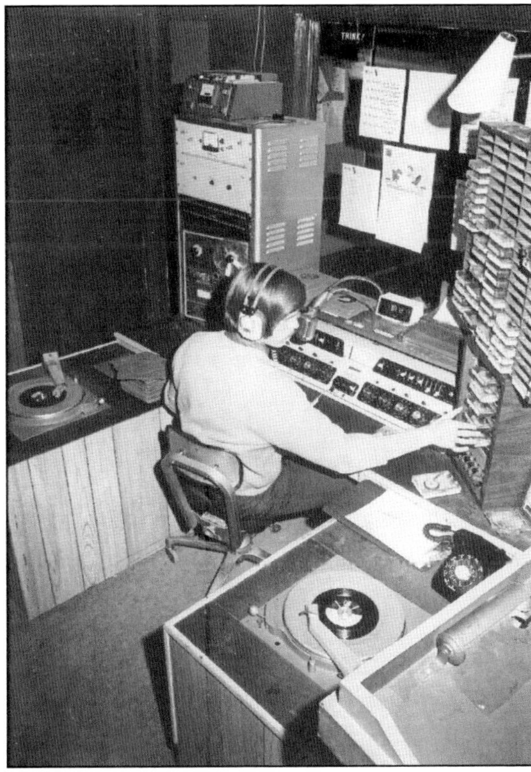

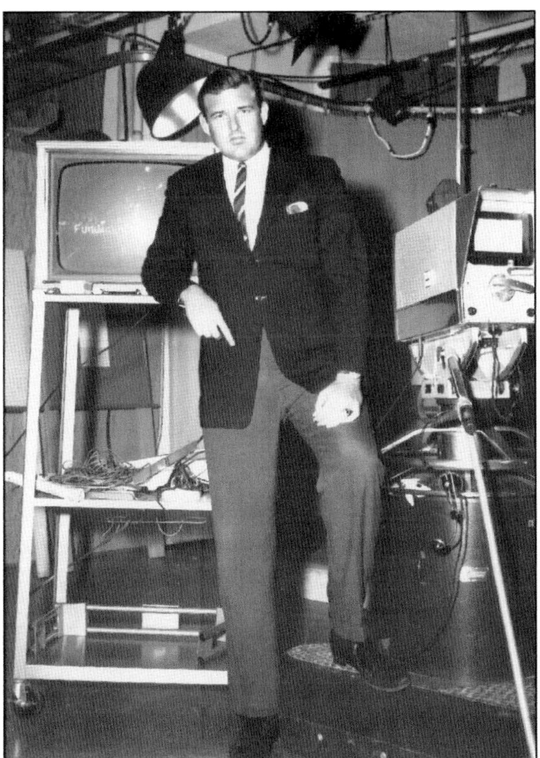

Televised courses were used to supplement the curriculum beginning in the late 1960s. The short-lived experiment was discontinued by 1974. Bob Wallace was the director of on-campus television and offered a course in television production.

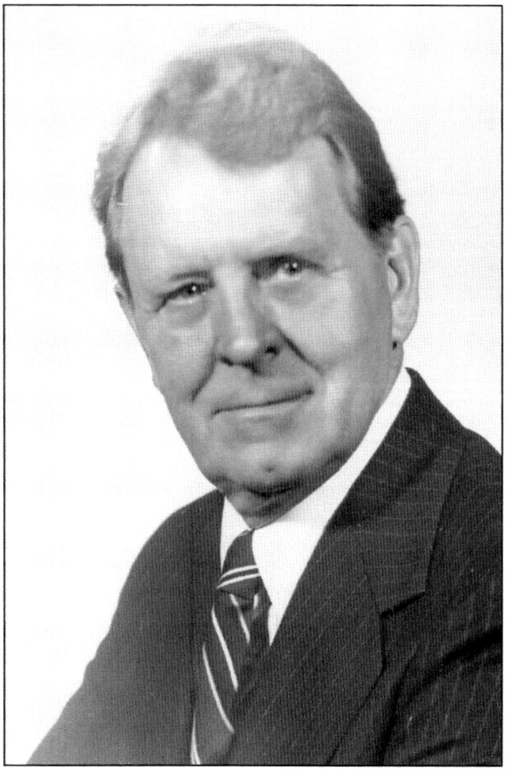

Dr. Chester McNerney served as president of Edinboro from 1966 to 1979. During his 13 years as president, 15 new facilities were added, including the Baron-Forness Library, McComb Field House, and a new student union. The student body grew from about 3,000 students to 7,000 students during that time, and 33 new undergraduate programs were added.

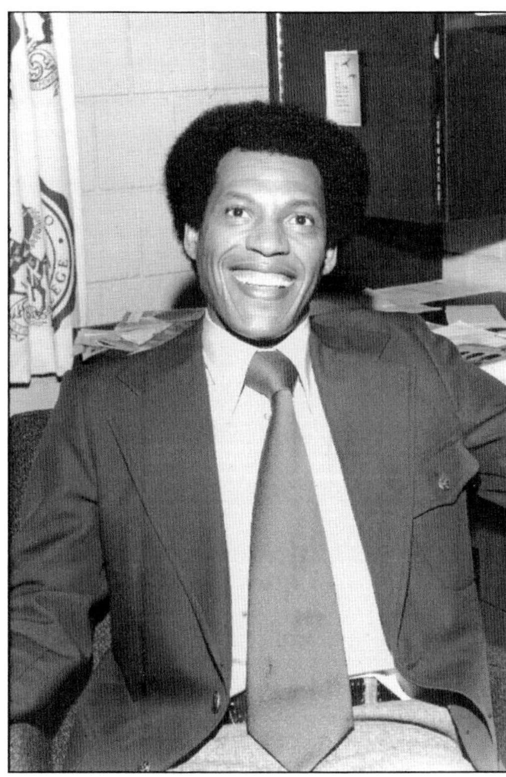

Aubrey Dillon graduated from Edinboro in 1961 with a bachelor's degree in secondary education and earned his master's degree in 1964. He later became the associate dean of students in 1972. Still active in his retirement, Aubrey is usually found on his sailboat or on the radio hosting a jazz program.

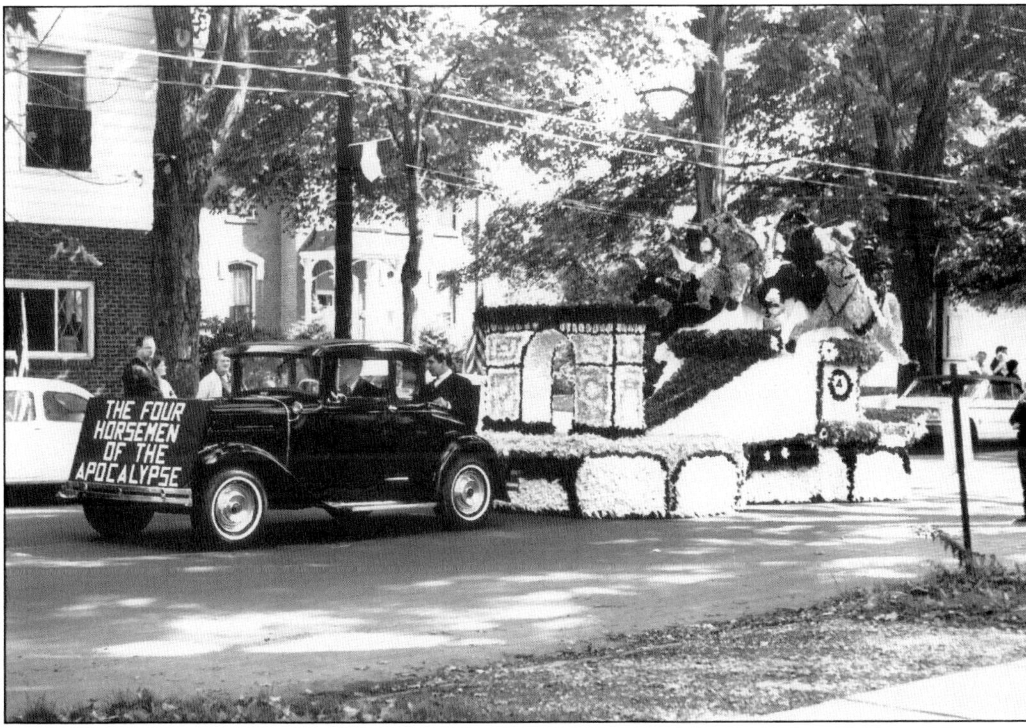

The Kappa Delta Phi fraternity entered "The Four Horseman" in the 1965 homecoming parade. Greek Societies continue to enter floats in the parade today.

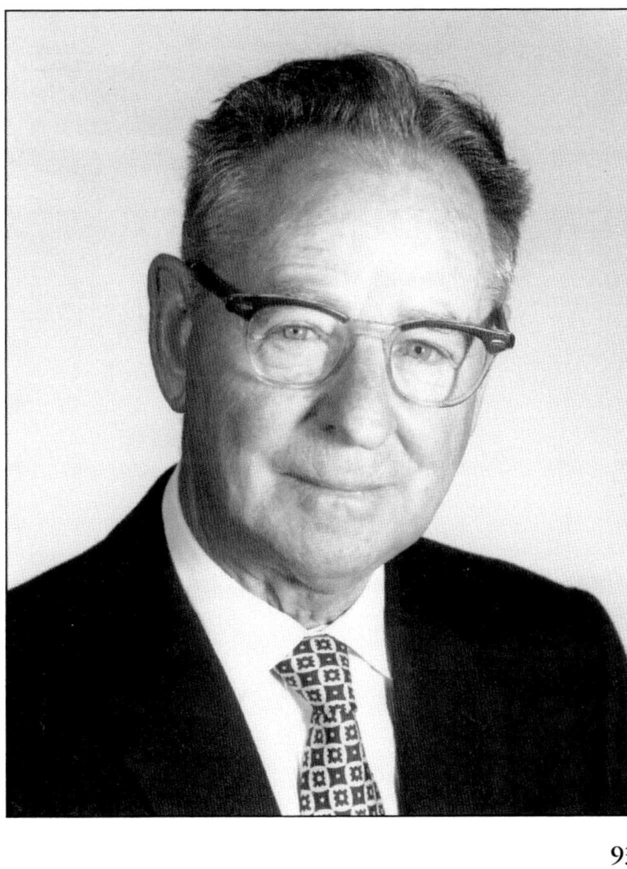

William Palen Rose, for whom Rose Hall dormitory is named, was on the board of trustees from 1940 to 1964. In 1926, he was a Republican candidate for state senator in Pennsylvania. In 1934 and 1936, he won the Republican nomination for congress for the Erie and Crawford County district. Rose was also the owner and publisher of Will Rose Newspapers in northwest Pennsylvania.

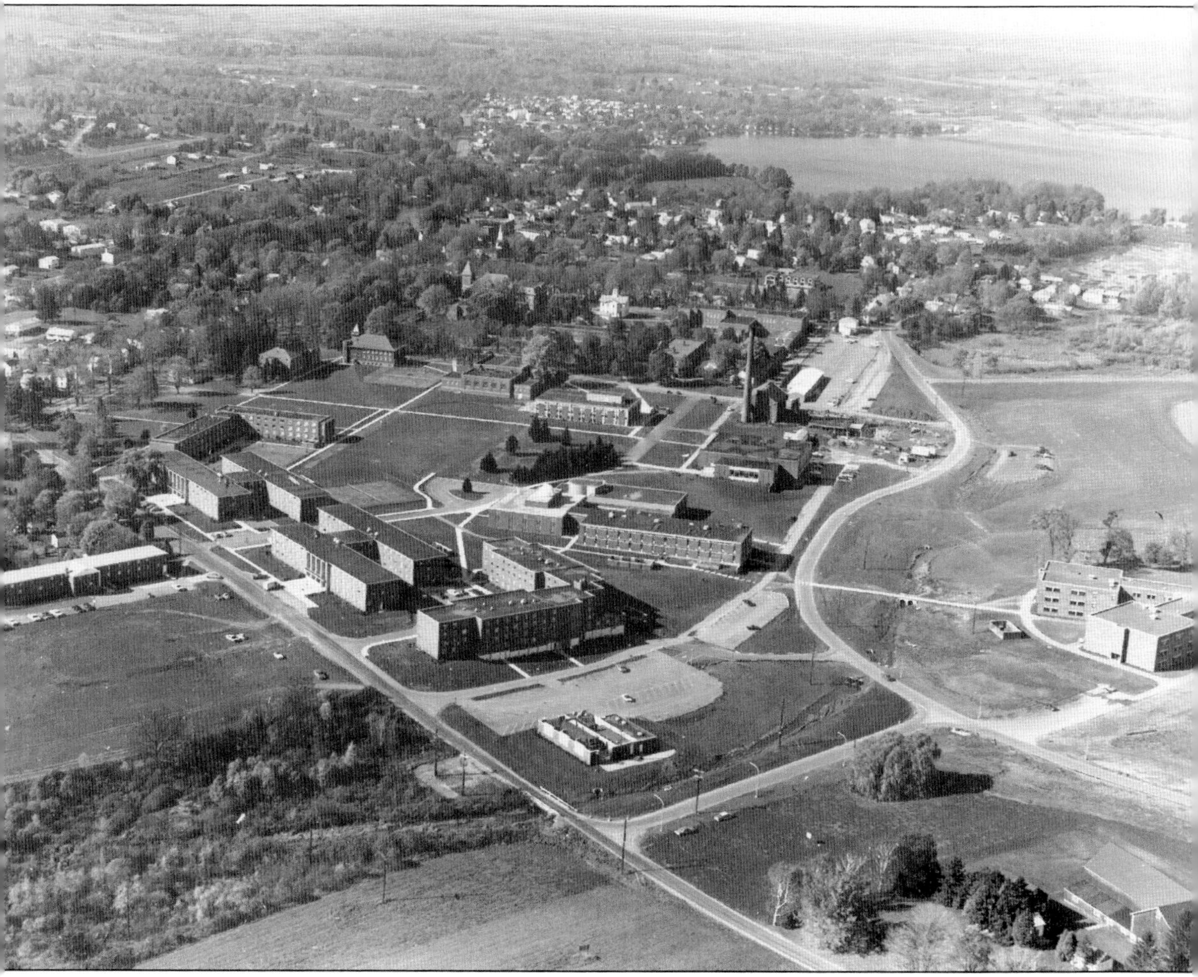

This aerial view of campus looks north from Darrow Road around 1968. The lake and town center are at the top of the image. On the right, Hendricks Hall, built in 1968, is still missing a parking lot. Rose Hall, Earp Hall, Dearborn Hall, and Centennial Hall are lined up on the left.

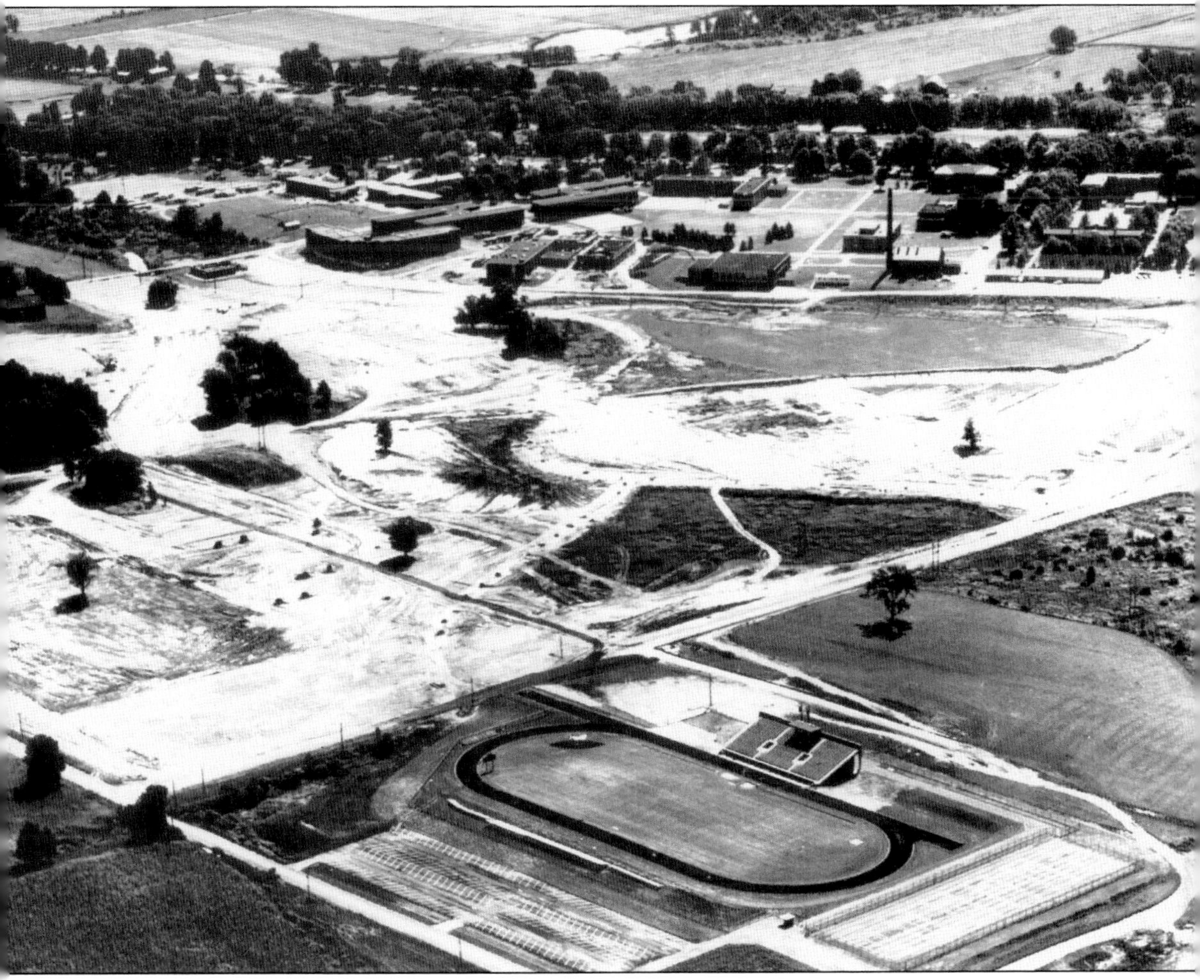

This aerial view of campus shows Sox Harrison Athletic Field in the bottom center. Built in 1965, it is the first structure on the east side of campus, which is now well populated. In this 1967 photograph, Electronic Hall is under construction. Electronic Hall was later connected to Cooper Hall and dropped its individual name.

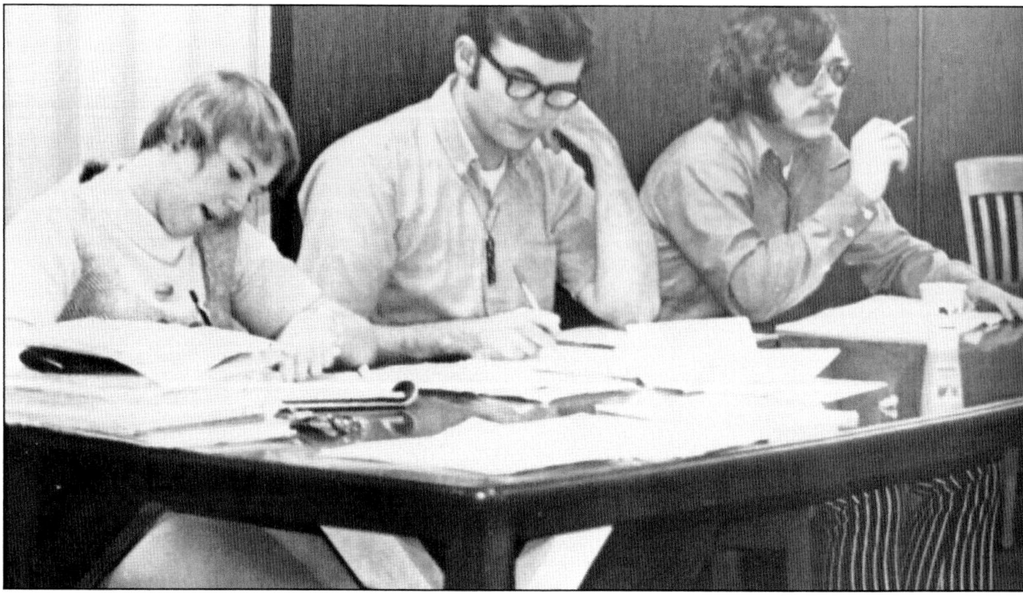

There was a student-faculty council until 1968, when the council recommended that the students form their own organization. The first officers, shown here from left to right, are Suzanne Schmidt, Gregory Pickens, and Jack Williams.

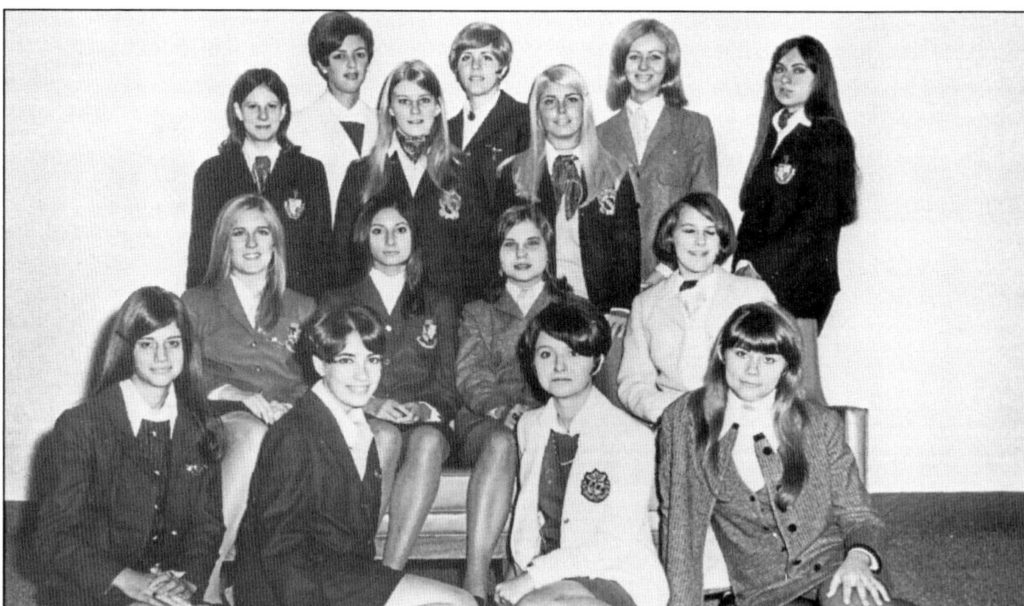

Greek organizations have been popular since the 1960s and have grown in numbers since then. To help coordinate the activities of the Greeks, two organizations were formed: the Pan-Hellenic Council, shown here in 1970, to help coordinate sorority activities, and the Interfraternity Council to help the fraternities.

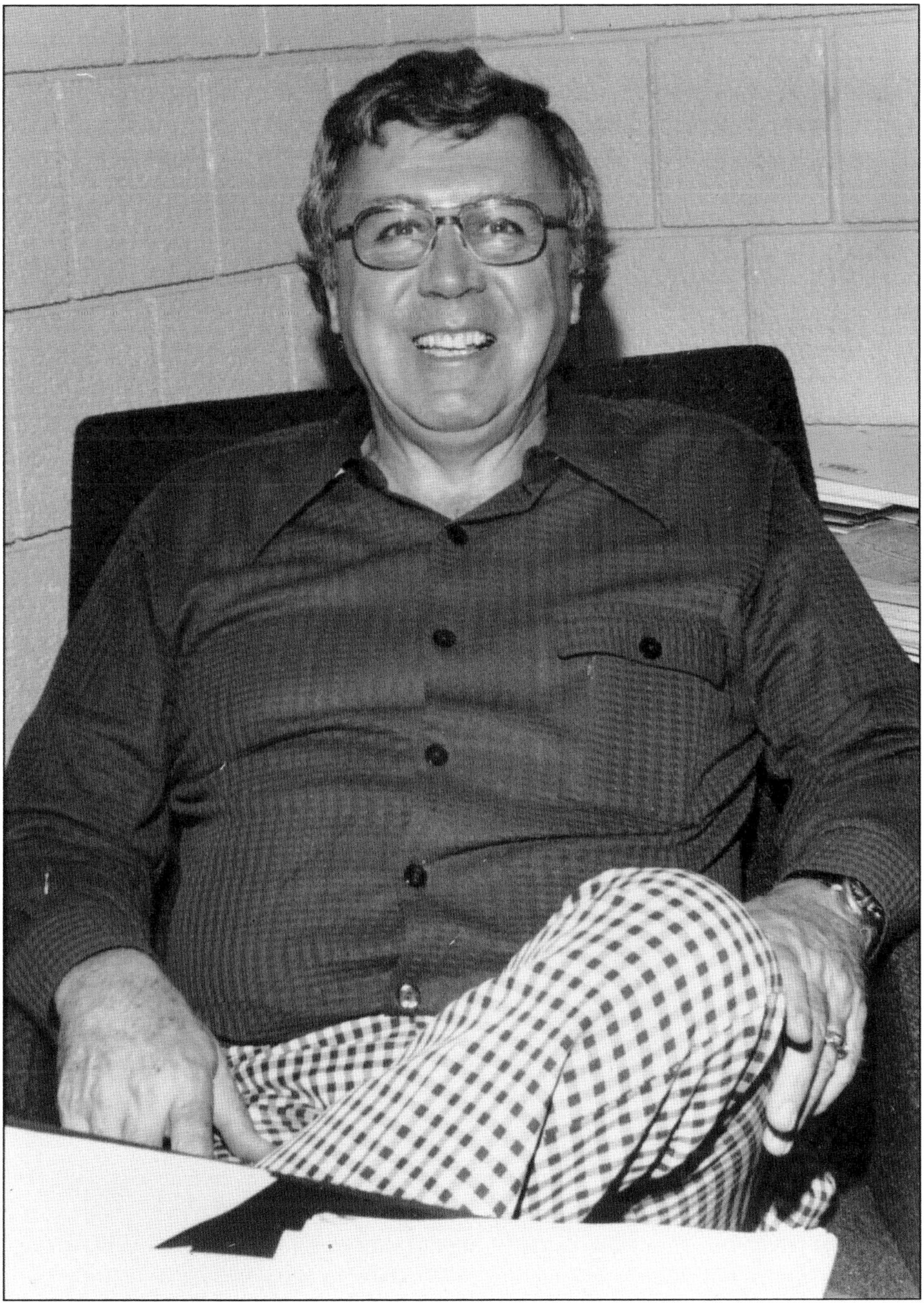

Jim Harrison, the son of Sox Harrison, first served Edinboro as dean of men beginning in 1960. After the positions of dean of men and dean of women were combined into the dean of students, Jim Harrison held that position until he retired in 1982. In keeping with the student rights movement of the 1970s, Jim oversaw the development of a discipline committee. If a student was found guilty, he or she could appeal and bring a lawyer to the appeal hearing. Edinboro was among the first schools to include due process and a right to legal representation in its student handbook.

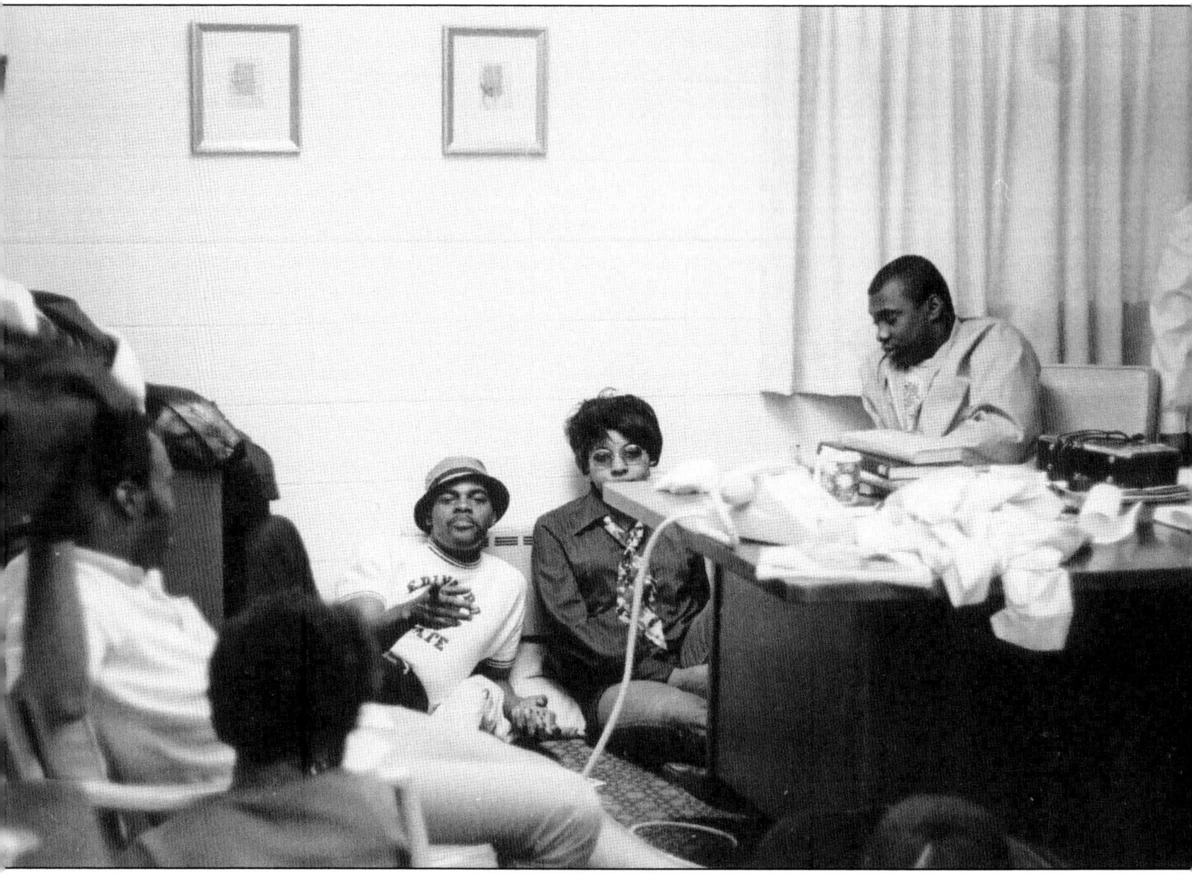

Edinboro escaped most of the campus unrest in the 1960s and 1970s, although there is one notable exception: this sit-in at the president's office in 1970. A number of racist incidents led students to go to the president's office for a conversation. The president was out of town, and the students decided to wait in his office for him. Angry crowds gathered, and the police were called. When school president McNerney returned, he and Irv Murphy, chairman of the board of trustees, managed to talk the students into going home. In return, the president agreed to meet with them the next day.

John Marsh (left) and Karl Nordberg, both faculty members at the school who investigated and published pictorial histories of the town of Edinboro, are seen here at the Goodell farm.

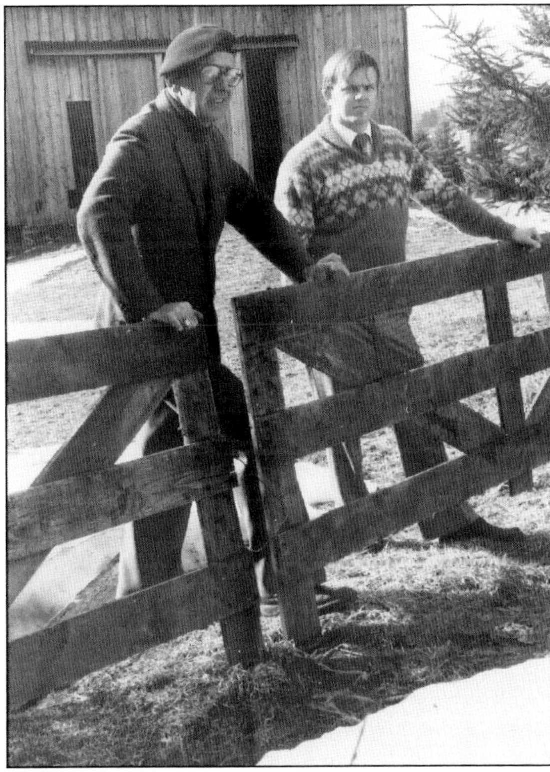

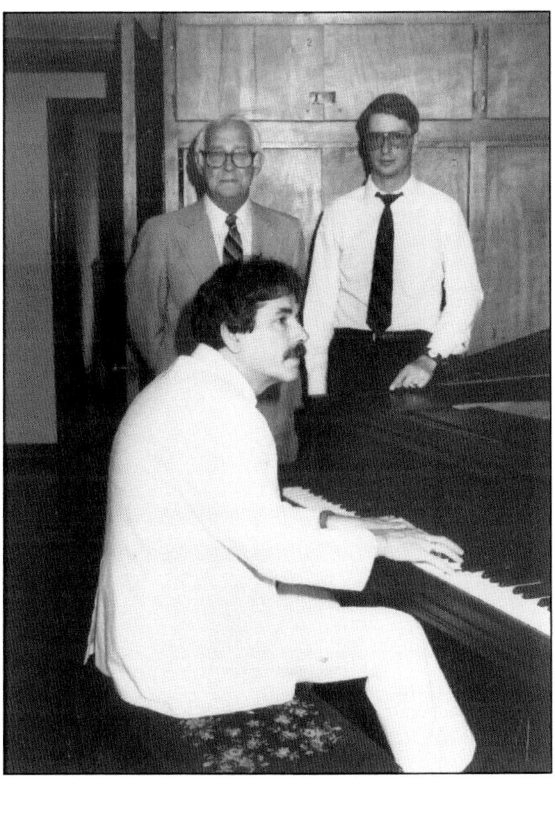

Dr. Paul Martin of the music department composed the current alma mater. It was first performed on May 5, 1970. Dr. Martin was also appointed director of cultural affairs. This program brought in nationally known speakers and performers and was funded by the student government.

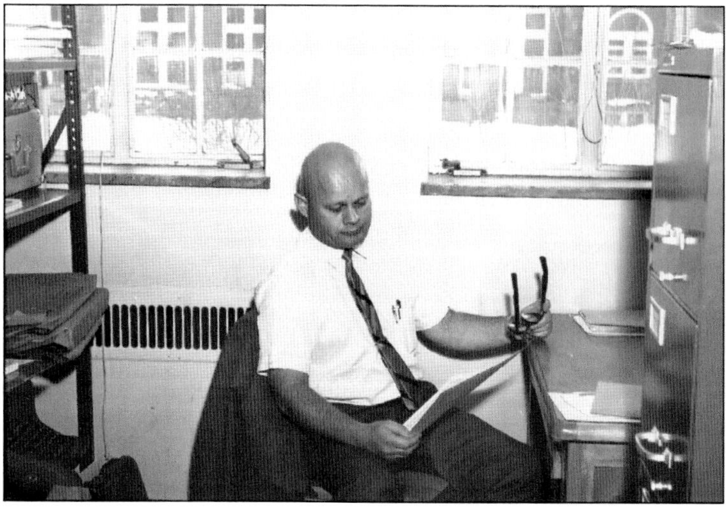

The Dr. William P. Alexander Music Center is named for the longtime chairperson of the music department. In addition to his chairperson responsibilities, Dr. Alexander led the school in developing an excellent cultural series.

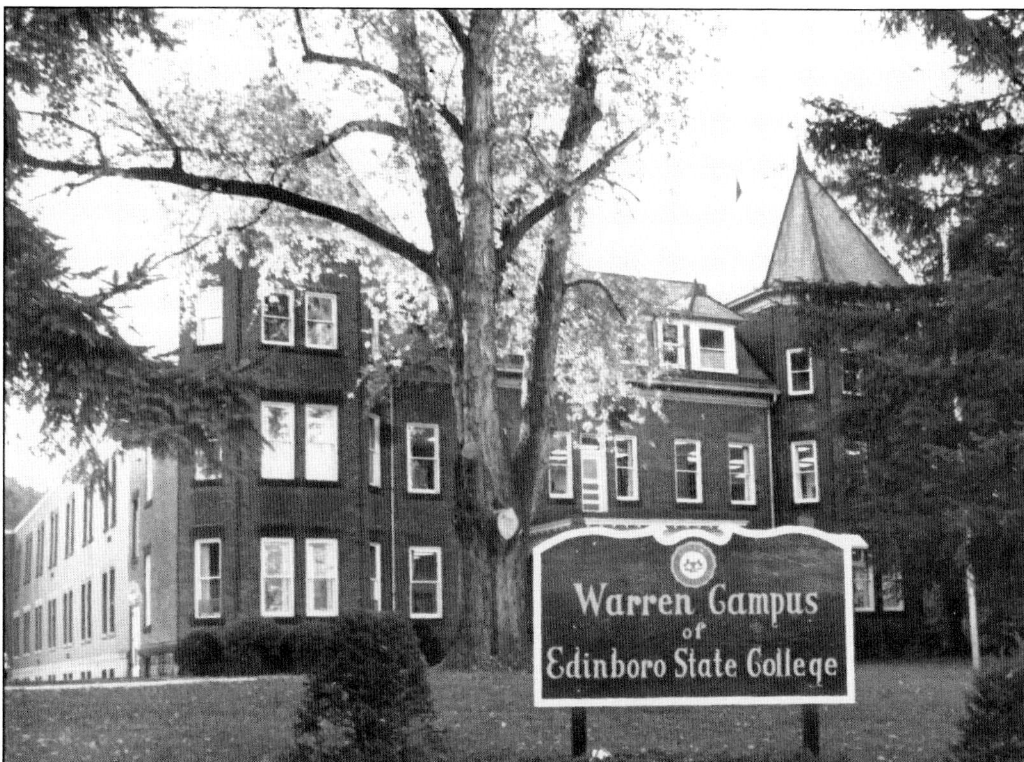

Edinboro had two campuses, both of which opened and closed around the same time. The Warren Campus opened in 1962 at Warren Area High School. Two years later, it moved to the East Street School. In 1971, Edinboro bought and renovated the Warren State Hospital farm colony and installed the campus there. The campus in Shenango had a similar start, beginning in 1961 at the Hickory Township High School and moving in 1968 to the junior high school, which it eventually owned. By 1977, both campuses closed.

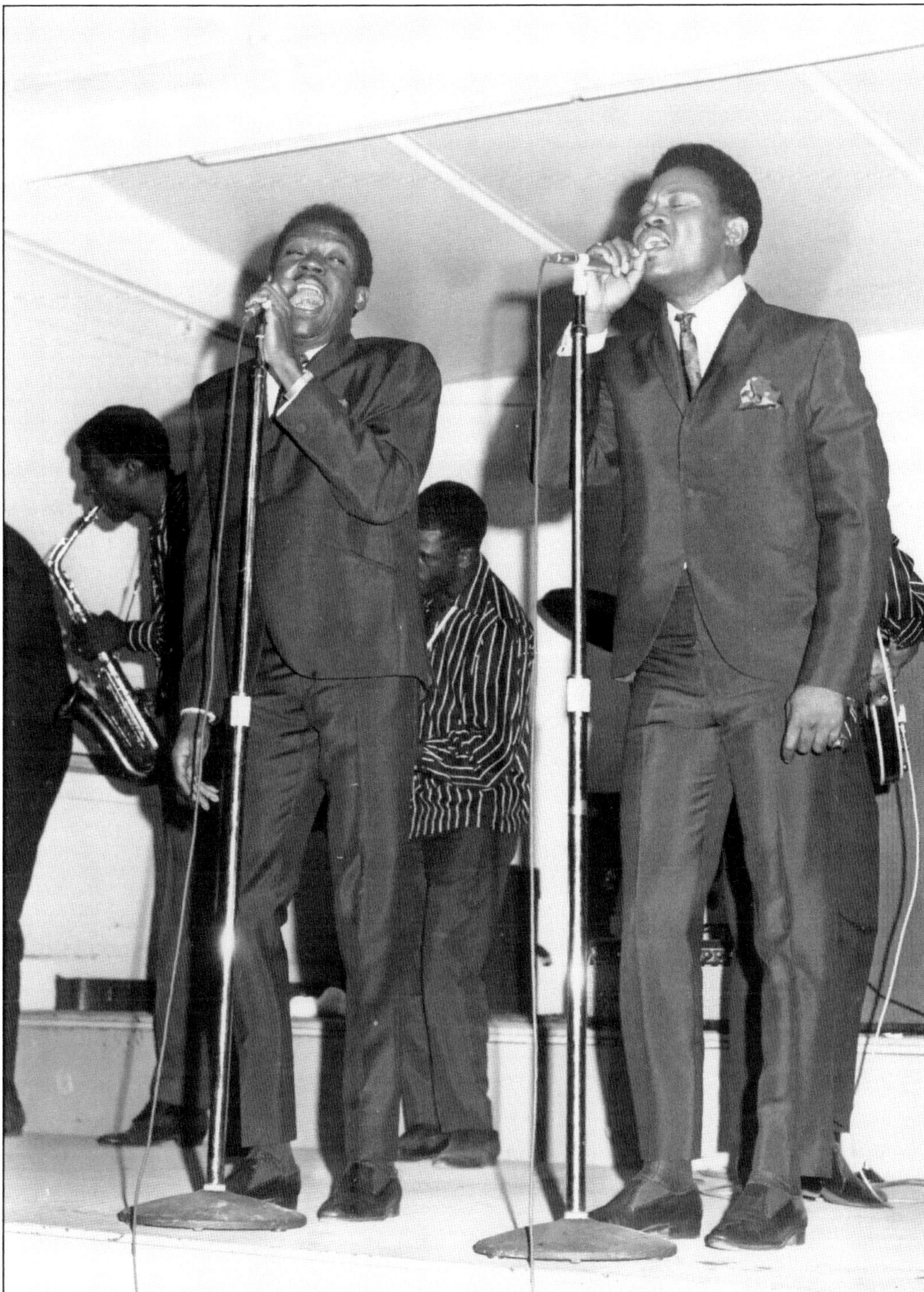

The late 1960s and 1970s saw a plethora of talent on campus. Along with Sam and Dave, pictured here, visiting performers included Frank Zappa, David Crosby, the Platters, the Beach Boys, Isaac Hayes, Muddy Waters, and Smokey Robinson.

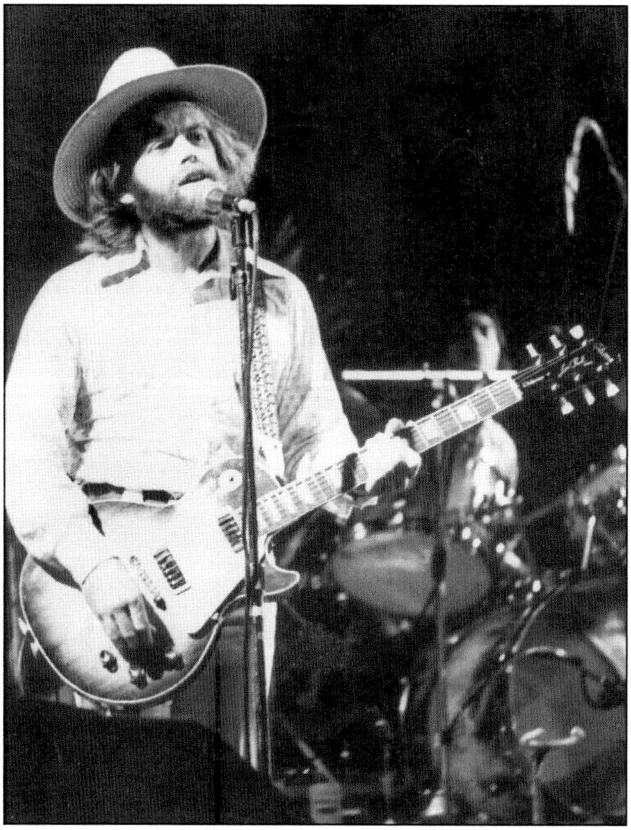

Al Jardine played guitar for the Beach Boys when they played on campus in 1974. Several other well-known bands came through campus, including Duke Ellington in 1971, Steve Miller Band in 1973, Robert Palmer in 1976, Charlie Daniels in 1978, Hall and Oats in 1982, and many more.

In 1971, in addition to hosting Duke Ellington and his band, Edinboro saw appearances by K. Leroy Irvis, the Erie Philharmonic, the Nitty Gritty Dirt Band, Frank Reynolds, and the National Ballet.

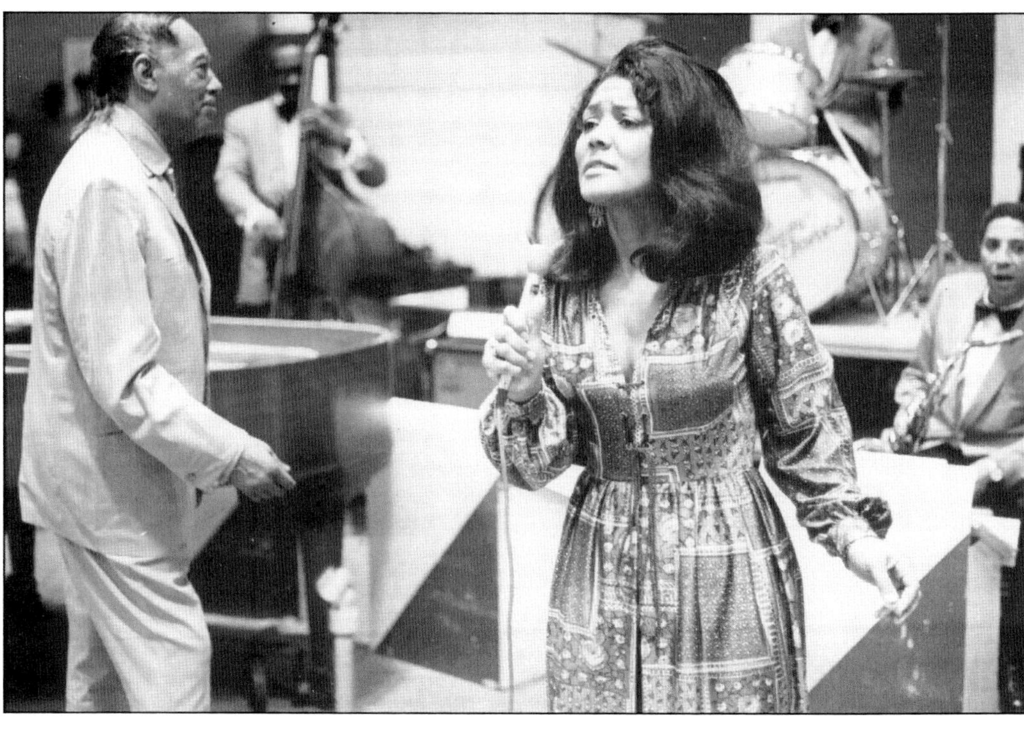

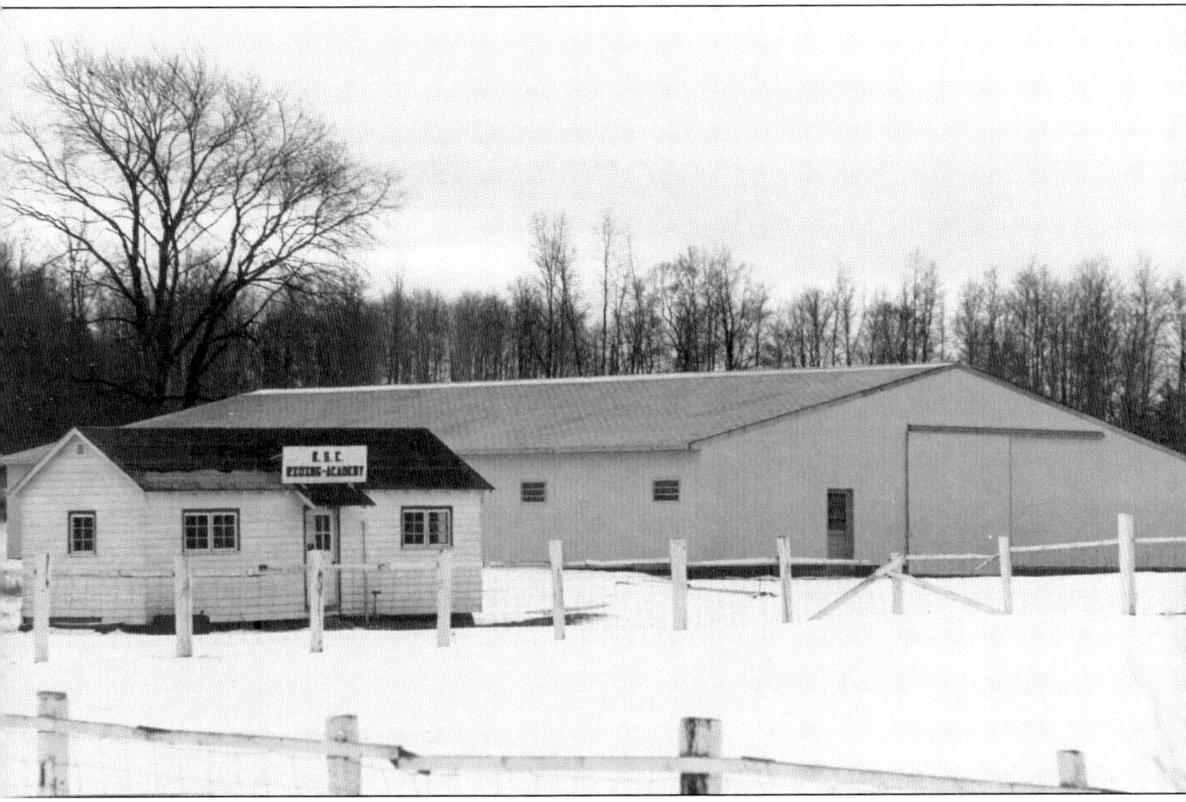

The Edinboro Riding Academy was next to the Dowling Equestrian Barn, which was built in 1974 and named after Debra Dowling, a former budget chairperson of student government. Today, the barn holds equipment for the facilities office.

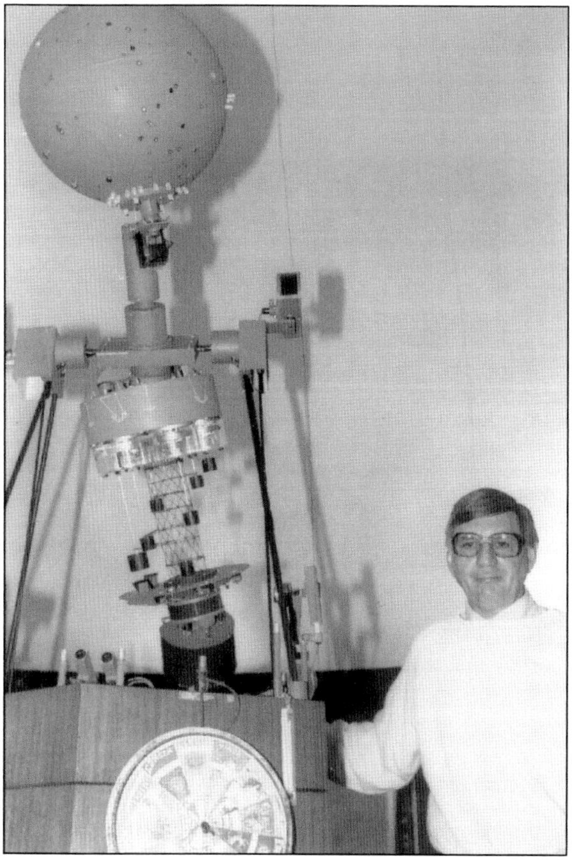

The Star Glow projector was installed in the planetarium in 1968. Dr. Merric Owen, who joined the college in 1970 to run the planetarium, is seen here with the projector. Students at that time paid a $125 basic fee, $306 for room and board, and a $20 activity fee.

Dr. Roy Stonesifer, (second from left) poses with students during a trip to a living history site for a hands-on experience. Today, the history department continues this experiential learning through travel learning, internships, and independent studies.

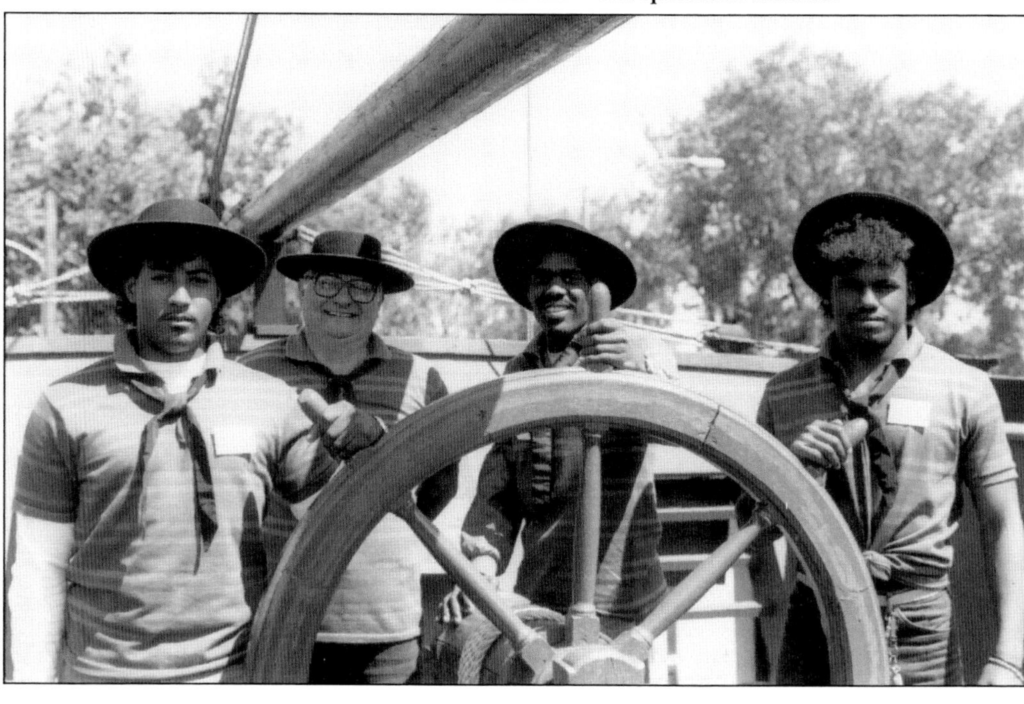

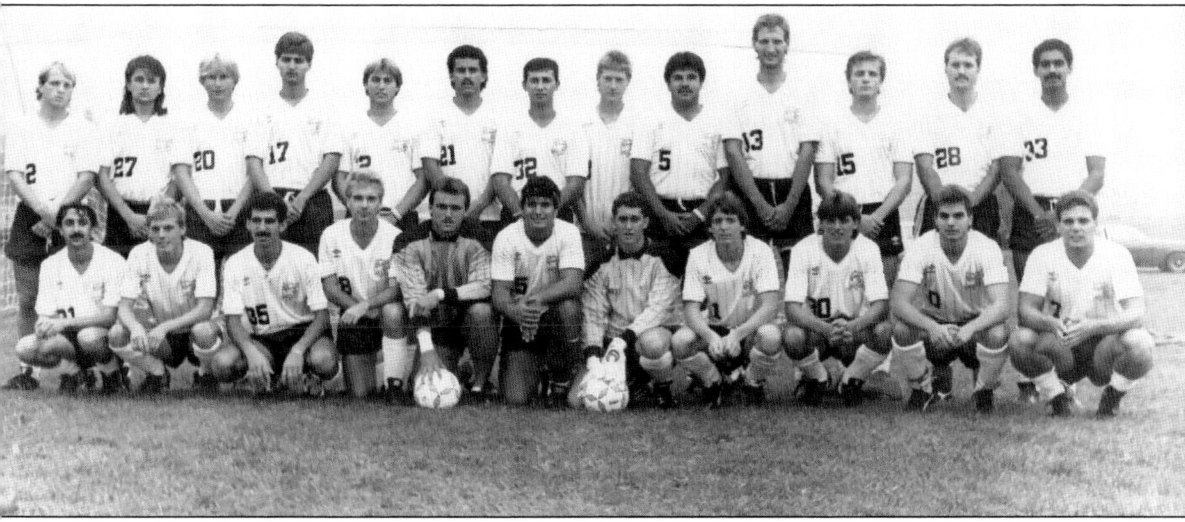

The men's soccer program began in 1969 and ended in 1987. Coached by George Shimpeno, the team played hard but were unable to win a championship.

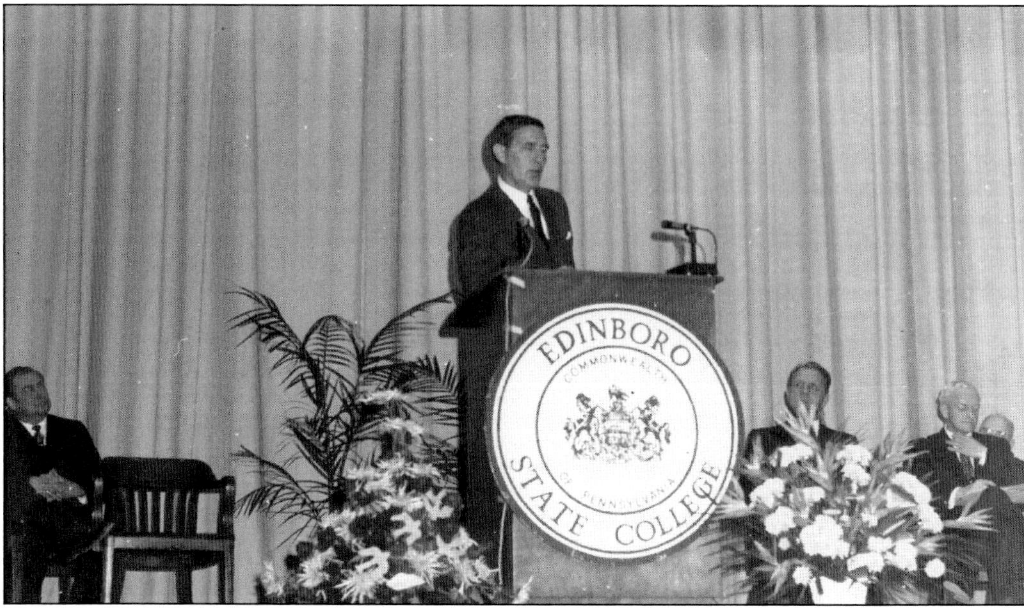

Morris Udall, a congressman from Arizona and a presidential candidate in 1980, spoke to the Edinboro community at the opening of the World Cultures Building in 1968. The structure is now named Luther V. Hendricks Hall. Reportedly, the faculty offices in the building are so small because Hendricks wanted to make sure each faculty member had their own office.

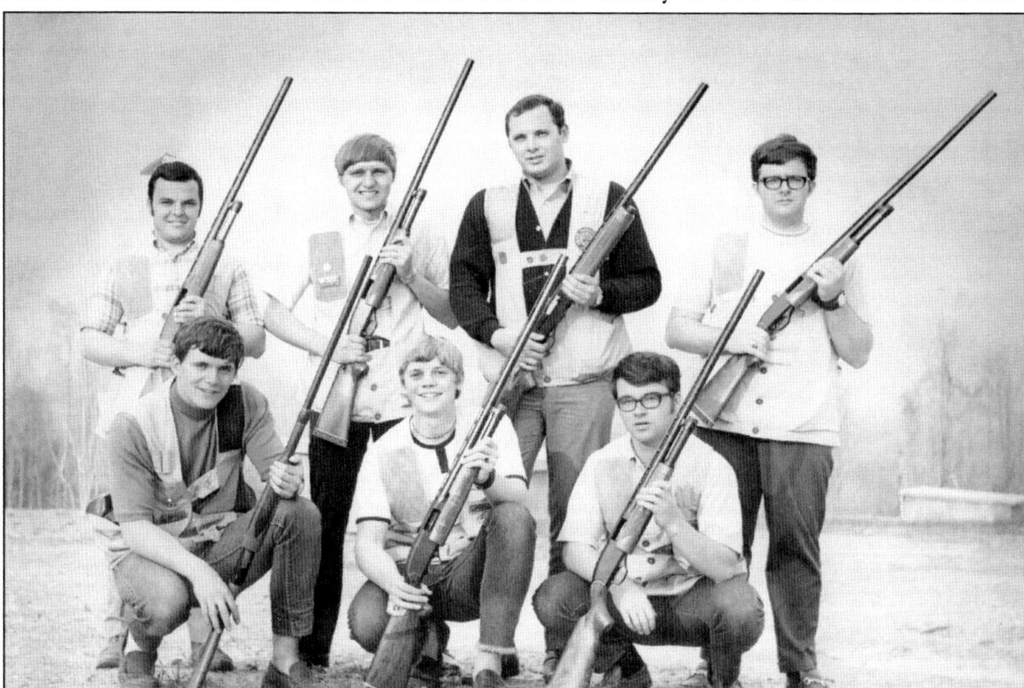

Coach Bob Orr led the Edinboro trapshooting team to the Eastern Regional Championship in 1970, earning them a bid to the national tournament, where they took fourth place. One shooter, Randy Barber, qualified for the world individual championship.

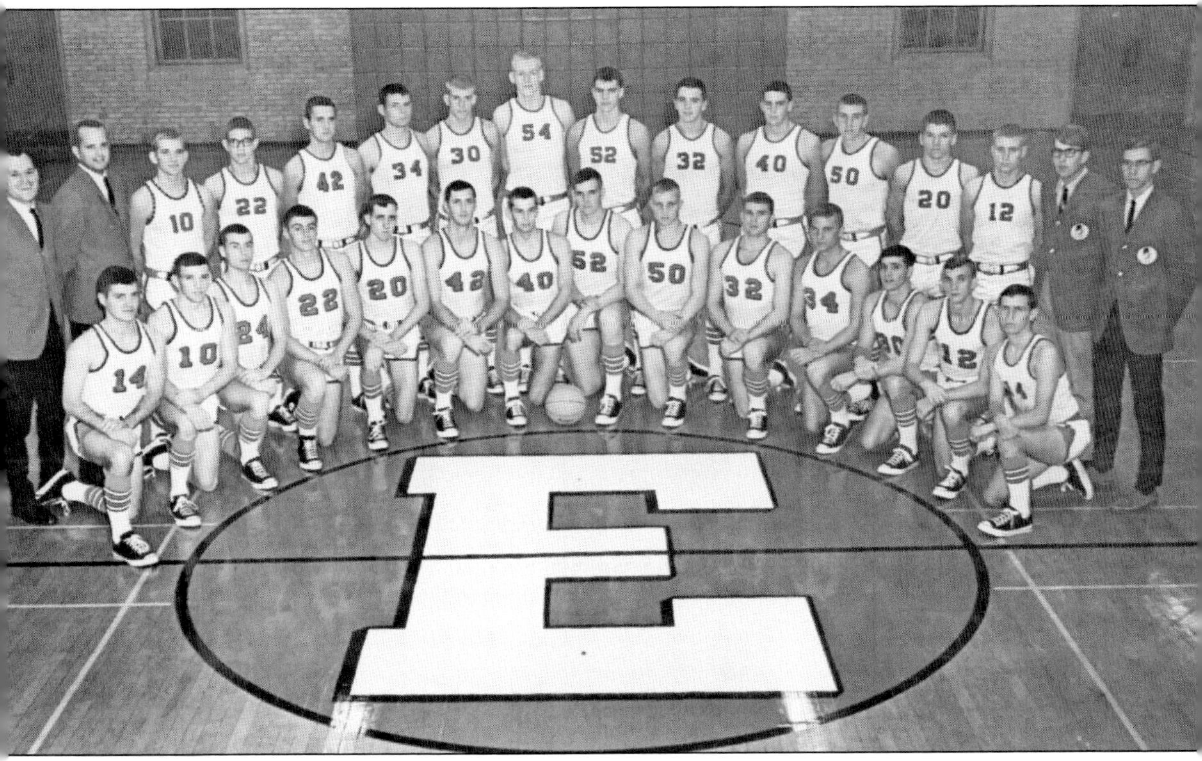

The 1967–1968 basketball team brought the first state basketball championship to Edinboro. They also set a new Pennsylvania State Athletic Conference record for points in one half with 75.

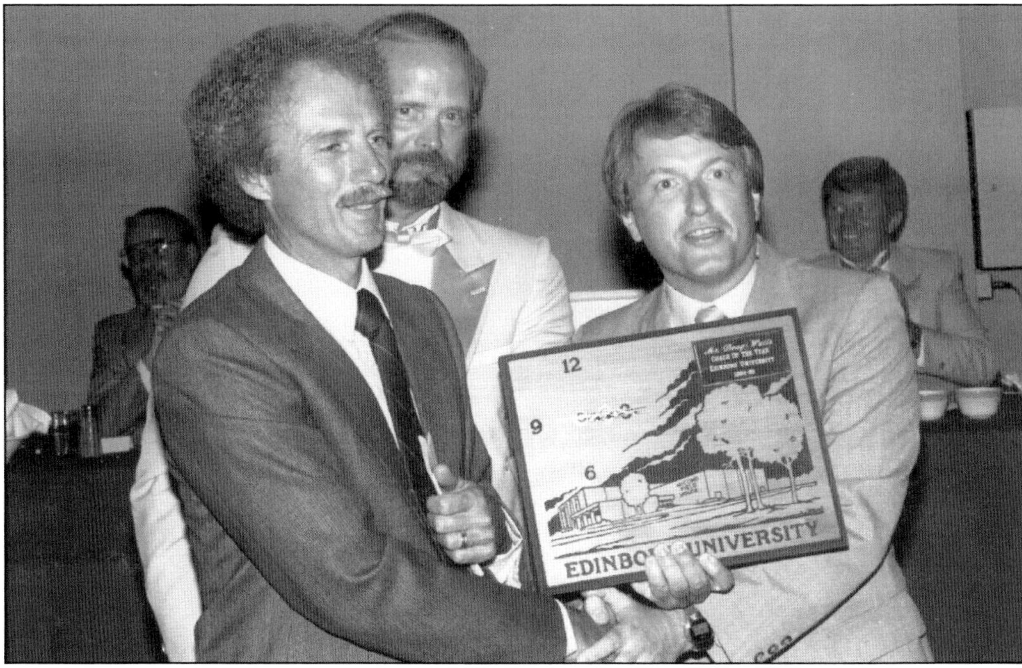

Coach Doug Watts has led more championship teams than any coach in Edinboro's history, and the cross-country course has been named in his honor. In addition to the 28 Pennsylvania State Athletic Conference (PSAC) team championships he has accrued, he has been awarded coach of the year nine times by the PSAC.

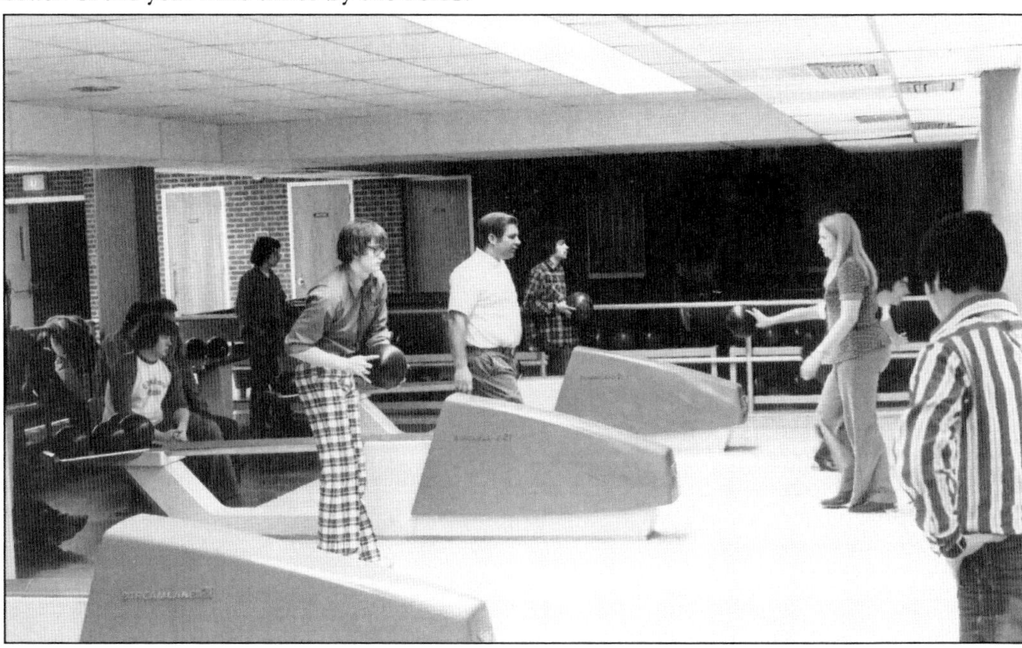

The student union has undergone several expansions. When the bookstore expanded on the ground floor, it took the space that had previously been a bowling alley. Aside from recreational bowling, Edinboro had also supported a bowling team, which was coached by Vernon Vogel.

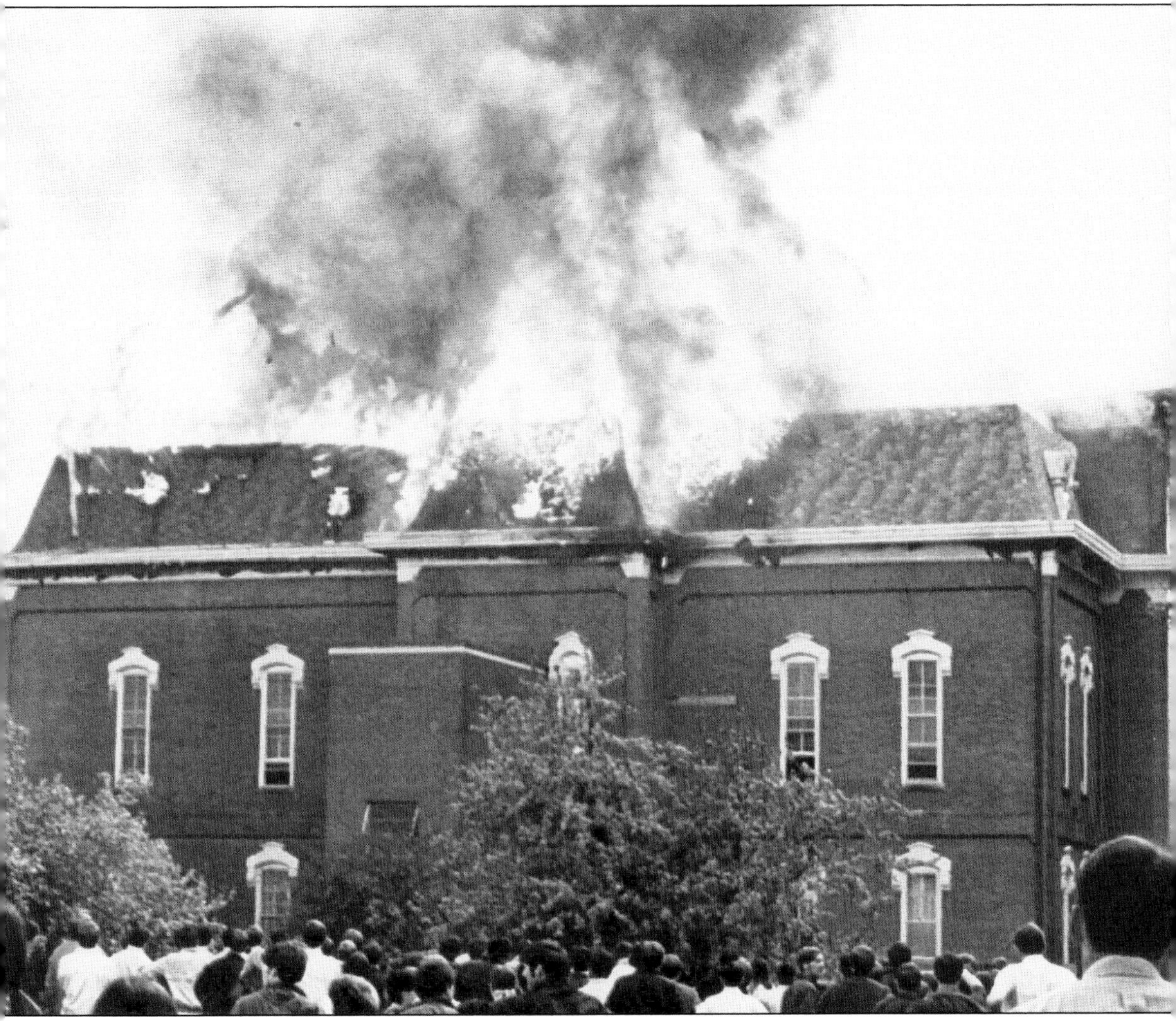

In 1969, the heart of the school was Normal Hall. It housed the president's office, business offices, classrooms, and more. On May 13 of that year, electrical sparks in the attic started a fire that could not be controlled. As the flames ate away at the building, faculty, students, and others formed a bucket brigade, passing the school's records out the front door. Without this heroic effort, the school may not have been able to continue as all the financial records, academic records, and personnel records would have been lost. In the midst of a national climate of campus unrest, Edinboro students came to the rescue of their school.

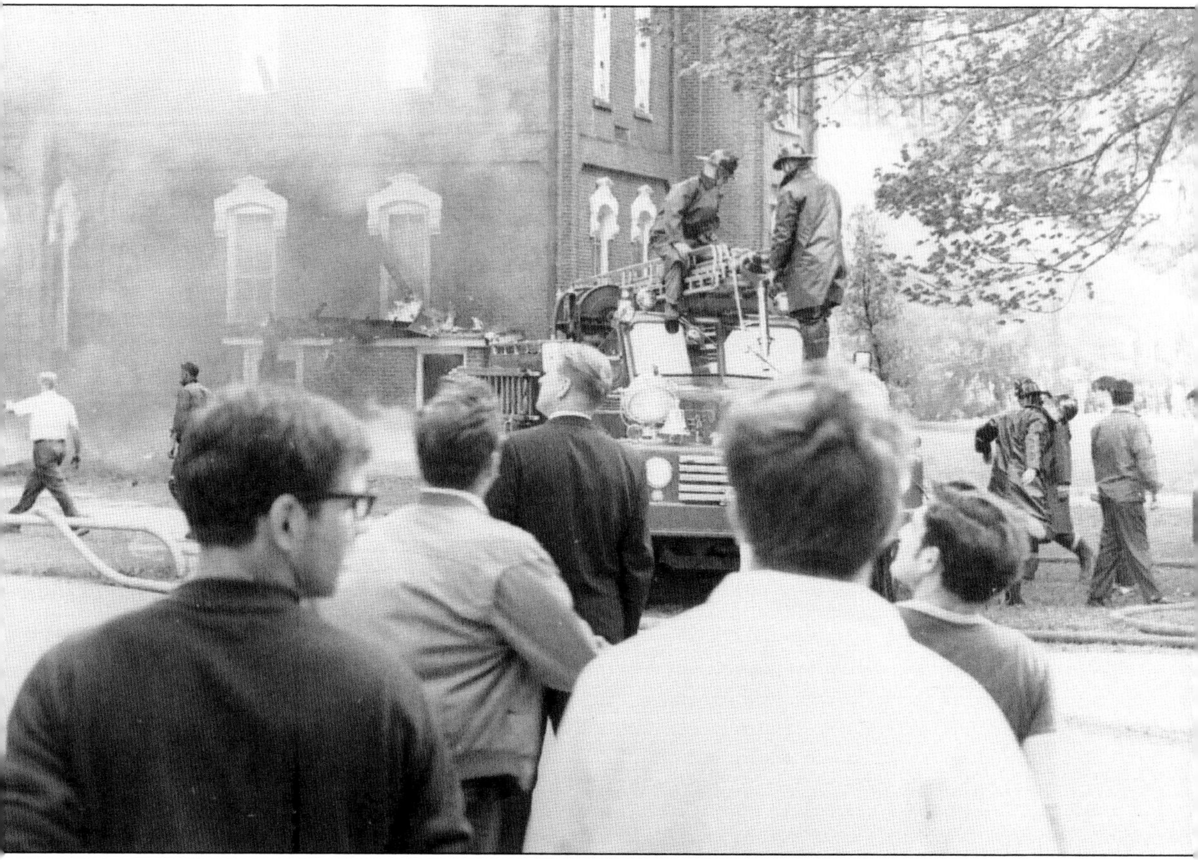

Edinboro president Chester McNerney (third from left, wearing a suit jacket) looks on as firefighters tried to control the Normal Hall fire. The building was completely lost, but fortunately, a new structure, Early Hall, erected as a maintenance building, had just been completed, and the administrative offices were moved there.

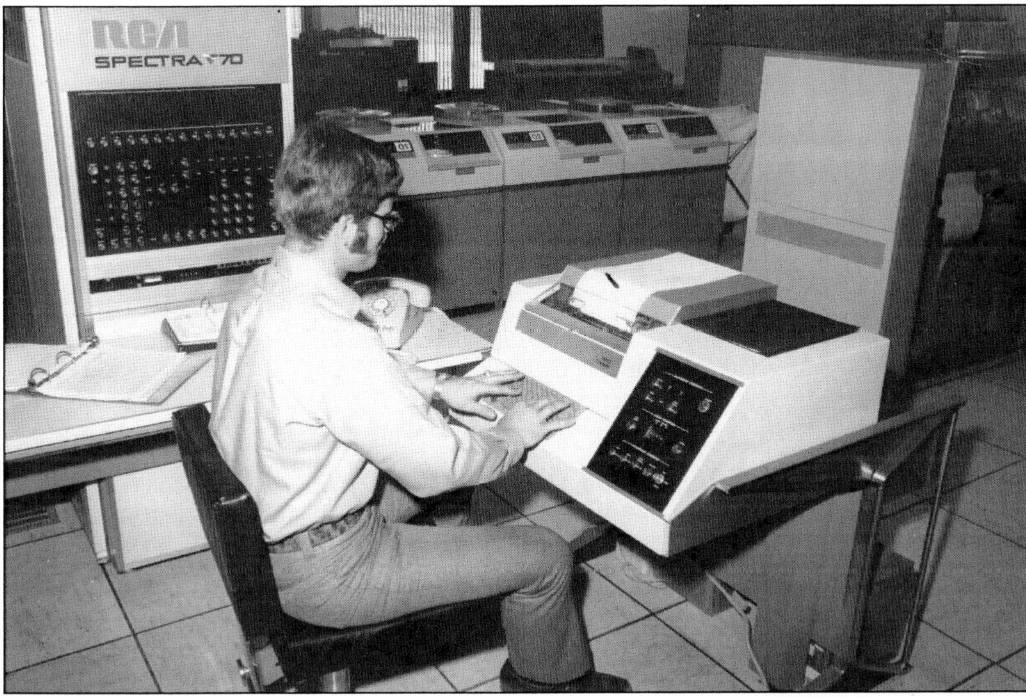

The first computers arrived on campus in 1965 and were housed in Normal Hall. When Hendricks was completed, the computer center moved there. They were later relocated to their current spot in Ross Hall.

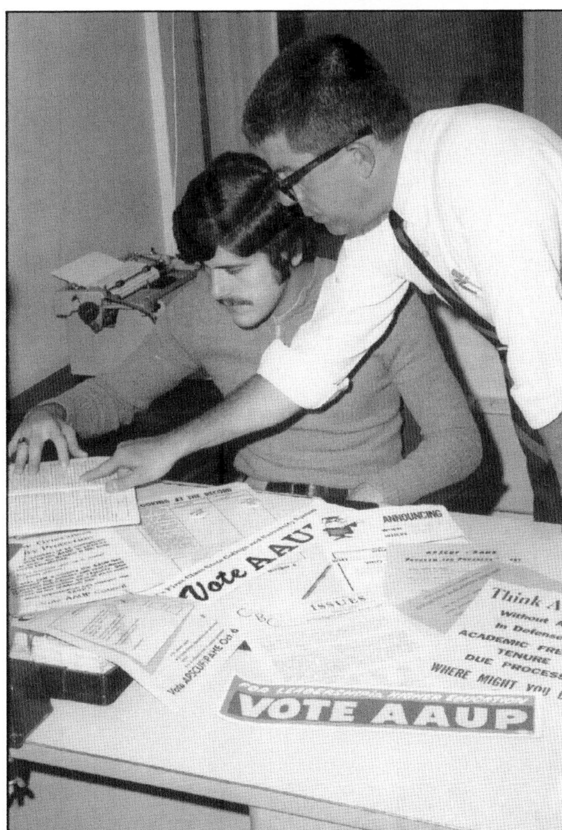

Originally founded as the State Teachers College Faculty Association in 1937, the organization is now known as the Association of Pennsylvania State College and University Faculties (APSCUF), and what began as a professional organization has since become a collective bargaining agent. When Pennsylvania passed Act 195 in 1970, state employees were given the option of unionizing. An election was held in 1970, and the state school faculty could vote for any of four choices: American Federation of Teachers (AFT), American Association of University Professors (AAUP), APSCUF, or no agent. Of the 4,000 votes cast, APSCUF received 2,010, the AAUP received 1,282, 169 voted for no agent, and 158 voted for AFT.

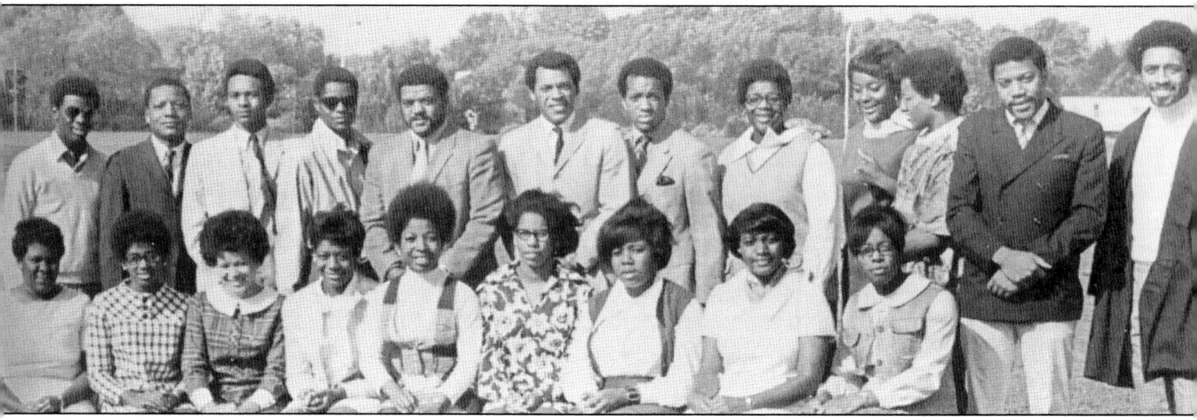

During the civil rights awakening of the 1960s and 1970s, Edinboro added black history courses and an African American section in the library. Members of the Association of Black Collegiates are seen here in 1970.

Four

STATE UNIVERSITY YEARS 1983–TODAY

The school has emerged from being a normal school, a state teachers college, and a state college to stand up as a university, which it has been for the last 29 years. In that time, much has happened.

Governance of the school has shifted from supervision by the department of education and is now overseen by the Pennsylvania State System of Higher Education. This push to be more independent of state government was meant to keep the schools free of political jockeying and to give the schools more control in charting their own course. At this juncture, the state-owned colleges became universities.

During this most recent era, the university has made strident efforts to engage the international community. Trips to China and Pakistan were regular occurrences under school president Foster Diebold. Today, international students on campus are commonplace.

Another hallmark of this era is a notable increase in significant contributions from donors. The Porreco Center opened as a result of a generous donation while the Meadville campus benefited from another large gift. Likewise, the Mike S. Zafirovski Sports and Recreation Center was built after a generous donation, and the Memorial Hall-Louis B. Cole Auditorium was remodeled thanks to another gift.

Edinboro has a well-deserved reputation as a campus for disabled students, which was recognized when the 1985 and 1988 National Wheelchair Games were held on campus.

Today, the university offers more than 100 programs. The School of Education still graduates teachers and school administrators. The School of Arts and Sciences graduates become nurses, speech therapists, policemen, museum directors, geologists, social workers, and various other professions. The School of Business graduates accountants, marketing, and management professionals.

More than 150 years of teaching students has turned a rural academy into a diverse university with an international footprint.

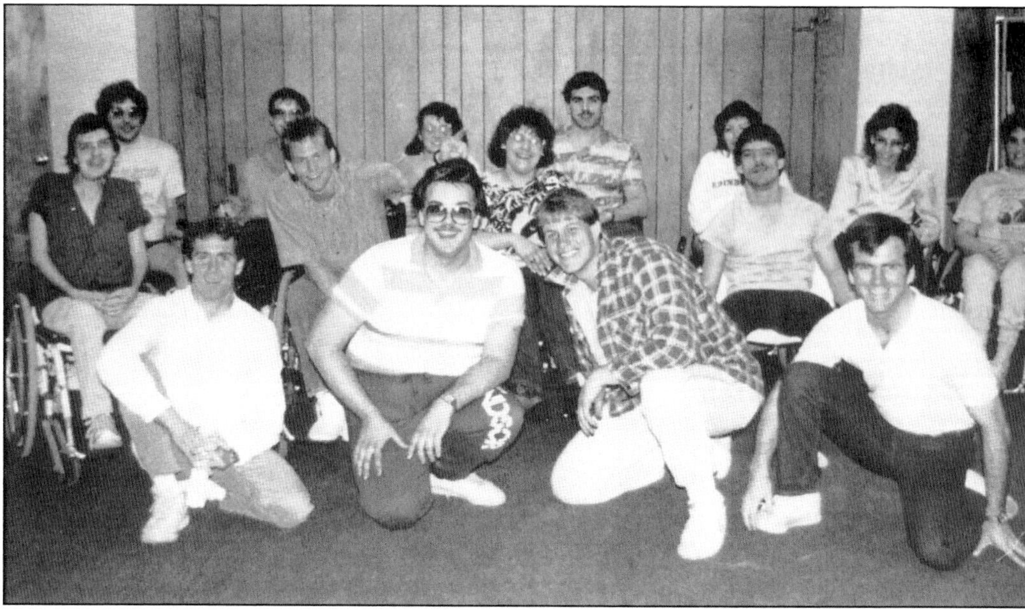

The Rolling Scots Wheelchair Athletic Team is seen here when they competed in the National Wheelchair Athletic Association and the National Association of Sports for Cerebral Palsy in 1987. There were a number of individual events, including table tennis, football, weight lifting, swimming, and other track and field competitions. Today, the Rolling Scots have a men's and women's basketball team.

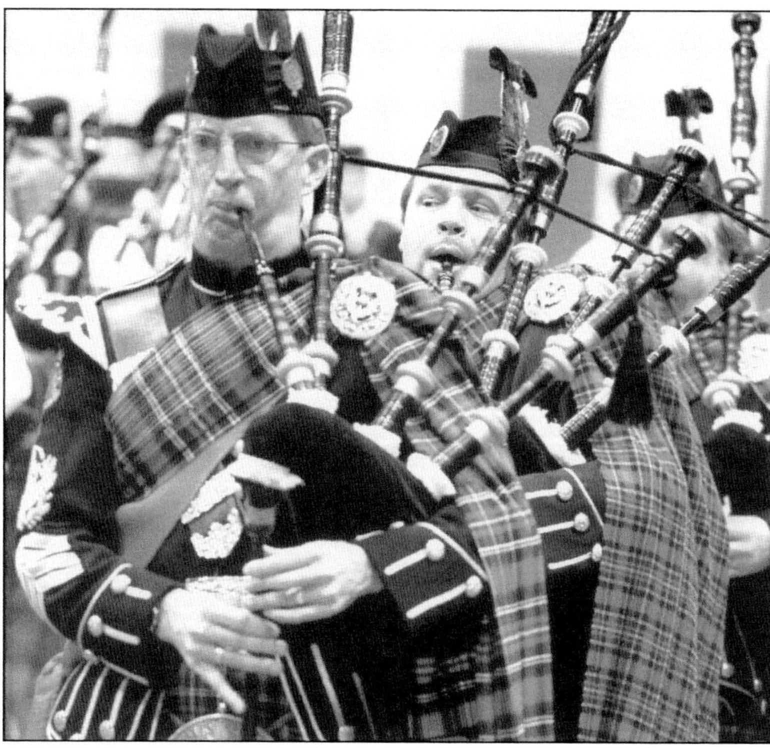

The Annual Highlands Games first opened in 1993 with Dr. Tim Thompson as the driving force. It began with a humble 500 attendees but is now attended by thousands. Bagpipers, Scottish dancers, and the traditional Scottish athletic competition bring people in from surrounding states to compete or just to be entertained.

Foster Diebold served as Edinboro's president from 1979 to 1996, through its transition from a state college to a state university. Among his legacies are the rehabilitation of Reeder Hall, the Biggers House, and the Taylor House and his ambitious international program.

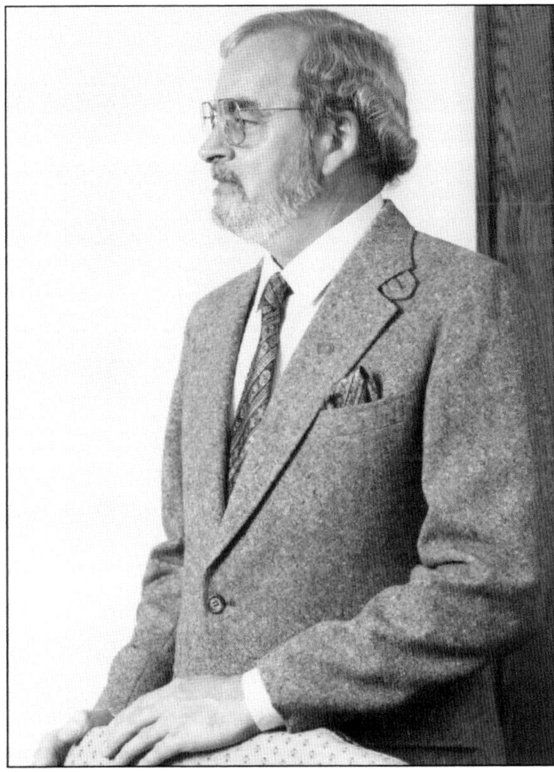

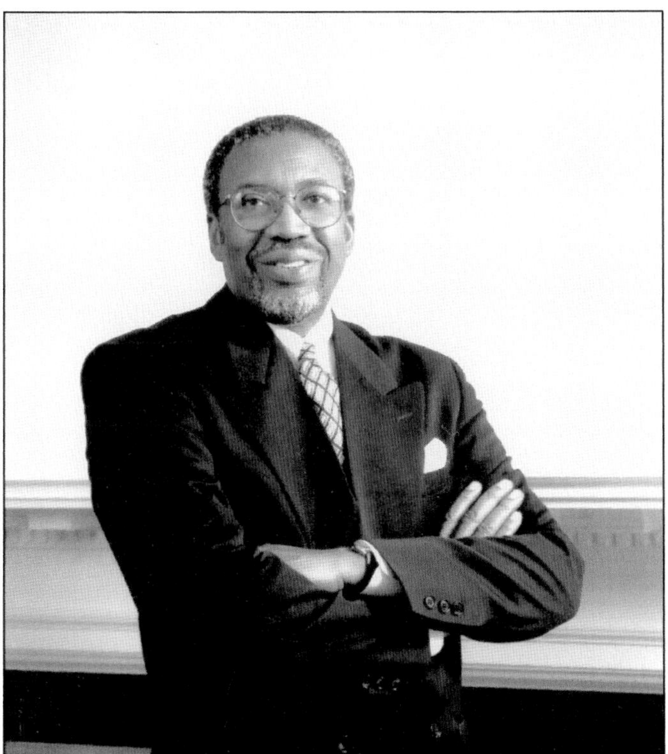

Dr. Frank Pogue came to Edinboro University from the State University of New York System Central Administration where he was vice chancellor for student affairs. He was president from 1996 to 2007 and promoted his philosophy of a student-centered university. During his tenure, the university adopted a master building plan, which is still being carried out.

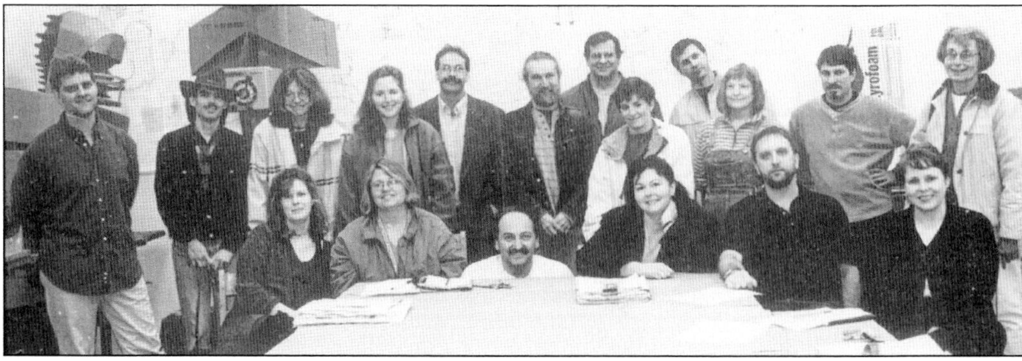

From Waldo Bates and Aime Doucette to an art department with nearly 50 faculty members, the art department has grown into one of Edinboro's largest departments. The animation program in particular has been a strong draw for students.

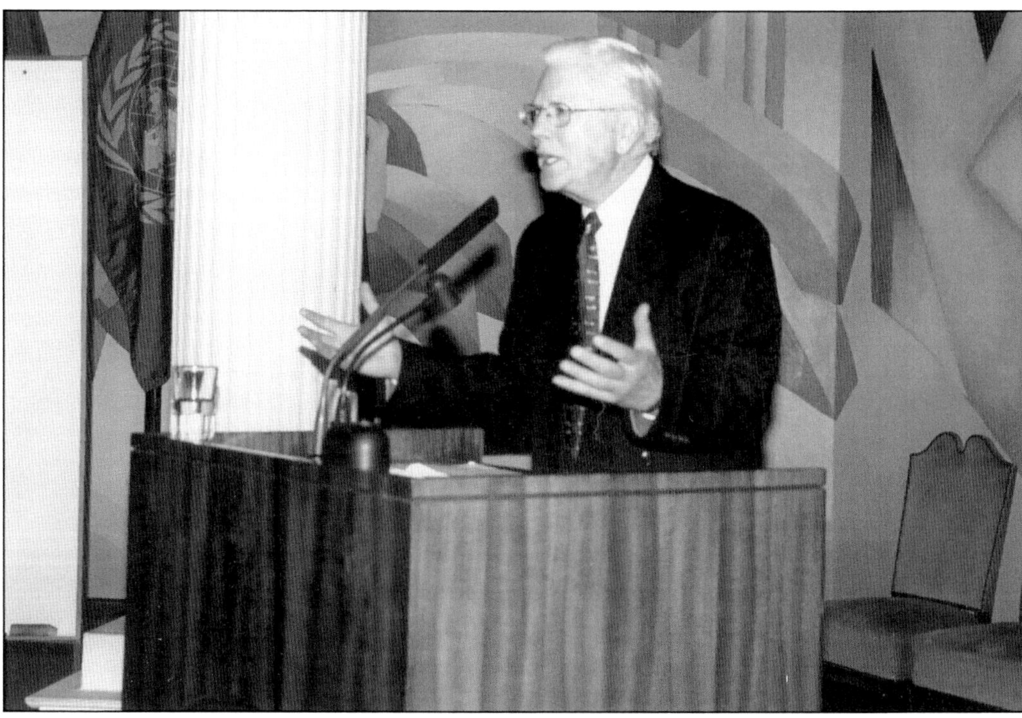

Dr. Jim Drane holds the first and only endowed chair at Edinboro University, the Russell B. Roth Professor of Bioethics, which was established to explore the ethical character of modern gains in biotechnology. Dr. Drane is a prolific author who has written 12 books and numerous articles on the subject. He is also a sought-after speaker on bioethics by countries around the world.

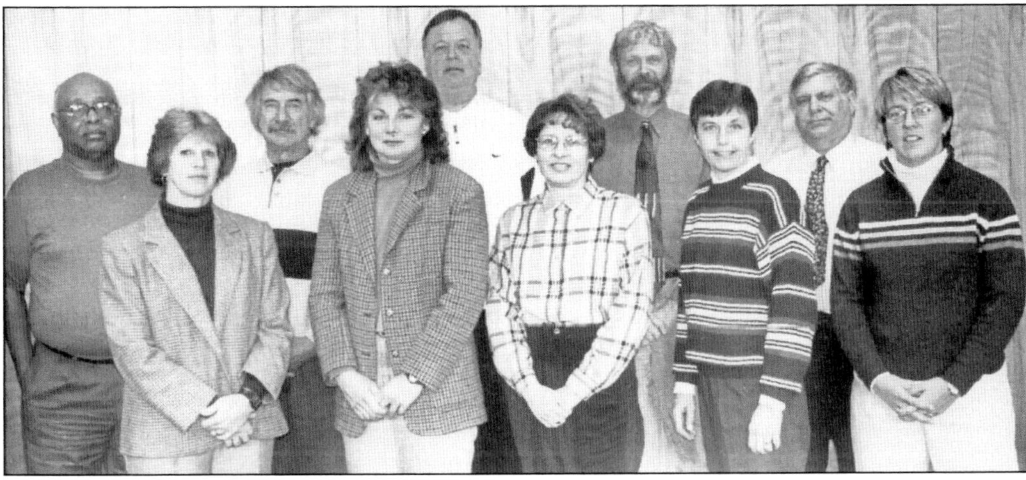

Edinboro's tradition of keeping a healthy mind and body is carried on by the health and physical education department.

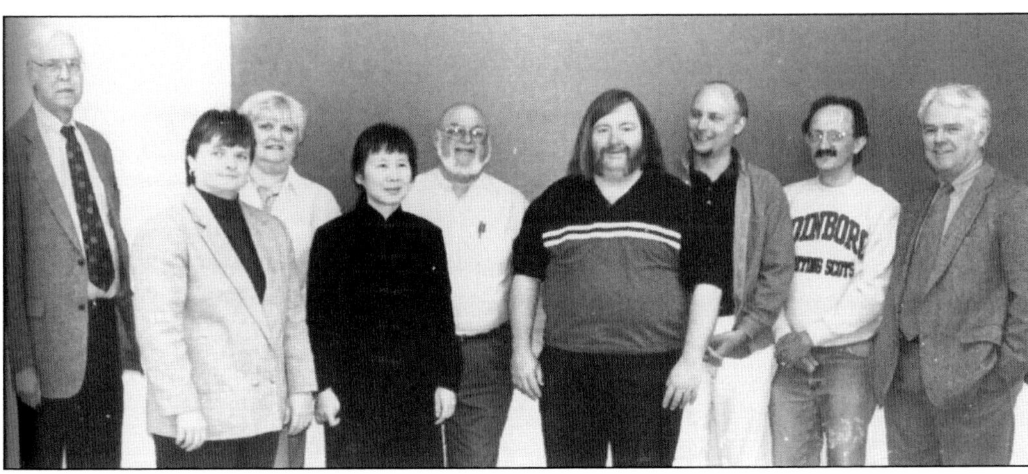

Edinboro no longer teaches penmanship or Greek and Latin, but US history has been taught since the beginning. The history department is seen here in 1999.

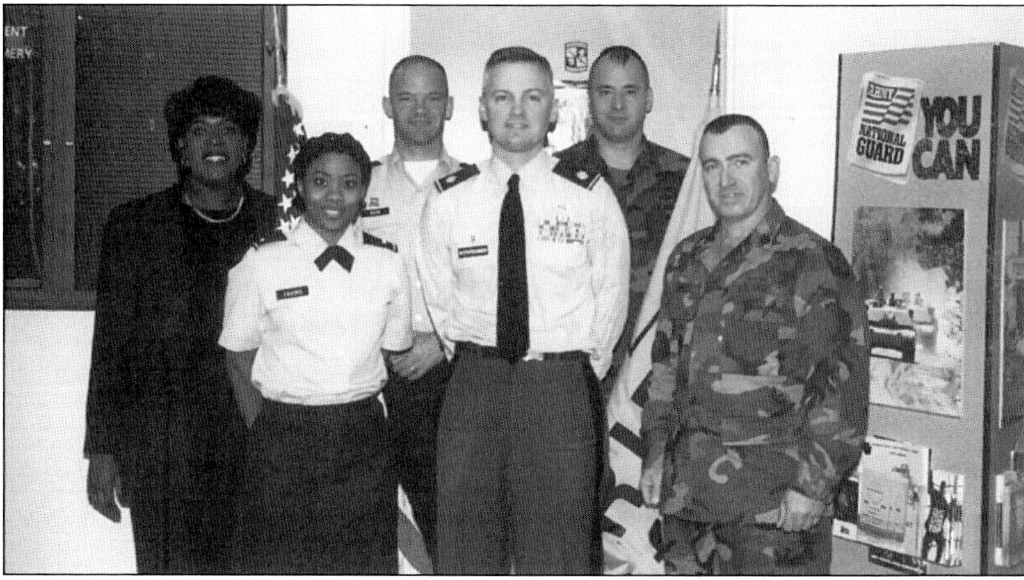

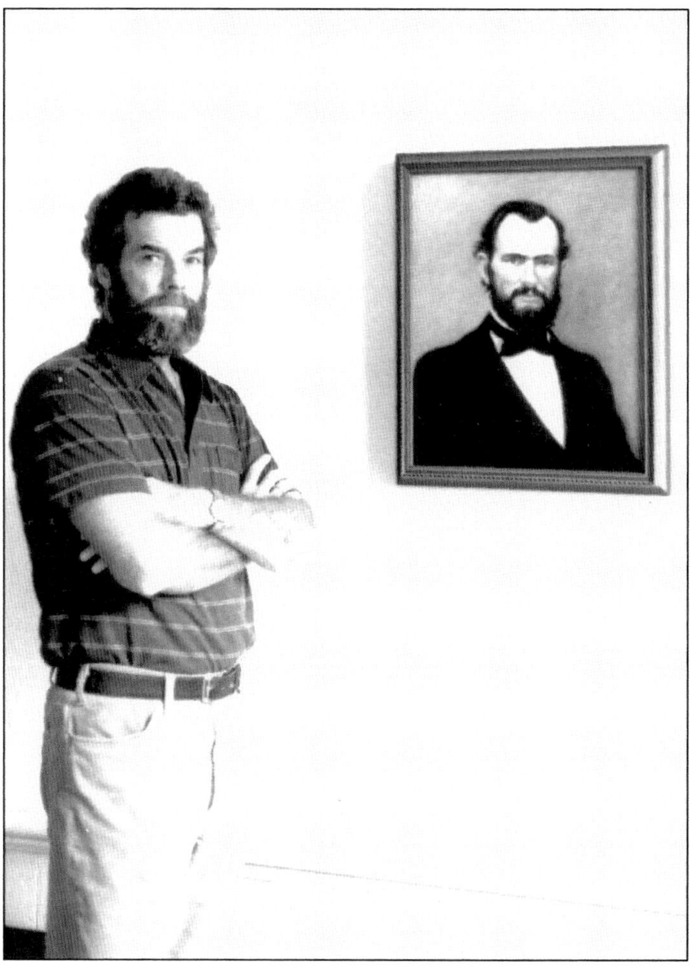

Reserve Officers' Training Corps (ROTC) first appeared on campus after World War II but was short lived. It next appeared in the 1970s, but because of the Vietnam War, some felt its presence would cause trouble; thus, a cooperative program with Gannon University was established. It was not until 1981 that Edinboro got its own program based on campus.

Portraits of all of Edinboro's principals and presidents were painted by professor James McMurray, who finished the portraits, commissioned by school president Foster Diebold, in 1986. The portraits hung in the lobby area outside the president's office until recently, when they were moved to the president's dining area. Since completing the initial commission, McMurray has been engaged to paint the succeeding presidents as well.

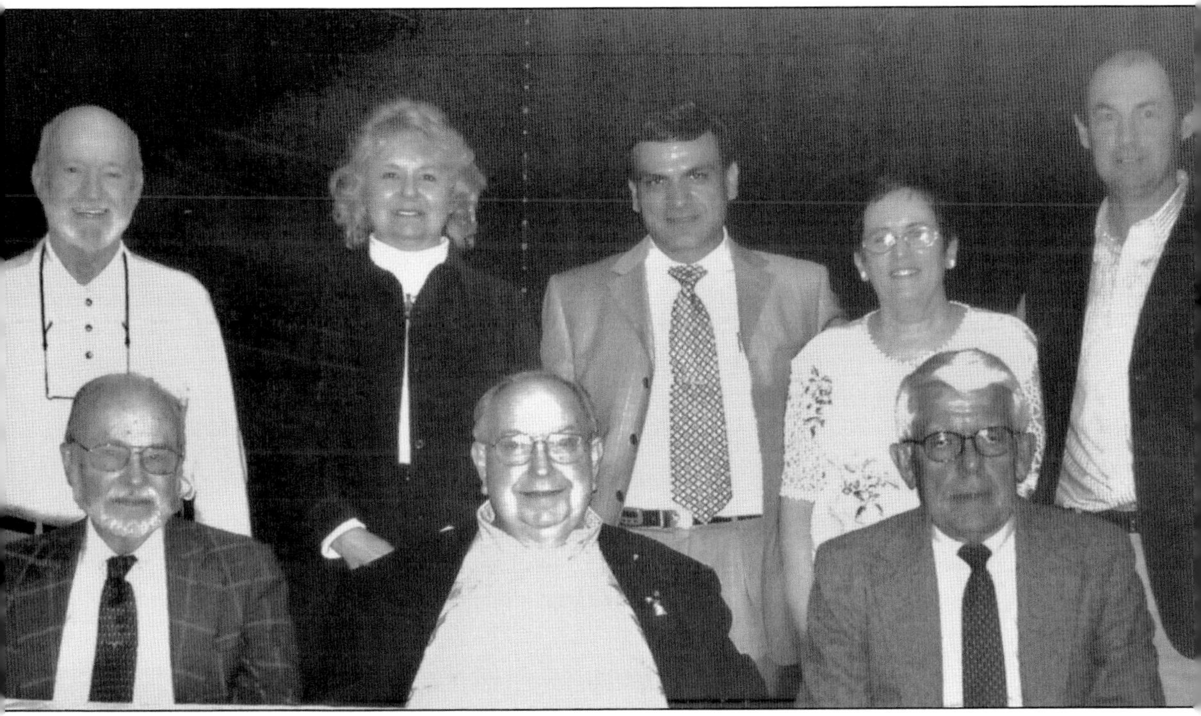

In 2006, a luncheon was held to honor all the presidents of Edinboro's APSCUF chapter. They are, from left to right, (first row) Russell Vance (1971–1973), Tom Heard (1983–1999), and Harvey Heath (1979–1981); (second row) Micque Brown (1973–1975), Marie Palmer (1975–1979, 1981–1983), Baher Ghosheh (1999–2001), Sherry Reynolds (2001–2005), and Dave Obringer (2005–2009). Current president Jean Jones is not shown.

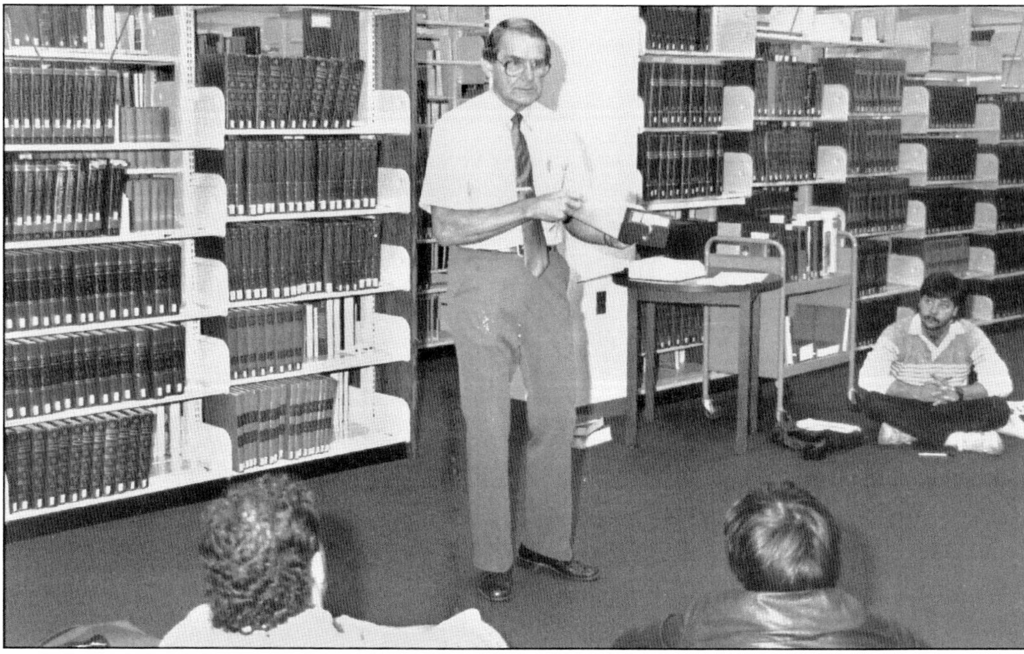

With journals at his back, the card catalog in his hand, and students at his feet, John Stonis demonstrates how to find materials in the library, which held around 300,000 books in the 1970s.

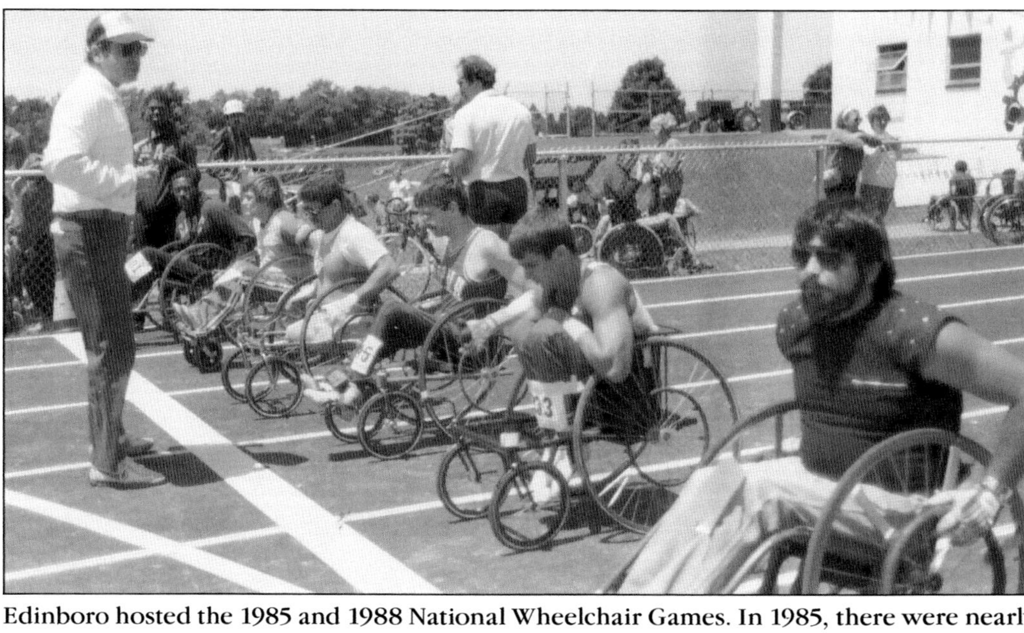

Edinboro hosted the 1985 and 1988 National Wheelchair Games. In 1985, there were nearly 350 athletes, and by 1988, there were close to 500. They competed in track and field, weight lifting, table tennis, swimming, archery, and air guns. Dave O'Dessa, Edinboro's vice president for administration, was the national chairman, coordinating the volunteers who made the games happen. O'Dessa said, "Suddenly my committee was 30-some people. All volunteers . . . It was a lot of work but we pulled it off . . . I can remember Doug Watts staying till three o'clock in the morning setting up all the eats."

Edinboro first recognized the need to support students with disabilities as early as 1970 with the admission of a blind student. This precipitated a planning process, which emerged in 1974 as the mainstream program. That same year, the Pennsylvania Department of Education named Edinboro one of three wheelchair campuses in the state. The program has advanced quickly to become one of the best programs for disabled college students in the nation. Here, a wheelchair student participates in the annual candle-lighting ceremony.

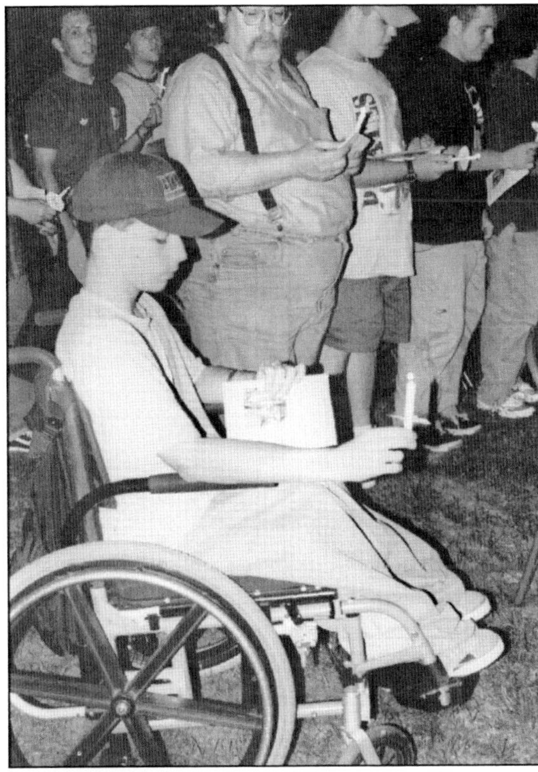

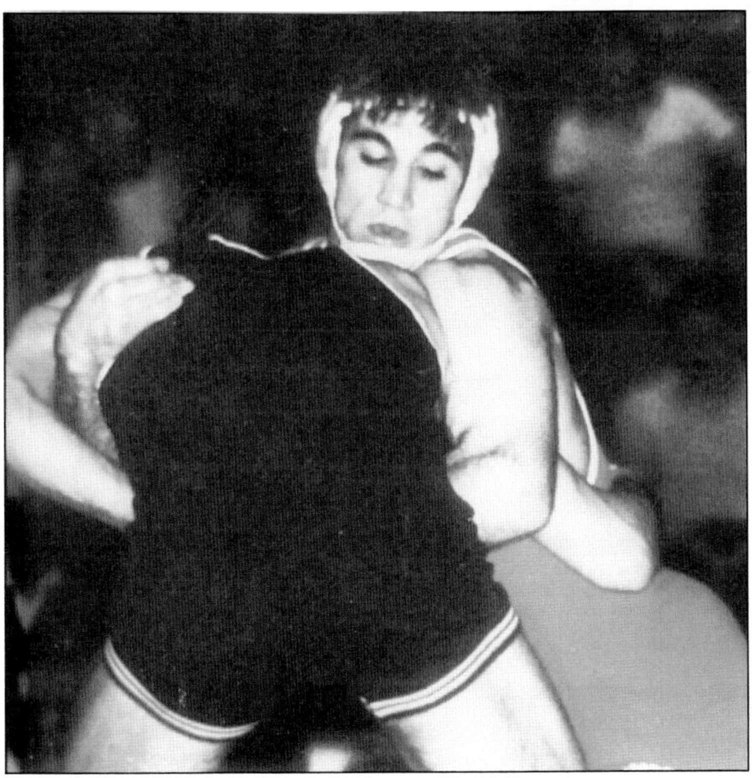

In 1981, the state schools decided to leave the National Association of Intercollegiate Athletes (NAIA) and become part of the National Collegiate Athletic Association (NCAA) Division II. Five years later, wrestling began competing as a Division I team. It remains the only Division I sport at Edinboro.

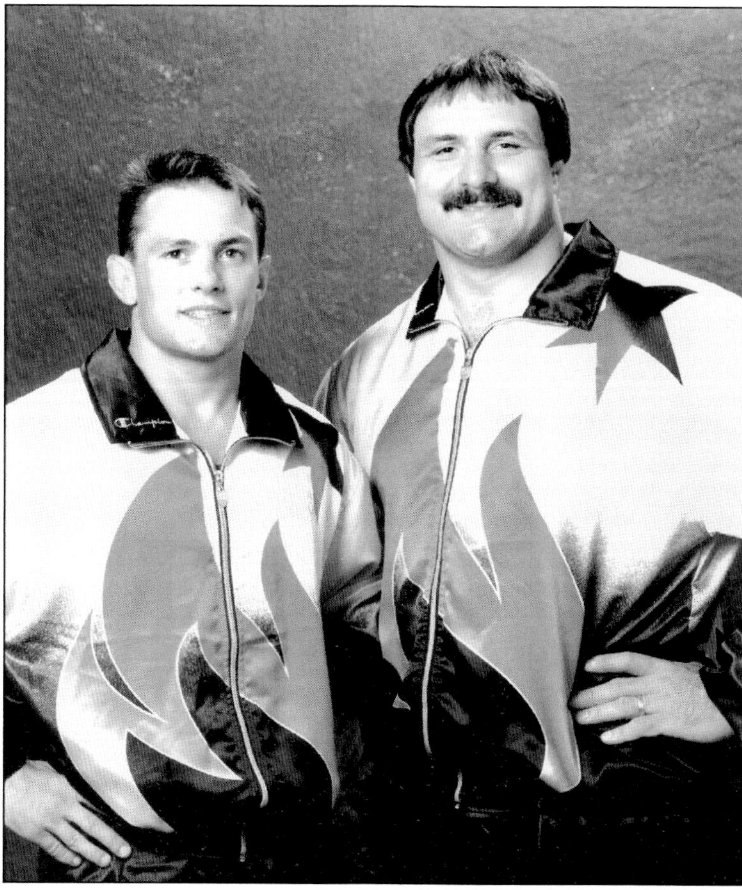

The Edinboro wrestling program has several connections to the Olympics, most notably Bruce Baumgartner (right), who has four Olympic medals, two of which are gold. Next to Baumgartner in this photograph is former Edinboro wrestling coach Lou Rosselli, who competed with Baumgartner in the 1996 Olympics. Two of Edinboro's athletic trainers have also participated in the Olympics: Gary Hanna and George Roberts.

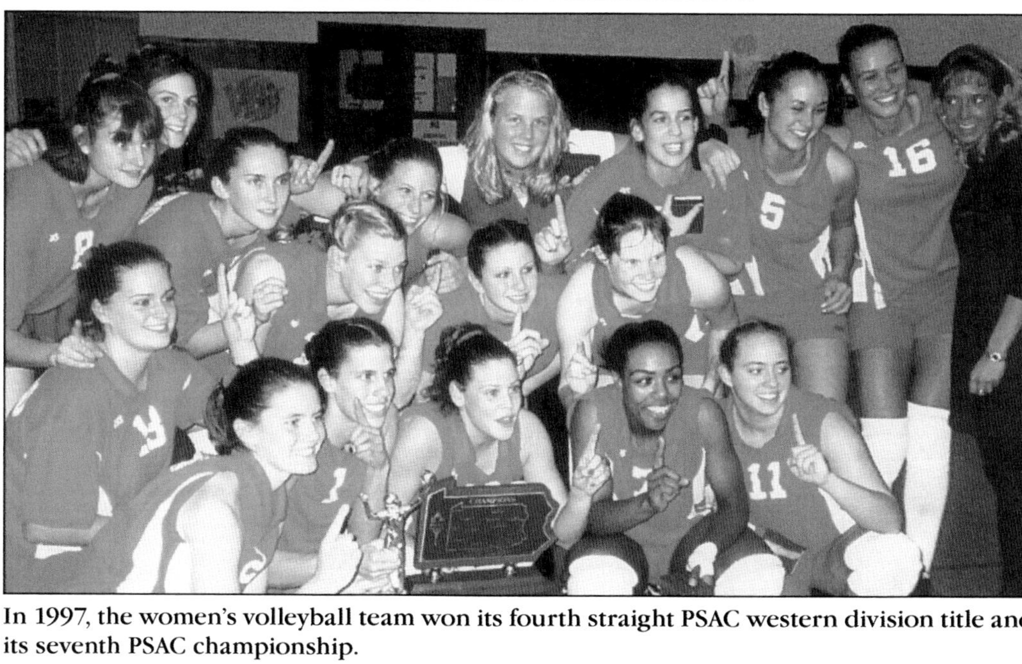

In 1997, the women's volleyball team won its fourth straight PSAC western division title and its seventh PSAC championship.

R. Benjamin Wiley was a local civic leader, serving as president of the Edinboro Council of Trustees and later on the Pennsylvania State Board of Governors. The Arts and Sciences Building is named in his honor.

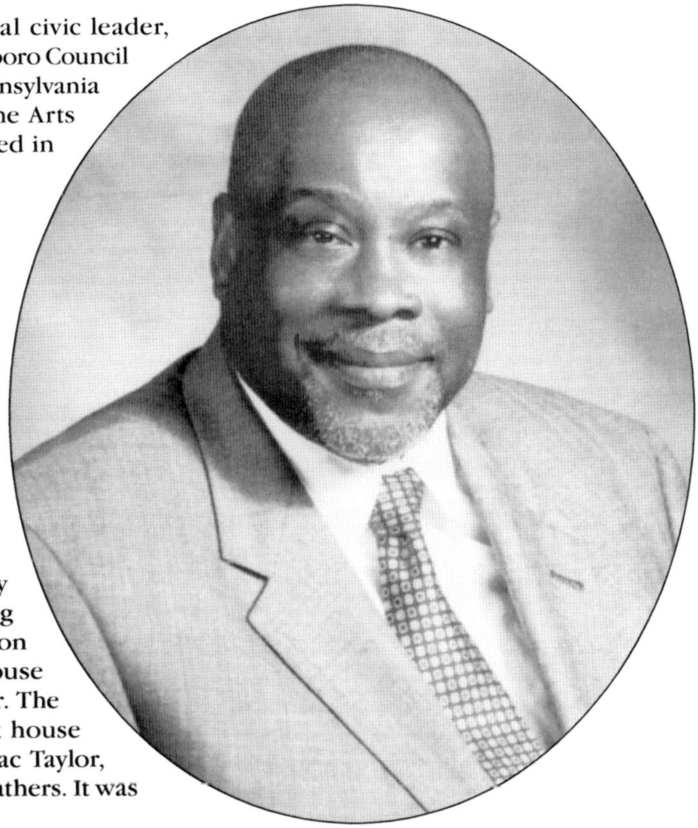

Taylor House was purchased by the university in 1986, during a period of building restoration at Edinboro. The Biggers House was purchased two years later. The Taylor House, the first brick house in Edinboro, was built by Isaac Taylor, one of the school's founding fathers. It was sold in 2011.

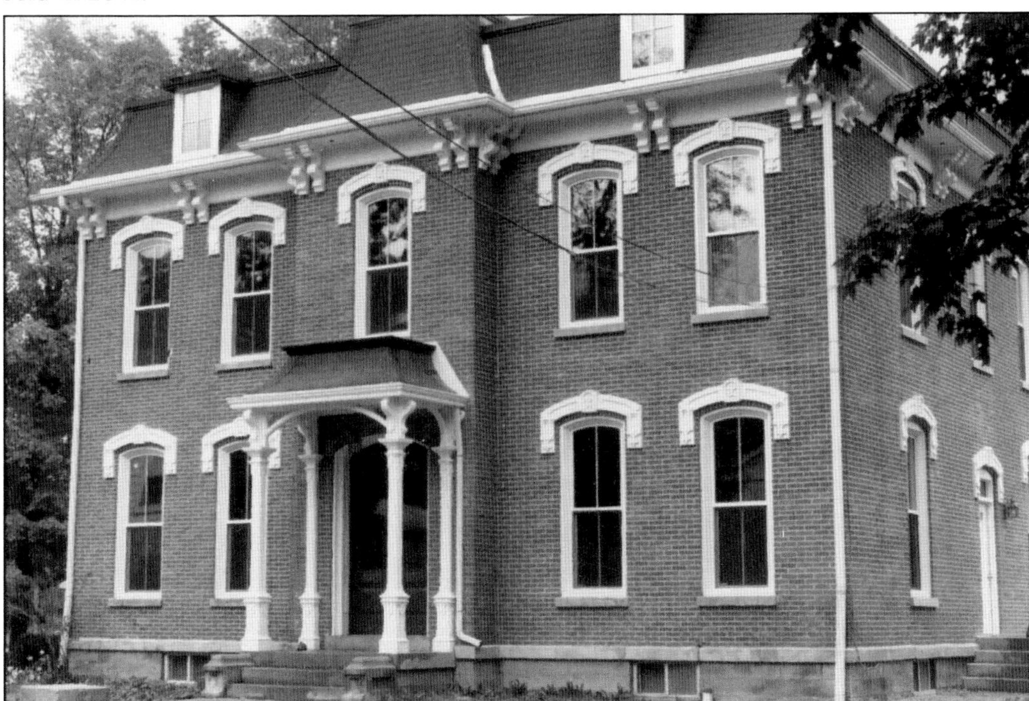

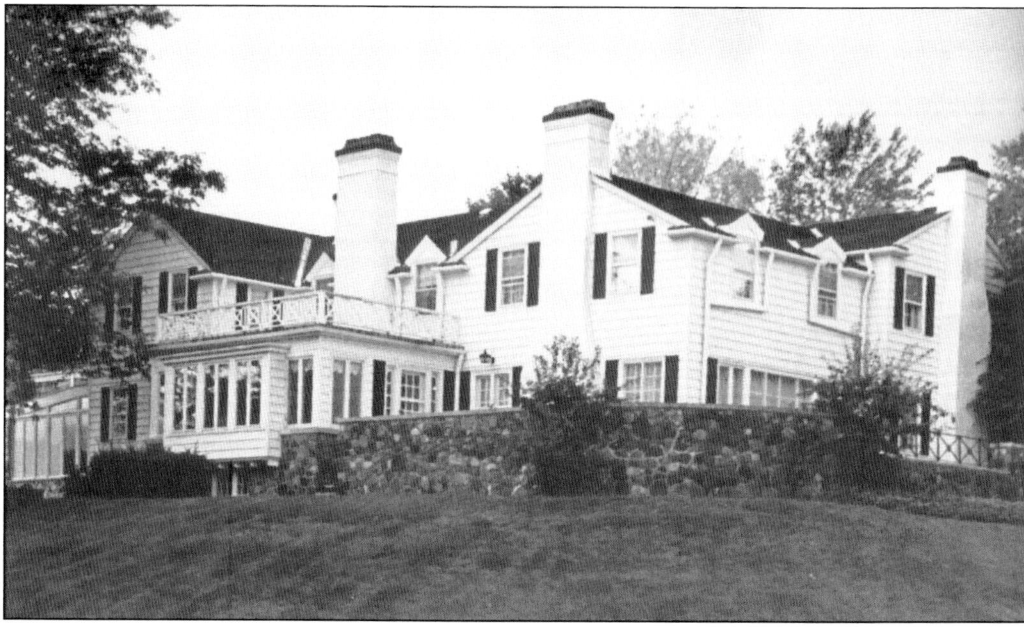

Edinboro University in Erie's Porreco Center was named in honor of Mary Porreco, who received her normal school certificate and master's degree at Edinboro. Her nephew Louis Porreco donated the 22-acre estate to Edinboro in 1986. Since 1980, Edinboro has also had a presence in Meadville, most recently at Meadville Access Center, located at the Bessemer Center. A new location will open in 2012.

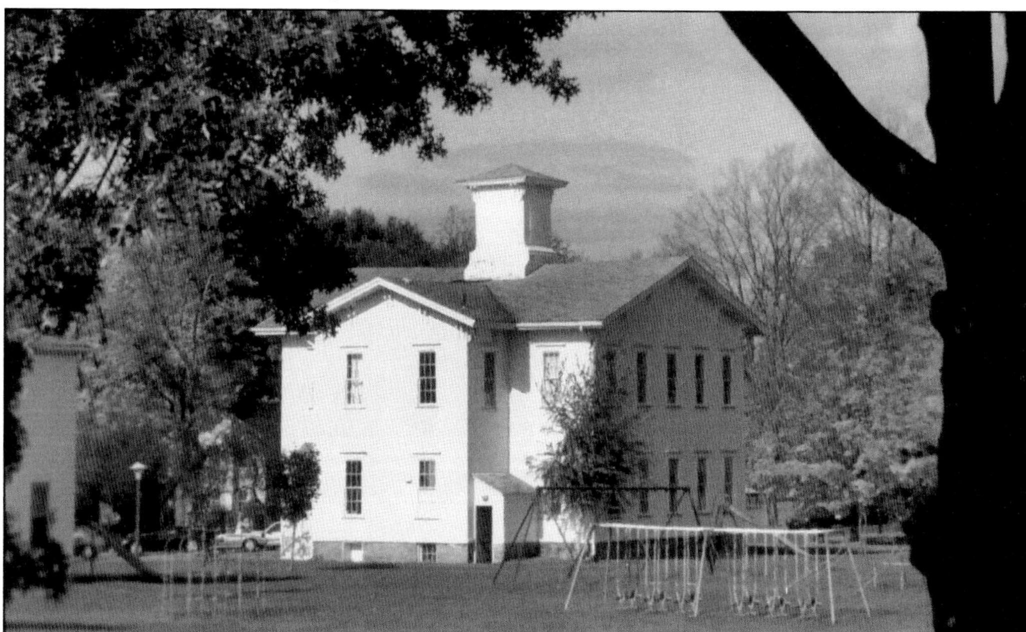

Before an effort was made to have the building listed in the National Register for Historic Places, Academy Hall, seen here around 1960, had fallen into disrepair. Academy Hall was listed in the National Register on November 21, 2006, has been restored, and is occupied by the admissions office.

Dr. Jeremy Brown came to Edinboro in 2007 and was president until 2011. A native of Manchester, England, Dr. Brown was proud to show his heritage. During his time at Edinboro, Dr. Brown carried out the master plan developed under the Pogue administration and added the Zafirovski Sports and Recreation Arena to it.

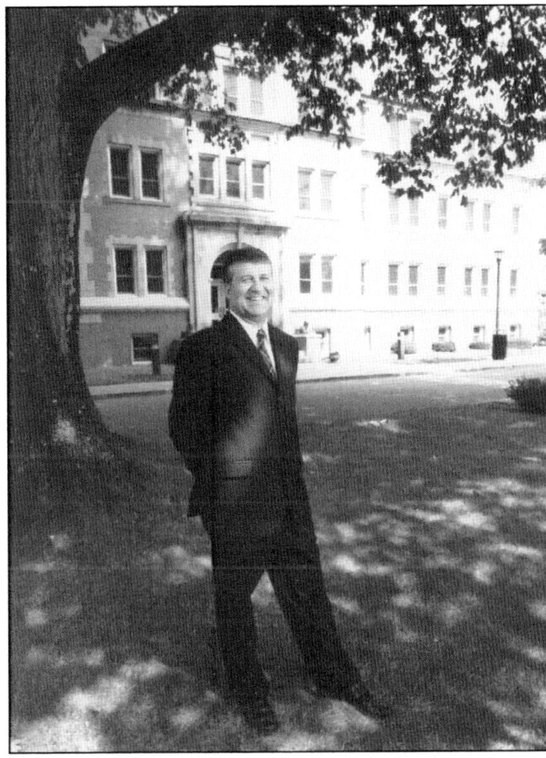

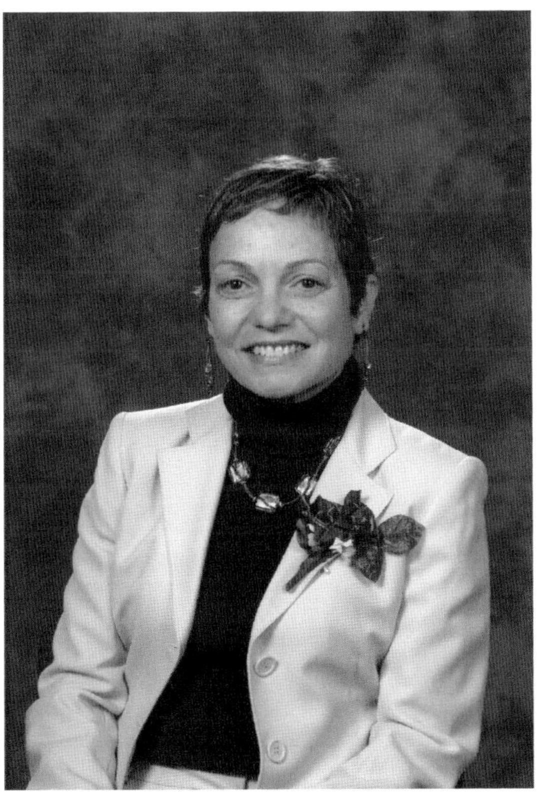

Dr. Jeremy Brown left Edinboro in June 2011. Dr. James Moran, vice chancellor of academic and student affairs for the state system, stepped in as interim president for one year. Dr. Julie Wollman, pictured here, became Edinboro's 17th president on June 1, 2012. Before her appointment at Edinboro University of Pennsylvania (EUP), Dr. Wollman was at Wheelock College in Boston, where she served as vice president for academic affairs.

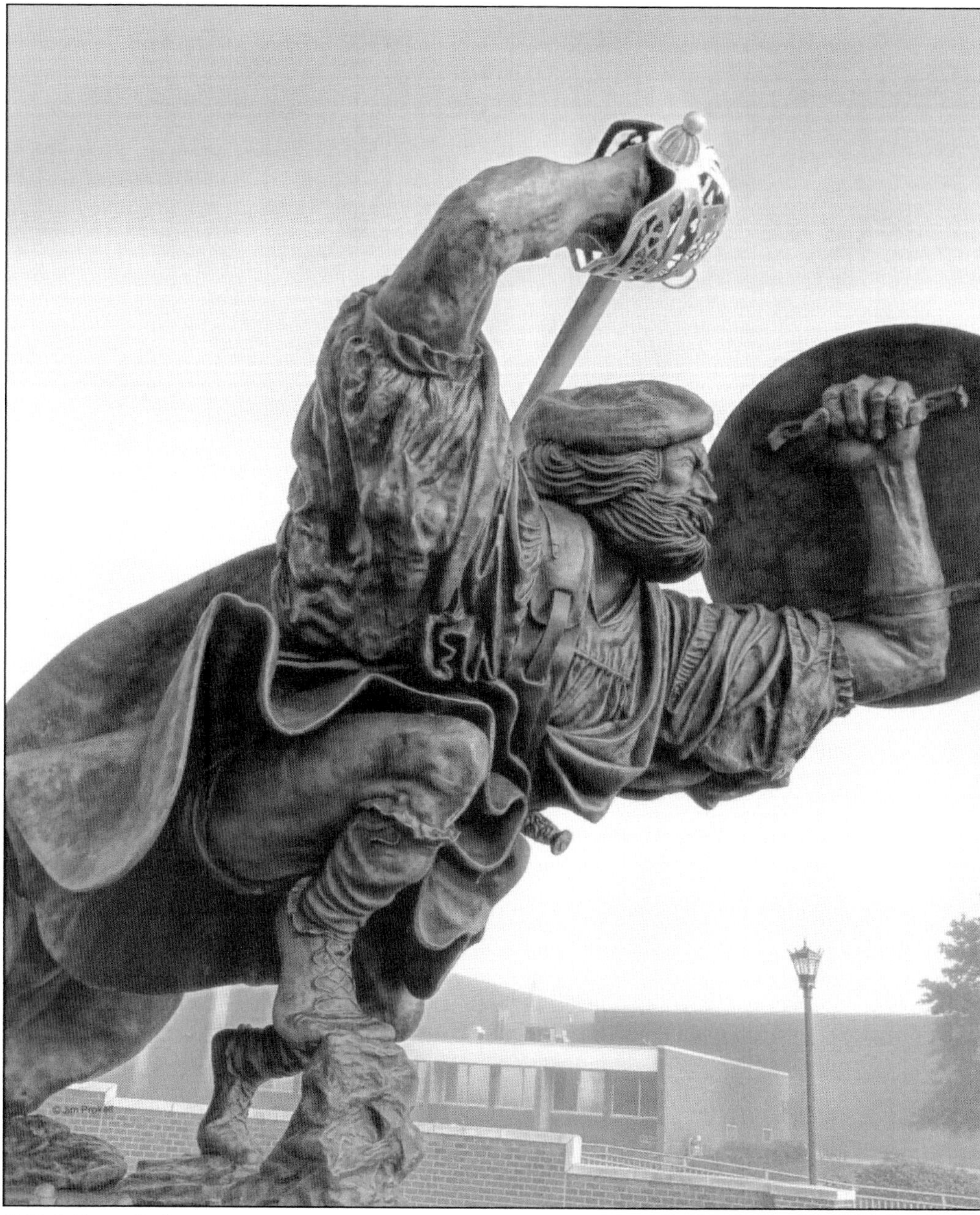

Officially, Edinboro sports teams were called the Highlanders, but sportswriters began to alternate Scots with Highlanders, and Fighting Scots evolved out of this. By 1971, it was being used by the Edinboro sports programs. Dan Higham, the man who did the casting, named the Scot statue "Angus." It was designed by Edinboro alumnus Jim Prokell.

BIBLIOGRAPHY

Edinboro University of Pennsylvania. *College Catalog*. Edinboro, PA: Edinboro University, 1860–2012.

———. *President's Office, Archival Records*. Edinboro, PA: Edinboro University, 1860–2012.

———. *Spectator*. Edinboro, PA: Edinboro University, 1935–2012.

———. *Spectator, Image Collection*. Edinboro, PA: Edinboro University, 1935–2012.

———. *University Archives, Media Collection*. Edinboro, PA: Edinboro University, 1860–2012.

———. *Yearbook*. Edinboro, PA: Edinboro University, 1910–2000.

Neel, George W. *A History of the State Teachers College at Edinboro, Pennsylvania*. New Brunswick, NJ: Rutgers University, 1950.

Strausbaugh, Roy. *Edinboro University: An Administrative History, 1963–1993*. Edinboro, PA: Edinboro University Services, Inc., 1997.

Vance, Russell. *A Portrait of Edinboro: From Private Academy to State College, 1856–1976*. Rochester NY: PSI Publishers, 1977.